FONDATION HARDT
POUR L'ÉTUDE DE L'ANTIQUITÉ CLASSIQUE

ENTRETIENS
Tome XVI

MÉNANDRE

ENTRETIENS SUR L'ANTIQUITÉ CLASSIQUE
Publiés par Olivier Reverdin
TOME XVI

MÉNANDRE

SEPT EXPOSÉS SUIVIS DE DISCUSSIONS

PAR

E. W. HANDLEY, WALTHER LUDWIG,
F. H. SANDBACH, FRITZ WEHRLI, CHRISTINA DEDOUSSI,
CESARE QUESTA, LILLY KAHIL

Entretiens préparés et présidés
par Eric G. Turner

VANDŒUVRES-GENÈVE
26 - 31 AOÛT 1969

CES ENTRETIENS ONT ÉTÉ ORGANISÉS ET CE VOLUME A ÉTÉ PUBLIÉ
AVEC L'AIDE DU FONDS NATIONAL SUISSE DE LA RECHERCHE SCIENTIFIQUE

AVANT-PROPOS

De tous les auteurs anciens, Ménandre est celui qui doit le plus aux papyrus et à l'ingéniosité de leurs interprètes. On ne possédait de lui que des lambeaux. Une première vague de découvertes, à la fin du siècle dernier et au début de ce siècle, ressuscita une partie de son œuvre. De nouvelles découvertes, depuis une quinzaine d'années, permettent de se faire désormais une idée précise et nuancée de son art. La plus importante est, sans conteste, celle du Codex Bodmer, contenant en son milieu, presque intact, le Δύσκολος, *publié en 1959 par Victor Martin, et, dans ses parties extérieures, moins bien conservées, la* Σαμία *et l'* Ἀσπίς, *dont l'édition princeps, établie par Rodolphe Kasser, avec l'aide de Colin Austin, a paru dix ans plus tard, en 1969. Entre-temps, grâce aux savants travaux de E. G. Turner, R. Kassel, E. W. Handley, le* Μισούμενος, *le* Σικυώνιος *et le* Δὶς ἐξαπατῶν *nous ont été partiellement restitués. Enfin, la découverte, en 1962, par S. Charitonidis, des mosaïques de la « Maison du Ménandre », à Mytilène, et celle, toute récente, de deux fresques, à Ephèse, ont renouvelé l'étude de l'iconographie des comédies de Ménandre.*

On le voit : Ménandre est à l'ordre du jour. C'est ce qui a incité la Fondation Hardt *à lui consacrer ses seizièmes entretiens, qui ont eu lieu en août 1969.*

Le présent volume contient les exposés présentés lors de ces entretiens et les discussions qui les ont suivis. E. W. Handley (Londres) y étudie les conventions du théâtre comique et la manière dont Ménandre les a utilisées ; Walther Ludwig (Francfort) examine le rôle des divinités dans l'action dramatique, chez Ménandre, et prend comme terme de comparaison la Cistellaria *de Plaute ; F. H. Sandbach (Cambridge) analyse les manipulations que Ménandre fait subir au parler attique et à la langue littéraire pour les adapter aux exigences du dialogue comique. Ménandre et la philosophie, thème souvent traité, est repris par Fritz Wehrli (Zurich) à la lumière des découvertes récentes. Mlle Christina Dedoussi (Jannina), qui avait édité la* Samienne *telle qu'on la connaissait avant la publication du papyrus Bodmer, a commenté à nouveau cette comédie. Comparer les structures dramatiques du théâtre de Ménandre et de celui de Plaute permet de fructueuses observations et conduit à une meilleure compréhension du génie de l'un et de l'autre poète. C'est à Cesare Questa (Urbino) qu'avait été confié le soin de le faire. Mme Lilly Kahil (Fribourg en Suisse), enfin, a traité de l'iconographie des pièces de Ménandre, sujet renouvelé par les découvertes de ces dernières années, en particulier par celle des mosaïques de Mytilène, qui n'avaient pas encore été publiées lorsque ces entretiens ont eu lieu. Grâce à l'obligeance de la revue* Antike Kunst, *à qui nous exprimons notre gratitude, on trouvera dans ce volume la reproduction en couleurs de quatre panneaux de Mytilène et d'une des mosaïques de Dioscouridès, à Naples.*

Le professeur Eric G. Turner, qui avait été chargé de préparer ces entretiens, les a présidés ; il a pris une large part aux discussions et il a revu les manuscrits. Le but de la Fondation Hardt était de permettre à quelques-uns de ceux qui ont le plus contribué, ces dernières années, au progrès des études ménandriennes de faire le point. Le lecteur jugera dans quelle mesure ce but a été atteint.

Prenant le relais de la Fondation du Jubilé de l'Union de Banques Suisses, qui avait largement contribué, financièrement, à la préparation, à l'organisation et à la publication des trois précédents entretiens, le Fonds national suisse de la recherche scientifique a accordé, pour ceux-ci, un important subside. Qu'il en soit remercié.

TABLE DES MATIÈRES

TABLE DES ILLUSTRATIONS

Les quatre planches se trouvent après la page 246

I

E. W. HANDLEY

The conventions of the comic stage and their exploitation by Menander

THE CONVENTIONS OF THE COMIC STAGE AND THEIR EXPLOITATION BY MENANDER

> I tried to keep in mind that in a play, from time to time, something should happen; that the audience should be kept in the constant expectation that something is going to happen; and that when it does happen, it should be different, but not too different, from what the audience had been led to expect.
>
> T. S. Eliot, *Poetry and Drama* [1]

Near the end of Act II of Menander's *Dyskolos*, the young hero, equipped with a borrowed mattock, sets off for a bout of hard work in the fields, hoping to meet and impress the misanthropic father of the girl he loves. The stage is left empty. Enter a cook, dragging after him a sheep, and cursing it as he goes. The sight of an angry man in a muddle with an animal is universal enough as a source of amusement to have its effect on audiences nearly two-and-a-half thousand years later, even if many of them have met the name of Menander for the first time when they decided to buy their tickets, and are not accustomed to being catered for by men who bring the meal on the hoof. The classical scholar in the audience is in a different position. He knows that *mageiroi* are quite a well-documented character-type in fourth-century comedy, thanks in part to the material collected by Athenaeus for his *Deipnosophistai*; back in his study, he can put a hand to a considerable bibliography of the topic, quoting parallels for the action and for points in the language, and perhaps invoking a visual aid or two from terracotta statuettes of men with animals [2]. In such ways, in spite of

[1] *The Theodore Spencer Memorial Lecture*, Harvard University, November 21, 1950 (London, Faber and Faber, 1951), p. 32.

[2] As for instance in my *Dyskolos of Menander* (London and Cambridge, Mass., 1965), pp. 199 f.

our very fragmentary knowledge of Greek Comedy in the two generations between the last of Aristophanes and the first of Menander, it becomes plain from sheer repetition that certain elements in Menander's comedies are in some sense conventional or traditional. That is to say that, whatever their status in relation to contemporary reality, their appeal to a theatrically conscious audience in Menander's own time is compounded with the effect they have as traditional or conventional elements in drama. In other words, the very appearance on stage of a man with an animal who is recognizably a *mageiros* creates certain expectations with which the dramatist must reckon.

The dramatist's reckoning may lead him in several ways. He may, for instance, attempt to outdo the convention by making his own treatment brighter and better, rather in the mood of Plautus, when he makes a slave boast that he has secured his young master a royal and golden fortune, and has no time for your Parmenos and Syruses with their frauds of two or three minas [1]. Or he may exploit the convention more subtly, realizing that he can recreate an expected pattern of words or action with no great displacement of effort; and then, perhaps with equal economy, marking a point or two of difference from the image in the detail of his own treatment. He may also want to link such a motif into a chain of expectation, giving the audience a hint in advance that such and such a thing is to happen, and then using it, when it does, to create further anticipation for something else. This seems rather closer to the doctrine which Eliot's words recall to us, and rather more like Menander; for it is, perhaps, by infusing the apparently

[1] Chrysalus at *Ba.* 645-50: it is amusing that in Menander's original he had the common name Syros, as appears from the Oxyrhynchus fragments of Δὶς ἐξαπατῶν discussed in my lecture *Menander and Plautus: a study in comparison* (London, H. K. Lewis, 1968).

familiar with the tension created by context and structure that he achieves some of his most successful dramatic effects.

Leading on from our example of something very familiar in Comedy, I should like to suggest recurrent motifs as one general heading under which we can consider conventions of the comic stage. Given New Comedy's links by descent from both the major forms of fifth-century drama, and the continuing influence of classical tragedy as well as earlier comedy, it is clear that exploitation of tragic as well as of comic motif may enter into this. Equally clearly, one could consider Menander's use of conventional topics in speeches and dialogue under a related heading. All this, at one end of the scale, could involve, or lead into, discussion of his use of conventions of language, even of metre and metrical forms; at the other end, it might run into questions about his approach to character-portraiture and plot-construction. Although I shall suggest that the critic of ancient comedy should beware of drawing lines too firmly between different departments of the comic playwright's art, there does seem to be here a group of conventions which can go together for our purposes as literary conventions, and reflect the point that comedy is a species of literature.

A second class (the order of enumeration is not supposed to be important), may be made of conventions which are to do with theatrical performance: conventions springing from the physical character of the theatre for which Menander wrote; the conventions of costumes and masks, in so far as we recognize them as established in his time; conventions in the use of a limited number of actors (however limited we think it was), and in the actual stage-management of action and spectacle in so far as we can reconstruct these visual elements from the available texts and illustrations left to us from Antiquity.

Thirdly, in a kind of drama which has had from Antiquity onwards a much treasured reputation for realism, there is a special sense of convention which comes in when we ask questions about the status of the comic representation in relation to real life; as when we ask how far events in plays are supposed to make sense in terms of real time and place, or how far the economic facts about characters' lives are ' true ' facts, with precise counterparts in the world outside the play, as opposed to facts only acceptable in a fictional context and with a conventional sense.

It might be objected that so comprehensive a scheme would allow us to turn the discussion to anything in Menander. That is, in fact, the idea. Comic poets of the fifth century, one recalls, sometimes took conscious pride in their novelties, and decried stock jokes and themes, even, as it might be, in the act of using them. At the opposite pole, Terence (admittedly in the course of a rather speciously angled answer to a literary controversy) was prepared to assert that the comic poet has no novelty left open to him [1]. The same is sometimes said nowadays about plots for novels. Yet they go on being published in quantity. Thus, whatever value one wants to put on sheer innovation in any particular form of creative activity, it is obvious that with some, at all events from the consumer's point of view, the pleasures of familiarity are considerable; and if there were any danger of our underrating this, the immense development of certain forms of drama as entertainment for mass audiences through cinema, sound radio, and television would rapidly rescue us. There are mass audiences not only for canonical types of screen play, for example Westerns and detective stories, each with its many familiar conventions of setting, characterization and incident, but also for the more extreme case which depends on the kind of frequent and regular access to the

[1] Novelties: e.g. Cratinus, *Odysses* 145K.; Pherekrates, *Korianno* 79K.; Ar. *Clouds* 547 ἀλλ' αἰεὶ καινὰς ἰδέας εἰσφέρων σοφίζομαι. Stock jokes: e.g. Ar. *Peace* 739 ff., *Clouds* 538 ff. and scholia, *Frogs* 1 ff. Terence: *Eun.* 41.

same audience which modern communications make possible: namely, the serial, consisting of a long sequence of more-or-less self-contained pieces of action in which the same principal characters go on appearing, and may take on, for their audiences, a curiously real and ageless existence of their own—the ideal child who never grows up, the ideal friend whose lasting idiosyncracies seem to give a ground bass of permanence in contrast to one's own shifting moods and affairs. Noticeably, the very fixity of convention which can be exploited to hold the audiences for which it was created is also something which can make a whole genre acceptable in a quite new environment: thus the ' Western ' idiom is known and liked by some large number of Europeans for whom the Old West of the United States is even more of a fictional entity than it must be for many of the present inhabitants of those lands. This is a factor which it may be interesting to remember when one considers the long life and the popularity of Menandrean comedy in places far removed from the Athens in which it evolved. And such analogies, however imprecise they may be, could also lead our discussions to reopen that old topic on Menandrean comedy, perhaps especially favoured by those who find it unattractive—how closely drawn are its conventions of subject, in terms of the range of human experiences which it reflects?

I have one more general observation to offer. Whatever opinion he may wish to express of the literary, dramatic or other value of Menandrean comedy, the critic who tries to appreciate and explain the means by which it achieves its effects is in a certain difficulty of presentation and perspective. It is difficult to avoid going on much too long; it is difficult to avoid sounding either hopelessly trivial or hopelessly over-refined, and the experience must in some sense be akin to that of the experts who try to say (though no doubt with batteries of statistical data) why one advertisement is immediately appealing and successful, and another not too different is an utter flop. It is perhaps even more related to the experience one has in the presence of a superbly successful comic performance by a star with a genius for delivery, timing, gesture and expression, when one asks : ' Could I explain how it was done, and why it was done like that? ' The answer, I suppose, is that there is nothing improper in wanting to know, but one must not expect the attempt to find out to be as enjoyable as the original reaction.

Let us return to our cook with his sheep. Even a simple incident can be used to illustrate the basic point that a single event in a play can simultaneously involve a number of dramatic conventions, some of them latent, in that they are accepted without special consciousness as part of the normal means of communication between dramatist and audience; others not so, in that, on the given occasion, a special and conscious use is made of them. Thus both dramatist and audience neglect the fact that, being someone in a play, the cook is wearing tights like a comic actor and unlike a real cook. He is recognized as a cook on sight, so far as we know, by his mask, and perhaps his cook's knife or other standard details of costume. This time the point does matter, and typically, it is reinforced by what he says, most directly in referring to himself as ' the *mageiros* ' and to the place where he is as ' the Nymphaion where we are to sacrifice ' (399-401). Moreover, he is given a variant on one of the very familiar stock-in-trade jokes of cook scenes, the word for to chop or cut up, κόπτω or κατακόπτω (in this case the latter), with its slang sense of giving someone a thoroughly unpleasant experience, as by hacking at him with criticism or battering him with sheer conversational boredom : this time, with all the struggle they have had, the notion is that the sheep has had the cook under the chopper : he is hauling it along ' like a boat up a beach '. Thus both visual and verbal conventions play their part simultaneously, and variants on both add, or seem to add, a spice of new interest.

Suppose we approach from another angle. The stage building, that place of many uses, is accepted as representing somewhere in a remote valley in the mountains of the Northern Attic borders for the very good reason that Menander has made it clear in advance that that is where the play is happening [1]. The point is gently reinforced by making the cook say '*fortunately* here it is' (he has come a long way, and his loaded companion Getas is trailing behind), and by inventing the notion that when carried over the shoulders, as animals commonly were and are in Greece, the sheep held up the march by reaching for leaves to eat on the way (400, 394 ff). Is one surprised to see a figure so commonly associated with town life in so remote a place? No: because we have already been told, in a context where the information had the air of an incidental detail, that Sostratos' mother is a woman who goes all round the district making sacrifices, and had sent Getas to hire a *mageiros* for one of her pious excursions (259 ff.). Do we worry about where the cook came from, to be fetched to so remote a place in time to sacrifice and cook for a mid-day meal? No: because the precise details do not enter into the matter. The general rule seems to be that provided the realities of place and time are not so conspicuously violated as to make the action ludicrous for that reason, the dramatist can expect to carry the audience with him in a little convenient stretching. If the cook was supposed to live in or near Athens (where, not surprisingly, he boasts of having an extensive practice), Getas would be supposed to have had a journey of around 25 miles since early morning to fetch him and bring him back (393n.). The point of this meticulous organization of detail is not of course, that it is some kind of private game between the dramatist and his

[1] 1 f.: see *Dyskolos of Menander* 20 ff. with further references.

more scholarly admirers, but that, if the audience is to be relaxed and properly attentive to the effect being created, they must be given just enough information to carry on their interest without irrelevant surprises ; and loose ends which may distract them from the main business in hand must be tied in or tucked out of sight. A puzzled or distracted spectator is, for the moment of being puzzled or distracted, a lost one [1].

Perhaps we can now extend our analysis a little further and make some comparisons. The whole comic episode of the entry of the cook in the *Dyskolos* makes an immediate contrast with the mood of romantic resolution given by Sostratos' departure with his mattock for toil and hot sun. Similarly in the *Misoumenos*, the moment of Thrasonides' resolve to confront the father of the girl he loves is succeeded by the entry of Kleinias with a cook, giving instructions on a very familiar topic—the number of guests to be catered for, and on the need for speed [2] ; in the *Aspis*, the moment in the first act when Daos makes a stand against Smikrines' determination to have his rights over the girl and the estate that goes with her is brought sharply up against—not the arrival of a cook, but the departure of one, from the household which was to celebrate a wedding and is now plunged in sorrow. Once again, familiar topics appear : theft, in the form of reproach to his assistant for failure to capitalize on the situation by filling the oil-bottle on the way out, rivalry between cook and *trapezopoios*, and, once more, a form of the κόπτω-joke [3].

[1] The point is nicely put at the beginning of G. H. Gellie's paper ' Motivation in Sophocles ' in *BICS* 11 (1964) 1-14.

[2] *Misoumenos*, *POxy* 2656, 270 ff. : ' number of guests ' motif as (e.g.) *Sam.* 287 ff. and Straton, *Phoenikides* [Page, *Lit. Pap.* 57] 6 ; ' hurry ' motif as (e.g.) *Epitr.* 206 [below, p. 14, n. 2] and *Dysk.* 943 σπουδὴ γὰρ ἦν.

[3] *Aspis* 216 ff. : theft, e.g. Euphron, *Adelphoi* 1K. ; Page, *Lit. Pap.* 59 (b) with Treu, *Philologus* 102 (1958) 215 ff. ; P. *Aul.* 553 f. ; *trapezopoios*, *Dysk.* 646 and n., H. Dohm, *Mageiros* (Munich, 1964) 82 f. On the κόπτω-joke,

Now one effect of these three scenes, placed as they are, is to bring the action down from a high point to which it has developed, and carry the act to a swift close on a new note : six lines are spent on this in *Misoumenos* ; 34 in *Dyskolos* ; the same, perhaps one or two more, in *Aspis*. The pattern of introducing a new development towards the end of an act is a recurrent one in Menander, and, naturally enough, the development is often brought by the arrival of a character new to the play, or new at least to the preceding sequence. For example, *Samia*, Act I, at 96, say about 30 lines from the end, Moschion has resolved to steel his nerves and go off and rehearse the social and ceremonial business for the wedding of which he is so nervous. Enter the two old gentlemen Demeas and Nikeratos, with their travellers' talk of the Black Sea, from which they turn, apparently casually, to the topic of the wedding which their return home has brought to mind. Or *Epitrepontes*, Act II, at the end of the Arbitration, at 206, enter Onesimos, 37 lines from the end of the Act : a brief reference to the slowness of the cook (it is because things are so slow that he has time to step outside), and then he notices that the ring which is just being looked at and talked about is the one his master once lost. Or *Sikyonios*, Act III, at about 120, some 30 lines from the end, enter Pyrrhias with the vital news, and the evidence, of Stratophanes' true parentage, on which the next stage of the action is to turn. Or, from Act IV, *Dyskolos* 775, after the climax of Knemon's major speech and Sostratos' betrothal, enter Kallippides, required for the next stage, but at this moment with his mind on being late for the party, just nine lines from the end of the act ; *Aspis* 491, some 30 lines from the end, enter Kleostratos, who is thought by

see below p. 15 with n. 2 ; and on the funeral feast (233) note Hegesippos, *Adelphoi* 1K., 10 ff. and Anaxippos, *Enkalyptomenos* 1K., 40 ff., quoted together by Dohm, *op. cit.* 78.

all but the audience to have died in battle by the river Xanthos in Lycia.

Thus if one function of the three cook-scenes which led us into this topic is to bring contrast and end the act on a lighter plane of comedy, the varied sample of instances we have taken from elsewhere suggests that their placing is unlikely to be an accident in the purely structural sense, but has something to do with Menander's use of the convention of act-breaks in relation to the progress of an action. We are, of course, exceedingly ill-informed about what happened in the breaks. Tradition enacts that the first entry of the chorus may have special treatment, even if it is almost or wholly disregarded as an entity elsewhere: thus, in the *Plutus*, in addition to providing that the chorus shall have some sort of performance before 325 (and probably, in composing the play, he had no need to think what sort), Aristophanes also devised a parodos for which the chorus is in character, and a special dance, parodying the *Cyclops* of Philoxenos, which they are to do with Karion before they come to their conventional ΧΟΡΟΥ [1]. This is the tradition which Menander preserves in his formulaic announcements of the chorus's first entry at the end of Act I, and we can digress to note two special variants: *Dyskolos*, where the drunken young men are given a special character, either as 'paean-singers', if, like myself, one is stiff-necked enough to hold on to the text; or as 'followers of Pan', by an easy and attractive conjecture; and *Aspis*, where they are not simply 'a crowd' but '*another* crowd'—the audience has seen one crowd already in the procession of captives led home by Daos, and, it may be, Menander is not merely

[1] Cf. *CQ* n.s. 3 (1953) 55-61, esp. 59 n. 4, and W. J. W. Koster, *Autour d'un manuscrit d'Aristophane écrit par Démétrius Triclinius* (Groningen, 1957) 117 ff., with further references. Doubts over the textual history and significance of ΧΟΡΟΥ in the *Plutus* need not radically affect our use of the play here to illustrate a kind of episodic structure.

alluding to this, but marking the contrast of mood and spectacle which he has created in this play [1]. What interests us, here, however, is a particular kind of plot-planning in relation to the discontinuity given by the breaks. Such a break may simply be treated as an interlude between episodes. An extreme case would be the breaks between episodes at the end of the *Plutus*, after 958, for instance, if it is right to think that the chorus performed there. But the break can have more of a dramatic function if something is done by the shape of the action or the words of the dialogue to create expectation for what will come after it, and it may then be used to mark a lapse of dramatic time, as in the *Plutus* after 626, where a night passes during which Plutus incubates in the temple of Asklepios. With a play of integrated structure, such as the *Dyskolos*, the problem, I take it, is to use the breaks as part of the design, so that they give intervals in the continuous action, but not destructive ones. Hence the tendency, there and elsewhere, to achieve a compromise between break and continuity by introducing a diversity of action near the break.

The content of our three short cook-scenes takes on another interest when viewed in this light. Let us take *Misoumenos* first. If these six lines were a fragment, we should perhaps only dare to observe that someone was instructing a cook in a not very surprising way: 'There's one stranger to entertain, cook, and myself, and for third, a girl of mine—if she's come in, for Heaven's sake: I'm worried about that myself. If not, just him: I shall be after her all over town. But come on in, cook, and make your motto Speed'. We have enough to know that what we are getting, in the rather simpler visual terms of the cinema,

[1] *Dysk.* 230; *Asp.* 247, cf. 88 f. The reference back to the procession of captives is doubtful, because ὄχλον ἄλλον may mean (i) 'another ὄχλος' as opposed to the present ὄχλος of cook and company (cf. Knemon at *Dysk.* 166) or (ii) 'others, a crowd' (cf. LSJ s.v. ἄλλος II. 8).

is a quite different camera angle on two of the principals. The word ξένος, which in the context of dinner-party means 'guest' has a particular function in this play in relation to Demeas, the stranger arrived from Cyprus. It has appeared prominently before; it will soon come in again, when, a few lines from the beginning of the new act, Kleinias asks Getas 'Has a *xenos* just come into your house?' and the verbal link helps the theme to take up again [1]. One could offer a contrast with what must be a near-minimal use of cook-motif at the end of Act II of *Epitrepontes*, which we mentioned just now: there of course, the main interest is on the discovery which Onesimos is to make about the ring, and it is the ring which makes the verbal link with the next act; the cook is not only not silent, but does not even show his face. Even so, words are not wasted. In eight of them, Menander shifts the focus of attention to Charisios' side of the story, suggests a motive for his character's entrance, and (as with the progress of the sacrifice and party through the *Dyskolos*) uses the reference to the meal to keep a time scale of the action going: English can only match in syllables, not words: 'No-one ever saw a slower cook: this time yesterday they'd been having their wine for hours' [2]. If this sounds, as it may, like a bad case of over-interpretation, the test is to put in some other form of words instead: 'I suppose I might as well go and sit on the porch for five minutes'. For many playwrights, that would have been quite good enough.

The effect of the new angle, as well as that of thematic contrast, is clear to see in the *Aspis* cook scene, and Menander's choice from the available store of conventional detail has clearly been made with that in mind. By putting

[1] *Mis.* 286, recalling 270, 273, and (more remotely) *POxy* 2657, 24, 27, 31 (*Menander and Plautus*, p. 20 n. 8).

[2] *Epitr.* 206: cf. T. B. L. Webster, 'Menander: Production and Imagination', *Bull. Rylands Library* 45 (1962) 235-272, at pp. 268 ff.

the death of Kleainetos so prominently to the fore at the opening of the play, and by providing him with an uncle of extremely grasping unpleasantness, Menander sets himself a problem which could well be pondered by those who expect comedy be to all jokes. Accordingly, just as this essentially serious theme is handled with an eye alert for the relieving humour of the human weaknesses which show through, so also the predominantly comic tailpiece with the cook has links and contrasts with the serious themes to give them perspective. For Daos, the situation has brought grief at the loss of his master, and of his own prospect of a comfortable retirement in old age. Grief comes to Kleainetos' sister, who was about to be married with a beneficent dowry from the nicer uncle, and for the women of the household preparing for the wedding. Instead of having a brother who could have endowed her handsomely from the spoils of his campaigns, she is an heiress, which could be a most unenviable position for a young woman to be in [1]. There is very perfunctory grief from Smikrines, as head of the family and with all the wealth now capable of being grasped. Now we are to have a cook's eye view : annoyance at losing his contract through the arrival of 'some corpse from Lycia', fury that the distraction of the women in their grief has not been exploited as an opportunity to steal oil; the thought the *trapezopoios* will come in to cater for the funeral feast; then, whether from the *trapezopoios* as the manuscript has it, or from the cook continuing, the play on κόπτω : the women are beating their breasts—'I shall be κοπτόμενος just like you if I don't get a drachma' [2]. Finally, there is contempt for the loyal Daos, who has brought all the wealth home and not

[1] See, for instance, on *Dysk.* 729-739, where the Attic law of inheritance is part of the background to Knemon's provision for his family, but is not an explicit issue as in *Aspis* and some other plays.

[2] If, as in B, the *trapezopoios* is the speaker at 233-235, the effect will be a little like that of the verbal echo at *Dysk.* 520-521. See further on *Dysk.* 397 f.

made off with it. A Phrygian, is he? Thracians, especially Getai, are the real men, not half-men like that. The joke on the slave's nationality (without dramatic context a conventional one, even if nicely turned) has an extra point from the fact that Daos has just turned his nationality to a quite different use in declining to help Smikrines' plans to get the estate : ' I am Phrygian ' he argues (a people who proverbially saw things the wrong way round) ' and a slave : you must not expect me to see things the same way as you do, or to help you in legal affairs which are above my station.' We do not know if the cook came back in the lost part of the play. He has served his purpose well here. He leaves at the end of the Act, as the chorus of revellers appear, and the next Act takes up from Smikrines' exit immediately preceding the incident.

A difference with the *Dyskolos* is, of course, that there the cook has a substantial part. A good deal has been said about him elsewhere, and we can take the remaining points we need from his entrance scene very briefly. The detail of his opening speech we have already considered. By the design of this play, two lines of action, each touched off by Pan, converge in the neighbourhood of the Nymphaion at Phyle. Sostratos has been made to fall in love with Knemon's daughter; the rest of the family is brought as a result of a dream in which Pan appeared to the young man's superstitious mother. The cook and the household slave Getas, complaining about their mission and discussing the omen which sent it, are part of the mechanism for bringing the two lines of action together. They show Sostratos' mother's superstitions in a different light from that which we had from her son. They talk of her dream; dreams are by no means a novel topic in drama, but this one has the excellent comic effect that its apparently alarming content refers in fact to the bout of digging for which the audience has just seen Sostratos leave. They talk of getting things ready, and their words, and the theme, will be echoed when the action is resumed the other side of the act-break, though not without the diversity of a sudden appearance by Knemon.

The topic of linking and transition over the act-break is one which could well be pursued further. Before we move on to something quite different, it will be useful to mention one passage as a control on our observations, namely the Oxyrhynchus Δὶς ἐξαπατῶν [1]. The pattern we have been considering is present. A very interesting sequence of action (of which we have an idea from Plautus' *Bacchides*), has put Sostratos in the position of being asked to reprove a trusted friend for being involved in an affair with someone who, to the best of his knowledge, is waiting for *him*. This turns him to the notion of handing over to his father the money he had proposed to divert in order to further the affair. Enter the father, some 34 lines from the end of the act. They go off to transfer the money : ΧΟΡΟΥ. Re-enter the same pair, and the theme of the conversation re-opens. After 27 lines of the new act, exit father. Sostratos returns to reflect on the girl and the friend who, as he thinks, have betrayed him. Eleven-and-a-half more lines of soliloquy, resuming with the aid of a verbal echo from where we left off, and enter the friend. Now here it is much more diffcult to get a clear idea of the function of the scenes on either side of the act-break, because much of the content is lost by damage, and we do not have the relevant part of the rest of the design except in Plautus' version. It is, however a point of some interest that Plautus, who had no concern to arrange

[1] What is said here depends on the reconstruction and interpretation set out in *Menander and Plautus*. The arrival of Sostratos' father at ii. 18 (= 30) is inferred from the remains of the pronouns ἐ̣κ̣ε̣ῖνο̣ν̣ and τ̣[ουτο]ν̣ί in that line; his exit at iii. 28 (= 90) is given by ταῦ̣[τ'] ἄ̣πειμι πρὸς ἀ̣γορὰν / [πρ]άττ̣[ων· ὅ]τι πράττ̣ῃς ἄ̣[λ]λο δέδοται τοῦτό σοι̣ (πραττ̣εις pap.). For a fuller discussion of Plautus' treatment of his original, see Questa's paper in this volume.

the action round a break, eliminated the two scenes, had the transfer of money made in a rapid off-stage transaction, and refashioned the move between stages of the action by conventions of his own.

One interesting effect which is given by a structure of exits and entrances such as we have been considering, is, perhaps, that of offsetting the fixity of the actual stage setting. Menander had little scope, so far as we know, for more than some quite simple alterations to the background for a country as opposed to a town play, and nothing of the flexibility and capacity for realism of a conventional modern theatre, not to speak of the infinitely more flexible capacities of the film-maker. As an aside to this, it is quite possibly true that the need for scenic effects grows with the capacity to produce them, and one has seen modern plays, or modern productions, where the urge for scenic variety is of positive dramatic detriment, where the imagination can do better with less artificial aid. None the less, Menandrean drama has means for conveying the character of a setting, and for distracting attention from its fixity by action and words; and there are occasions when something which should happen indoors is needed for public presentation to the audience, or when something important happens off stage and cannot be staged because to do so, rather than presenting it through narrative or dialogue, would be impracticable or uneconomical.

A very simple device which can be used to extend the stage momentarily to the inside of a house (if we may put it like that) is the device of having a character talk back through the open door as he is leaving. This convention is so common that it is normally completely latent (as we have called the cook's tights). So in the Δὶς ἐξαπατῶν (102) Moschion, whom the audience cannot have seen for some time, enters from the house of the twin sisters saying ' So he's heard I'm here—where on earth is he? ' This is apparently enough for Menander's audience to reconnect with the situation. Plautus, adapting the passage and using the same device, evidently thought his audience should have more. It comes out as (*Ba.* 526): 'I will put your instructions before everything else, Bacchis, to look for Mnesilochus and bring him with me to you. I am surprised indeed at his delay if the message from me has reached him. I will go to his house here and see if he is at home'. Another example might be the case of the bibulous midwife, for which we depend in part on Terence's version of *Andria.* 481, the midwife Lesbia comes out of the house giving instructions to an old woman Archylis at the door. The incident is known to be Menandrean, since we have the Greek for part of the instructions—Terence, not untypically, has simplified some of the detail. The primary dramatic point is to confirm to the audience that Pamphilus' baby son is now born. Simo, standing outside, remarks 'she didn't say face-to-face what should be done with the girl after the birth, but after she'd come out, shouting back inside from the road. Oh, Davus, do you think so little of me? Do you really think I'm a man you can set about tricking so openly?' He thinks that the whole thing is a put-up job, purely for his benefit, to convince him that there is a baby when there is not. Now if the midwife is to say anything at all that the audience hear, outside is where she must say it. The dramatist perfectly well could have let her give her instructions on leaving, and have made no more of it; but he chooses, in this instance, to play with the convention by making someone on stage give it a 'real-life' value. But once attention is drawn to the behaviour of the midwife, it needs some sort of naturalistic motivation, or the audience will share the viewpoint of Simo and wonder why she is behaving like that. That, I believe, is why, when we first heard of the midwife, at 228 ff., she was given a character which is perfectly conventional for an old woman, but usefully relevant to the incident we are discussing : she is, were were told ‘ imprudent and fond of a drop of drink ’, and the Archylis, with whom she has her doorstep conversation, we know of as a drinking companion of hers (232). It is partly because of this unostentatious preparation for the incident that I incline to think the design of it was Menander’s rather than Terence’s [1].

The same principle of ‘ special use when needed ’ can be seen to apply to conventional details of setting or costume. The altar to Apollo Agyieus at the house door is an expected part of a setting which can be ignored if and when it is not wanted. But it comes into special use in the *Samia*, at 444 ff., when Demeas appeals to his Apollo to help him carry through the wedding and sing a good wedding song in spite of himself and the feelings he wants to conceal. Or, in the *Dyskolos*, there is nothing surprising in the fact that a rich and elegant young man like Sostratos should go out hunting wearing a *chlanis*. But in a country context, it makes him conspicuous for what he is, he is ‘ the man in the *chlanis* ’ when seen by Gorgias at 257, and Menander still has more use of the point to make later [2].

A somewhat more difficult exercise with conventions is given in the *Dyskolos* by the staging of Knemon’s major speech. The old man has been badly shaken by his experience in the well, and wants to call the family to his bedside for what is, in effect, his will and testament. He has himself

[1] This is to be read as a tentative view of a passage which has provoked plenty of diverse and interesting discussion over the years : if nothing else, it could well illustrate the difficulty of arriving at critical agreement on so delicate a matter as comic technique from the limited and perplexed evidence we often need to use. See especially H. Marti, *Untersuchungen zur dramatischen Technik bei Plautus und Terenz* (Diss. Zurich ; publ. Winterthur, Schellenberg, 1959) 71 f. and *Lustrum* 8 (1963, publ. 1964) 57 f., together with brief comments by Shipp (1960) ad loc., and, among earlier work, A. W. Gomme, *Essays in Greek History and Literature* (Oxford, 1937) 260 n. 1.

[2] *Sam*. 449 f. ἀλλά τὸν ὑμέναιον ᾄδειν εἰσανάγκασόν με σύ / οἷον οὐκ ἄριστ’ ἔγωγ’ ἄν, ὡς ἔχω νῦν· ἀλλὰ τί;, with Webster’s conjectural restoration of 450, *BICS* 16 (1969) at p. 105 ; on Sostratos and his *chlanis*, see *Dysk*. 257 n.

carried outside. Menander does not attempt to motivate that naturalistically. Instead, he treats Knemon like a stricken hero of tragedy, perhaps underlining the point with an echo of Euripides' *Hippolytus* at the beginning of the scene, and alluding to the convention when Knemon asks to be 'wheeled in' at the end of it[1]. If this case is valid, it belongs to the class of uses of tragic convention for special effects. That class, as has often been pointed out, is in itself a compound one; for certain kinds of borrowing from tragedy are by Menander's time so well established in the comic tradition as to be, in some sense, part of the fabric, while others seem to represent fresh inspiration. Thus it is conventional in New Comedy, as earlier, for the tone to rise to that of high poetry when characters express specially strong emotions, and there is a whole range of effects from actual quotation through kinds of parody or adapted quotation to the much less pointed kind of effect which is given by a choice of elevated rather than strictly poetic words, or by the effect of tragic strictness in the verse—all of which effects could no doubt be underlined by voice and gesture. So much is common ground, though one may well argue about the nature of the tragic allusion in any particular context; one may well find that it is compounded of several elements, visual as well as verbal; and that Menander, on the whole, is less interested than Aristophanes in the purely laughable or satirical possibilities of the incongruity between the foreground comic situation and the background tragic one, and more interested in gaining an extra dimension to his comic action by referring it implicitly to a classic standard. A slight, but I think possible case of the compounding of verbal and visual elements, which I have thought of as remembling that of Knemon in bed, would be the entry of his daughter at *Dyskolos* 189: in distress—οἴμοι τάλαινα τῶν

[1] *Dysk.* 690, 692 and 758 with nn.

ἐμῶν ἐγὼ κακῶν—and carrying a water-pot, she recalls the Euripidean Electra; and if the audience took the point, they will have had an extra dimension to the comic situation, and an extra touch of amusement when Sostratos says of her ἐλευθερίως γέ πως / ἄγροικός ἐστιν (201 f.). There is no such doubt about the allusion to the messenger speech of the *Orestes* in the long narrative by the man from Eleusis at *Sikyonios* 176 ff., for it is clearly given by reminiscence of Euripides' own words; but the function of the speech in relation to dramatic convention and dramatic effect is a much more speculative topic. The debate over the slave Dromon and the girl Philoumene was evidently to be a major feature of the plot. To stage it in full, even if resources in actors could have permitted that, would have taken a great deal of time and would have been uneconomical of effect. And so the scene is carried elsewhere in imagination by dramatic narrative, which has the great capacity of being able to select, and to call on the imagination to supply what the eyes do not. An extreme case of the vivid and important, but unstageable, would of course be Daos' long narrative of the Lycian campaign and the death of Kleainetos at the beginning of the *Aspis*. But there are also vivid and impressive narratives of more domestic scenes, which might somehow have been presented in direct action. Such is Demeas' long narrative, beginning Act III of the *Samia* (206 ff.), in which he tells of the wedding preparations in his house, and how he overheard a conversation about the baby which has aroused a suspicion he will not voice. The further dramatic point here is that the personality of the narrator itself enters into the effect, and may in turn be illuminated by the way in which he tells his story. In the *Sikyonios* speech, Menander learnt from Euripides to let the narrator characterize himself at the start, so that we have some impression of the quality of our outside witness which we can test by what he says; precisely because he is in the position of an outside witness, his descriptions of the characters we know already give an extra dimension of interest, just as, on a small scale, the action we examined in the three short cook-scenes has an indirect value in relation to our other knowledge of the situation. In the *Aspis* and the *Samia*, we already know enough of the narrator for the story to help build up a portrait of him as well as of what he is telling. A further variant on this technique of indirect presentation is given by the *Misoumenos*, when at 284 ff. Getas paces round the stage narrating to himself and turning over in mind the quarrel he has witnessed between Demeas and Krateia and his master Thrasonides. Here we have not only the extra dimension of a slave's eye view of the matter, but the further comic effect of a very puzzled Kleinias pacing after the slave and cutting in with comments on Getas' recollection.

Returning now to the *Sikyonios* speech, we can be clear that there is much more point to it than some kind of diluted Euripidean echo. I should like to think that the Euripidean echo does two things other than give the audience the pleasure of recognizing the allusion. I should like to think that it points to the analogy of situation between the slave and the girl and the heroic Electra and Orestes; and that it does something to justify dramatically the very long uninterrupted speech, by placing it in a dramatic tradition of descriptions of assemblies of which the *Orestes* was a classic case, one which had already made its dramatic influence felt before Menander wrote this play, and continued to be remembered because the *Orestes* continued to be a popular classic [1].

The question then is, when Menander gives a hint that he is writing in a convention untypical of his usual manner, is this a sign that the normal criteria of realistic presentation do not apply? The point could be considered not only of

[1] Cf. *BICS* 12 (1965) 47 ff.

scenes explicitly in the tragic manner, but of the ending of the *Dyskolos*, where several critics have wondered about the relation of the farcical ragging of Knemon to the carefully constructed and not wholly unsympathetic portrait of the character which the play has built up : part of the answer may be given by the change of convention which comes with iambic tetrameter lines delivered to flute-accompaniment [1]. An opposite problem of convention, perhaps, is presented by the opening of the *Aspis* : how can a death in the family be comic? Clearly it would not be if the opening were handled entirely naturalistically, and without the aid of any expectations created by convention. But just as the ending of the *Dyskolos* depends for its effect in part on the tradition of farcical revel at the ends of comedies, so the opening of the *Aspis* depends in part on the long tradition of surprise openings, of teasing the audience's expectations, as Aristophanes sometimes does, before explaining the truth in a prologue speech deferred until after the opening scene. It is consistent with this tradition, perhaps, that the first event should be a spectacle, that of the procession of the old paidagogos carrying his master's shattered shield ; the captives and booty ; and—the diversifying element—Smikrines in attendance. One wonders if the effect was heightened by the implied comparison with tragic spectacle, and it may be worth remembering that according to a scholiast on Euripides, *Orestes* 57, productions of the play of which he knew were augmented at the beginning by a procession in which Helen arrived with the spoils of Troy. The campaign narrative is also something with a respectable literary pedigree, and therefore a conventional value as well as its actual one : it is interesting that its counterpart in the

[1] See, for instance, *Dyskolos of Menander*, pp. 283 ff. ; W. G. Arnott, *Greece and Rome* 10 (1963) 140 ff. ; A. Schäfer, *Menanders Dyskolos : Untersuchungen zur dramatischen Technik* (Diss. Berlin, publ. Meisenheim am Glan, Hain, 1965 = *Beitr. z. klass. Phil.*, Heft 14), 66 ff.

Amphitruo (203 ff.) is treated in the grand martial manner by Plautus, and that Menander's narrative concerns the affairs of an ordinary soldier, not a king, and as seen by the elderly ex-tutor—which is the best approach to a military servant that can be made by this not-very-well-off young man who has become a mercenary in order to provide a decent dowry for the sister in his care. If consistently elevated in tone, or consistently natural, the opening would lack comic effect. Its working depends partly on the audience's built-in willingness to be surprised at the start of the play, and partly on the blend of conventions, with the added interest of the insincerity of Smikrines' grief gradually showing through and turning at the end of the scene into naked but disclaimed self-interest. The prologue-speaker, Tyche, makes sure that true perspective is given, and she herself reminds the audience of the force of convention when she begins: 'If something unpleasant really had happened to them, I, a goddess, would not have been likely to follow': she would, perhaps, have removed herself from the scene of misfortune and grief, like a latter-day Artemis leaving the deathbed of Hippolytus (1437 ff.).

Beginning from what seemed to me some of the most obvious conventional material in comedy, I have tried to show something of the complexities which arise when we try to translate our observations of recurrent themes and stage-practices and so on into an evaluation of dramatic effect. The overall result, if one can dare to suggest it from such a miscellany of instances, is that in Menandrean comedy it is not so much what happens that matters, but how. That is why, I suppose, plot-summaries such as one reads in text-books often sound so extremely trivial and novelettish. It is, of course, easy to say that his subject-matter is too closely confined to love-affairs and family relationships, but, whether rightly or not, these *oikeia pragmata* are things which a large part of mankind are preoccupied in for a large part of their time, and it is not necessarily reprehensible to weave them into amusing and sometimes, perhaps, genuinely enlightening patterns. What seems to distinguish the use of conventions such as we have been considering is not only the novelty that is given them by an unconventional selection, or an unconventional context, but the general sense of design which calculates the ingredients of comic appeal with an instinct both for immediate effect and for dramatic structure. Worlds apart in many ways, Menander might almost have said of himself with Pindar: καιρὸν εἰ φθέγξαιο, πολλῶν πείρατα συντανύσαις / ἐν βραχεῖ, μείων ἕπεται μῶμος ἀνθρώπων, ἀπὸ γὰρ κόρος ἀμβλύνει / αἰανὴς ταχείας ἐλπίδας.

DISCUSSION

M. Turner : I should to congratulate M. Handley on giving not lists or bare statements of theatrical practice, but a psychological interpretation of the significance and utility of conventions founded on an analysis of the complex way in which the audience would take them. A question which immediately springs to mind is whether all members of the audience would share the same preconceptions, sensitivity and education. Would they all or even many of them make the comparison of the κόρη in *Dysk.* 189 ff. with Electra in Euripides (a fairly recondite allusion)? On this point more needs to be said.

I also wish to comment on the most interesting analysis of Menander's timing of new developments or the entry of new characters just before the end of an act (i.e. the break marked ΧΟΡΟΥ). The ancient theatre lacked a curtain. Therefore the climax of an action could not easily come at the break itself. In fact the climax seems to come shortly before such breaks. If one takes the house-doors of the houses on a Greek stage as answering in function to a curtain, one can trace great play made with them. Characters wish to call someone else from inside (the mocking scenes, such as *Dysk.* 456 ff. and often) ; or to obtain entry ; or to shut someone out, as in *Samia* 398 Austin, where Demeas' ἕσταθι to Chrysis, her maids and her baby, attempting to come in again, makes the whole scene graphic and visual. But the " climax " is followed by Niceratus' discovery of Chrysis ; and when he gives her shelter in his own house, the way is paved for further development. In the interval supposed by ΧΟΡΟΥ the action may continue to ferment, and repetition of narrative of events to the audience can be avoided.

M. Ludwig : Ich möchte an zwei von Herrn Turner angeschnittene Probleme anknüpfen.

1. Das Publikum, das Menanders Komödien sah, hatte natürlich keinen einheitlichen Charakter. Es liesse sich grob in zwei Klassen einteilen : auf der einen Seite der naive Zuhörer, der dem Bühnengeschehen unmittelbar mit Auge und Ohr folgt und sich von ihm gefangen nehmen lässt. Das ist sicher die Mehrzahl und in manchen Augenblicken sind es vielleicht alle. Dieser « naive » Zuhörer achtet nicht auf die Konventionen der Bühne, ist sich ihrer im Augenblick nicht bewusst (selbst wenn er sie sich bei anderer Gelegenheit klar machen kann). Er bangt immer wieder um den Helden und ist über das Ende im Ungewissen, obwohl er bisher in jedem anderen Stück den Helden am Ende hat siegen sehen. Er geniesst und würdigt nicht das Spiel zwischen traditioneller Konvention und dem eigentümlichen neuartigen Dreh, den der Dichter dieser Konvention abgewonnen hat. Dieser Blickwinkel ist der des erfindenden Dichters und der des reflektierenden, distanzierten, kritischen Zuhörers. Das sind zwei verschiedene Weisen, dem Stück zu folgen. Das Stück kann deshalb auch vom Philologen in verschiedenen Ebenen interpretiert werden. Vielleicht kann man sagen, dass dem « naiven » Zuhörer die Konvention als solche immer erst dann bewusst wird, wenn der Dichter ausdrücklich mit dieser Konvention spielt, sich über sie lustig macht, sie durch Illusionsbruch als Konvention herausstellt. Die beiden Interpretationsebenen sind möglich, obwohl der « naive » und der « kritische » Zuhörer selbst Abstraktionen sind, und in Wirklichkeit diese Typen kaum rein vorkommen.

2. Der Hinweis auf die Einleitung einer neuen Entwicklung am Ende eines Aktes durch Auftreten einer neuen Person oder durch Einführung eines neuen Motivs war sehr interessant. An sich bedeutet die Bildung von Akten ja gerade die Bildung von Szenengruppen mit einer relativ geschlossenen Handlungseinheit. Die Tendenz geht hier in Richtung auf gesonderte, in sich geschlossene Teile. Aber es bleiben Teile eines Ganzen. Es bedarf einer Verbindung, eines Bindeglieds zwischen ihnen. Die Einführung eines neuen Moments kurz vor Aktende stellt ein Gegen-

gift gegen die Grundtendenz, die überhaupt zu den « Akten » führte, dar. Das « neue Moment » darf allerdings nicht zu stark hervortreten, da die an sich gewünschte Einheit der einzelnen Akte dadurch zerbrochen würde und der dramaturgische Gewinn wieder verloren ginge. Diskontinuität und Kontinuität müssen im richtigen Verhältnis zueinander stehen. Wie behandelt im übrigen Euripides seine « Aktschlüsse »? Findet sich auch bei ihm ein « neues Moment » in Herrn Handleys Sinn öfters vor dem Ende eines Episodion?

M. Handley : The point about different sorts of people in the audience is a very good one, and there are, I think, a number of passages in Comedy which suggest that dramatists were well aware of the different demands and capacities they tried to satisfy. One might think of the parabasis of Aristophanes' *Clouds* (518 ff.) on intellectual comedy and low comedy, or of the jokes about the audience and their books in the *Frogs*, which Professor Turner has discussed (*Athenian Books* ... (London H. K. Lewis, 1952) 21 ff.) ; but I have in mind especially Aristophanes' appeal to both σοφοί and ἡδέως γελῶντες in the same play at *Eccl.* 1155 ff. I should like to suppose, but cannot claim to prove, that we have a similar appeal in Menander in the fragment *POxy* 1239 (cf. *BICS* 12 (1965) 62 n. 22 ; C. Corbato, *Studi Menandrei* (Trieste, 1965) 89 ff.).

Granted, however, that successful comic poets must have known their audience's capabilities quite well, it remains worth asking how far a given comic effect can appeal to different levels of appreciation at once.

M. Turner : In connection with Herr Ludwig's reference to Euripides, it is interesting to note that the phrase ἐν ἡμέρᾳ μιᾷ (which, in effect, means " during the course of this play ") had certainly been used in this sense in tragedy, and especially in Euripides (so e.g. *Hippol.* 21-2, and see also the references collected by E. W. Handley on *Dysk.* 186 ff.). Apart from *Dysk.* 187 and 864, we can now trace this phrase in Menander in *Karche-*

donios, *POxy* 2654,8 ; *Samia* 709 ; *Aspis* 417 (where it is quoted from Karkinos).

M. Questa : La relazione del collega Handley ed il dotto intervento del collega Ludwig hanno toccato punti molto importanti. Il problema del ' distacco ' di un poeta, specialmente di un poeta di teatro, rispetto ai mezzi tecnici da lui stesso usati (mi riferisco specialmente a questioni d'intreccio e di determinate ' scene fisse ', come quelle di ἀναγνωρισμοί) si pone per molti autori comici. Aristofane fa già ironia sull' ἀρχαία al principio delle *Ranae* ; senza dubbio Menandro ironizza la tipologia della νέα, per es. negli ἀναγνωρισμοί del *Sikyonios* (v. 357 sgg.) e della *Perikeiromene* (v. 349 sgg.). Anche Plauto (per es. *Bacch.* 1072-1075) scherza su quanto il pubblico si aspetta da lui ed egli a bella posta non gli dà (' scena del trionfo ' nelle *Bacchides*, probabilmente ' anticipata ' — con doppia ironia in tal caso — nel grande *canticum* di Crisalo : v. 925 sgg.). La consuetudine di ironizzare su certe situazioni fisse riappare in un tipo di teatro che si ricollega a temi della νέα attraverso la *palliata* : l'opera buffa del Settecento italiano e del primo Ottocento (fino a Rossini), senza escludere il *Singspiel* (*Entführung* e *Zauberflöte* di Mozart, per es.). Ironia musicale non ha risparmiato Rossini (*Turco in Italia ; Italiana in Algeri*), la cui azione può sembrare une curiosa *contaminatio* di *Rudens* [' motivo del naufragio '] e *Miles* o ... *Elena* di Euripide [motivo della ' fuga per mare '] ; III atto del *Barbiere*, dove Figaro ironizza, quasi *extra fabulam*, su Rosina e il Conte che non si decidono a fuggire : ironia, qui sul ' tema della fuga ', e siamo ancora al *Miles* ! Ma, come ha detto giustamente Ludwig, queste sono riflessioni di dotti, di filologi, o considerazioni che solo uno spettatore colto può fare, e anche questi le fa *dopo* lo spettacolo, quasi sempre. Ad ogni modo è certo che quanto più un pubblico è colto e soprattutto abituato a un certo tipo di spettacolo, tanto più *avverte* intuitivamente (anche se non coglie subito razionalmente) il gioco allusivo e, diciamo, la strizzata d'occhio del poeta. Occorrerà distinguere, quindi, tra pubblico e pubblico. Per es. il pubblico di Terenzio (o meglio, quella minoranza di spettatori per cui sembrano idealmente scritte le commedie di quest'autore) è presupposto come perfettamente cosciente della fissità di personaggi e scene nella *palliata* (cfr. *Heaut.* 35 sgg. ; *Eun.* 19 sgg. ed il passo dell' *Andria* che citiamo appresso). E se non il suo pubblico, certo Terenzio ha quello che vorrei definire ' possesso strutturale ' degli intrecci della νέα-*palliata* (cf. *Andria* vv. 9-12 : *Menander fecit Andriam et Perinthiam : qui utramuis recte nouit, ambas nouerit* ecc.). Terenzio adattò al teatro latino commedie greche quando la produzione teatrale greca era conclusa da un pezzo, ed egli ha sì di fronte a sé una miniera ricchissima da scavare, ma una miniera che non si accresce più (lo stesso atteggiamento è già sensibile nel prologo dei *Captiui*, vv. 53 sgg. e non è senza preannunci nella stessa νέα : vedi quanto osservato dal Bianco in *Riv. cult. class. e med.* 1961, p. 91 sgg. a proposito del fr. 60 dei *GLP* di Page). Terenzio ha il senso delle ' funzioni ' dei personaggi nella trama di una commedia. Non a caso ho citato una parola tipica degli studi di Wladimir Propp sulla fiaba (*Morfologia della fiaba*, trad. ital., Torino 1967). Partendo dalla fissità degli intrecci e delle « funzioni » di questo o quel tipo comico (*leno*, *uirgo*, *meretrix*, *senex*, *adulescens*, in tutte le specificazioni a noi note da Polluce) possiamo da un lato intendere il ' distacco ' e l'' ironia ' dei poeti stessi, dall'altro tentare uno studio in base a nuovi criteri — quello delle ' funzioni ' appunto — capace di sviluppi interessanti, anche in rapporto alla questione della *contaminatio*. Come primo esempio, e sia pure nell'ambito di altro genere letterario, si veda l'esame strutturale che F. della Corte ha fatto del tema del *perfidus hospes* (*Mélanges Renard*, Bruxelles 1969, pp. 312-321).

Mlle Dedoussi : When the cook first comes in with Parmenon at *Samia* 282 ff. Austin, his entry has the effect of lowering the emotional temperature. To Demeas this is annoying, it causes delay in unfolding of the action, but it brings the traditional joke of the cook to the audience. Similarly the traditional jokes connected with the parasite at *Dysk.* 58 ff. are annoying to Sostratus, but amusing to the audience.

M. Handley : In the *Dyskolos* the delay is dramatically important because the play is about a young man in a hurry.

Mlle Dedoussi : When the cook enters the second time, at *Samia* 356 Austin (where Wilamowitz refused to allow him to participate in a three-cornered exchange), the delay prolongs the tension of the scene.

M. Turner : In this case the " delay " has a different dramatic effect. Demeas is a man in inner torment, and he cannot finish what he is determined to do, to expel Chrysis.

M. Handley : One has the impression that even when Menander does use traditional motifs to introduce a character (as with Chaireas in the *Dyskolos*) he still uses them very economically. Comparison with fragments of other poets suggests that such economy was far from universal among his rivals and contemporaries. Yet caution is necessary here, for our fragments lack context, and we cannot be sure how far their detail was functional or how far its apparently greater scale was in place in a whole play. Latin analogies (for example, the cook scene in Plautus, *Pseudolus* 790-893) give some sort of control and suggest that traditional material was sometimes developed for its own sake much more than in the Menander we have so far. But there is always the possibility of expansion by the Latin poet to reckon with, even the possibility of interpolation by Greek actors before the version was made (cf. *Menander and Plautus* 17 f. with n. 18, quoting Webster, *Hellenistic poetry and Art* 263, 268 ff.).

M. Sandbach : The cook of comedy is traditionally loquacious, and is often listened to with apparent respect by the slave who has hired him. Menander has hinted at the loquacity in *Samia* 287-292 Austin, and in the phrase ἱκανὸς γὰρ εἶ λαλῶν κατακόψαι πάντα πράγματα. Parmenon, however, is not ready to let this cook have his way, but cuts him short and stands up to him (292-5). He is pleased with himself and his self-satisfaction is further expressed by the orders he shouts back to Chrysis through the door when he returns from depositing the basket. Is « banging » the door as he comes out another sign of insolent self-confidence? Then the ground opens under his feet when Demeas says " Listen now, Parmenon : there are a lot of reasons why I don't want to give you a flogging." The scene with the cook is part of the preparation for this reversal.

M. Ludwig : Mich würde noch eine andere Frage interessieren. Im Blick auf die Bühnenhandlung, also auf das, was auf der Bühne geschieht, könnte man die Szenen einteilen in Sprech- und in Handlungsszenen. « Sprechszenen » wären solche, in denen Personen auf die Bühne kommen und miteinander sprechen ; « Handlungsszenen » würden Szenen genannt, in denen die Personen darüber hinaus eine sichtbare Handlung vollbringen (z.B. ein Opferschaf auf die Bühne tragen). Das Ursprüngliche und bei Aristophanes vorherrschende dürfte die « Handlungsszene » sein. Eine längere Folge reiner Sprechszenen wird dem Publikum leicht zu langweilig. Welchen Raum nehmen eigentlich Sprechszenen in diesem Sinn bei Menander ein? Wie umfangreich sind, proportional gesehen, die Handlungsszenen? Wobei die Handlungsszenen natürlich noch mehr oder weniger äussere Handlung enthalten können. Liesse sich von einer Konvention sprechen, immer wieder eine Handlungsszene einzufügen? Oder sind die Sprechszenen immer noch in der Minderheit? Wieviel äussere Bühnenhandlung konnte das Publikum bei Menander erwarten? Wie verhalten sich Sprache und Aktion? War mindestens ein lebendes Tier auf der Bühne sozusagen ein *must* für ein ordentliches Stück?

M. Handley : Professor Ludwig's distinction might work out interestingly if we began from the special case of exposition scenes at the beginning of a play, where one may pass quite suddenly from the dialogue of exposition to the beginning of part of the action, indeed to some particular piece of stage action which would qualify the scene as a *Handlungsszene* in Professor Ludwig's sense. Exposition can however include another element, that of display ; and I have sometimes used the term " display-scene " for places where this element is prominent. It is of course very prominent in the opening of Plautus, *Mostellaria* ; and in the " make-up " scene, which displays both situation and characters, verbal as well as visual effects are present.

Curculio and *Dyskolos*, where the opening is similar in design, both have their element of " display ", but—from the point of view of advancing the action—these two plays both proceed more economically than *Mostellaria*. A difference, of course, is that the serenade-motif of *Curculio* lends itself to visual display rather more readily than the opening of *Dyskolos*.

So far as exposition is concerned, the distinction we have in mind seems to be like that of Terence in the *Adelphoe* (23 ff.) : *senes qui primi uenienti partem aperient / in agendo partem ostendent.*

M. Reverdin : La première représentation moderne du *Dyskolos*, à Genève, en 1959, a mis en valeur les scènes où l'action tient plus de rôle que la parole. Cette représentation a été donnée en plein air, dans un théâtre construit à l'antique, avec cavea, gradins, parodoi, scène, la nature — en l'occurrence le parc de la Grande-Boissière — formant le fond du décor. Les photographies qui illustrent la plaquette publiée en souvenir de cette « première » (*Cnémon le Misanthrope*, *comédie de Ménandre*. Version française de la première représentation moderne, accompagnée de la musique de scène et de quinze planches hors texte. Editions du « Journal de Genève », 1960) permettent de se rendre compte de ce qu'elle fut.

Orner un autel de guirlandes, faire paraître devant les spectateurs des animaux, dresser les tables d'un banquet, rassembler les convives, tout cela prend du temps, constitue en fait des sortes d'intermèdes entre les scènes parlées; les uns correspondent aux intermèdes choraux; d'autres se situent à l'intérieur d'un acte.

Premier éditeur, Victor Martin a eu le privilège d'être invité à la plupart des représentations du *Dyskolos* dans les années qui ont suivi sa publication. Une chose l'avait frappé : certaines de ces représentations, en particulier celle d'Epidaure, en 1960, n'avaient duré qu'à peine plus d'une demi-heure. Chœurs et scènes d'action sans paroles ou avec peu de paroles avaient été sacrifiés. La pièce sortait défigurée de cette expérience qu'on est tenté de qualifier de barbare; réduite aux dimensions d'un lever de rideau, elle portait peu sur le public.

Ailleurs, au théâtre romain d'Augst, par exemple, où le *Dyskolos* fut joué, en allemand et en vers, avec masques, à l'occasion du cinquième centenaire de l'Université de Bâle, la représentation avait duré près de deux heures, et le succès n'avait été été que moyen: le rythme de l'action était visiblement trop lent.

Parlant de ces diverses expériences, Victor Martin, pour autant que je me souvienne de mes conversations avec lui, insistait sur la fonction à ses yeux importante des scènes qui font appel aux yeux du spectateur plus qu'à ses oreilles ou à son entendement. Un cuisinier poussant devant lui une brebis récalcitrante, pour peu qu'il soit un bon acteur, tient plusieurs minutes le public en haleine, sans prononcer mot, et la pièce, agrémentée de tels spectacles, les uns grotesques, les autres attendrissants, devient plus familière et plaît davantage.

J'ai le sentiment qu'en lisant Ménandre, nous devons laisser notre imagination créer ces images sans lesquelles la pièce manquerait de couleur. Le texte, d'ailleurs, nous y invite constamment : nous sommes enclins à nous laisser griser par la langue ; n'oublions pas pour autant les « tableaux vivants », ni les intermèdes lyriques, qui donnaient à la comédie son équilibre.

Mme Kahil : En ce qui concerne l'action scénique des comédies de Ménandre, par opposition aux monologues narrant un événement, les documents figurés me semblent bien indiquer que certains épisodes, que l'on croyait jusqu'ici racontés, étaient en fait joués. Je pense particulièrement à la scène par laquelle s'ouvraient les *Synaristosai*. La mosaïque de Mytilène, (Pl. II) et celle de Dioscouridès, (Pl. III), nous apprennent qu'une réunion de trois femmes, prenant leur petit déjeuner, et auprès desquelles se tenait un petit serviteur muet, devait probablement constituer le début de la pièce. Je reste persuadée que cette scène muette était vue par les spectateurs avant que les personnages ne se lèvent et ne se mettent à parler. Il en va de même, je crois, pour le *Phasma* ; la scène d'apparition de l'acte II, figurée sur les mosaïques de Mytilène, ne me paraît pas être une scène simplement *racontée* : elle était vraisemblablement représentée : la jeune fille apparaît dans une embrasure, devant le jeune homme (qui l'a déjà vue une première fois) et devant son père (qui la voit pour la première fois). Je me rends bien compte qu'il est malaisé d'expliquer cette apparition du point de vue scénique, mais la difficulté ne me semble pas insurmontable.

Ces « tableaux vivants » avaient certainement une grande importance chez Ménandre. On peut encore citer le « setting » du *Dyskolos* (qu'on pourrait rapprocher de certaines fresques de Boscoreale, avec un petit sanctuaire rupestre, entre deux maisons) : certainement très pittoresque, il devait frapper les spectateurs.

Par ailleurs, M. Handley a eu raison d'attirer notre attention sur la scène du *Dyskolos* où l'animal récalcitrant fait son apparition comique sur scène.

M. Sandbach : If the scene at the table was represented on the stage in *Synaristosai*, the actors need not have walked on to take their seats in the tableau vivant. Although there was no curtain, there may have been screens behind which they took up their position and which were removed by stagehands at the beginning of the play. Dover is inclined to believe that Socrates' pupils, supposedly indoors, were so concealed in the *Clouds* (ed. lxxv) and the same device might have been used at the beginning of that play to reveal Strepsiades and his son in bed.

M. Questa : La scena del banchetto poteva senz'altro essere rappresentata sulla strada. È una convenzione scenica accettata dal pubblico antico, che rende possibili situazioni come quella della *Mostellaria* (vv. 157-312), in cui la *toilette* della cortigiana Filematio, assistita dalla vecchia ancella Scafa, avviene sulla strada, per l'appunto, sì che il giovane innamorato Filolachete può vederla e commentarne le fasi. Aggiungo che, pur non essendo la cosa decisiva, il titolo a participio presente (Συναριστῶσαι) fa pensare che la scena del banchetto venisse in qualche modo presentata direttamente agli spettatori.

M. Turner : Mme Kahil has put her case very eloquently, and I must admit the dramatic impact of a version of Menander's *Phasma* in which the movements through the passage and through the wall could be presented visually to the audience. But the case for the other view seems to me too strong. It is based on

1. The positive difficulty of showing in *front face* a passage giving communication through a party wall between two houses, the two (front) doors of which face the audience. A very special surrealist perspective would be called for if one supposed the party wall somehow to be folded outwards, so that it could be presented in a central position to the spectators. The idea that such a passage could be so shown is, however, held by Professor Webster not to be inconceivable, since the passage was disguised as a *shrine* ; and it is a shrine which occupies the central position in the scenic arrangement of the *Dyskolos*.

2. Demeas' monologue at the opening of *Samia* Act III tells of what he heard from his " hiding-place " in the ταμιεῖον of his house : he is describing what took place indoors in the house. It would not have been beyond the wit of Menander to arrange these events out of doors in the street. But their natural locale is indoors, and it seems to me that Menander accepts that fact and in his virtuoso description of the scene writes so as to make the audience accept a description as entirely natural. Similarly in the new, as yet unpublished, Oxyrhynchus fragments of *Phasma*, I would see a *report* (i.e. not a visual presentation) of the way the young man used the opportunities of being alone with the girl

who came innocently through the concealed passage. I have argued the whole case in *GRBS X* (1969), pp. 307 sqq. "The *Phasma* of Menander."

M. Ludwig: Mir scheint, dass in den *Synaristosai* / *Cistellaria* eine spezielle Schwierigkeit besteht. In der plautinischen *Cistellaria* ist das *prandium* vorbei, als der Text beginnt (es wird im Praeteritum von ihm gesprochen). Das Dioskorides-Bild stellt die drei Frauen beim ἄριστον dar. Das stellt zunächst vor die Alternative: a) erst Plautus hat das Mahl von der Bühne weggenommen und ins Praeteritum versetzt, bei Menander begann das Stück mit dem Mahl; b) Plautus hat den Beginn des Stückes in dieser Hinsicht nicht verändert. Die Wahrscheinlichkeit spricht für b) (M. Turner weist bestätigend hin auf Men. fr. 385 Koe). Wie ist dann aber das Dioskorides-Bild zu verstehen? Ich dachte früher an die Darstellung einer Szene, die so nie auf der Bühne zu sehen war, die man sich aber als der sichtbaren Bühnenhandlung vorausgehend vorstellen konnte. Dioskorides hätte dann etwas gemalt, was nur in der Imagination des Zuhörers existierte, evoziert durch die rückweisenden Worte des gesprochenen Szenenbeginns. Oder wie soll man sich sonst das Dilemma erklären? Bot der Beginn des Stückes einen Blick ins Innere des Hauses, wo die Frauen beim ἄριστον sassen, worauf sie herauskamen (Mme Kahil)? Oder war der Tisch auf der Strasse vor dem Haus aufgebaut, zu Beginn nahmen die Frauen dort Platz, nach einem dialoglosen Bild standen die Frauen auf und sprachen miteinander (M. Handley)? War das Bild der speisenden Frauern zuerst durch eine Kulisse verdeckt, die zu Beginn entfernt wurde (M. Sandbach)? Das Präsens Συναριστῶσαι (M. Questa) ist wegen Περικειρομένη nicht entscheidend.

Mme Kahil: On vient d'évoquer des difficultés d'ordre scénique. Pour la scène des *Synaristosai*, il n'y a en fait pas de difficulté si on admet que la scène se passe à l'intérieur de la maison et qu'on la voit par la *porte ouverte* (et c'est l'hypothèse que me paraît suggérer la présence de bandes de couleurs dégradées sur la mosaïque de Dioscouridès) ; si la scène se passe dans la rue, la difficulté n'est pas insurmontable (comparons la scène de toilette de la *Mostellaria*) ; mais on doit, en ce cas, expliquer le cadre de la mosaïque de Dioscouridès. Pour le *Phasma*, le problème est plus complexe ; il faut que le *passage* entre les deux maisons, passage par lequel apparaît la jeune fille, soit visible pour les spectateurs. Mais je ne crois pas que, pour la scène hellénistique, cette difficulté ait été insurmontable. Enfin, à l'appui de ma thèse, je voudrais insister sur le fait que les tableaux de Mytilène semblent bien reproduire des moments de *l'action* et même des événements capitaux (c'est le cas pour la *Samia* et les *Epitrepontes*, que nous connaissons le mieux), et non pas des épisodes rapportés.

M. Handley : The inference that the meal was finished when the play began in Menander's version, as well as in Plautus's, will be strengthened if we admit the genuineness of the line ascribed to the beginning of *Synaristosai* by Thierfelder, *Studi Urbinati* n.s. B 35 (1961) 113 ff. (= adesp. 421 K. ; Meineke V. 1, p. ccclxix) :

ἐγὼ μὲν ἠρίστησα, νὴ τὴν Ἄρτεμιν,
μάλ' ἡδέως.

I should still think it possible that the play began with a silent tableau of the end of the meal. By some modern standards it would be odd for actors to walk on and sit down at a table at the opening of a play—but hardly odd to an audience whose theatrical traditions included (for instance) the opening of Euripides, *Orestes*, where, before the play begins, two actors have to appear and take up their positions at the outer door of the palace : Orestes lying asleep, Electra watching over him.

M. Questa : Ancora una domanda : un personaggio, uscito per andare all'agorà, può essere supposto, dopo la fine di un atto, come ritornato a casa senza riapparire sulla scena ?

M. Handley : This is a difficult question to answer in general terms. But judging from extant plays in Greek, the convention appears to be that when characters are seen to leave the stage, they re-enter by the same way, equally visibly to the audience. If, in Menander, it were necessary for someone to enter or leave unseen, one would expect some explanation or motivation to be provided, as is done, for instance, in Plautus, *Mostellaria,* when Tranio makes it clear that he has taken the two young men and their girls out by a back way (1044 ff.), so that the appearance of Callidamates from a wing entrance at 1122 is no surprise. At *Aspis* 391 ff. Austin, one might suppose that Daos has (notionally) taken the *apographe* to Smikrines during the act break, but a likelier explanation is that Smikrines is speaking ironically.

M. Wehrli : Die Behandlung des Überkommenen in einer so stark traditionsgebundenen Kunst wie derjenigen Menanders ist geeignet, Grenzen und Möglichkeiten der Neugestaltung aufzuweisen. Von der neuen Funktion, welche Menander den formellen Bühnenkonventionen zuwies, ist gesprochen worden. Er stellte sie in den Dienst einer dramatischen Geschlossenheit, welche die Episodenhaftigkeit der früheren Komödie weit hinter sich lässt. Ebenso erhielten mimenhafte Nebenfiguren wie der Koch oder der Sklave eine neue Sinngebung, sei es im Dienste der dramatischen Spannung oder des Kontrastes zu den differenzierteren Hauptfiguren, soweit sie mehr als eine Konzession an ein schlichtes Publikum waren. Die Untersuchung all dieser Neuerungen stellt uns vor die Frage, wie weit sie die gattungsgeschichtliche Kontinuität wahrten. Bekanntlich hat die antike Theorie Menander, genauer gesprochen die Dichter der Nea überhaupt an Euripides angeschlossen, was den Tatbestand allerdings zu sehr vereinfacht. Die tragischen Einflüsse mochten noch so stark sein, vollständig haben sie die Komödie sich selbst nie entfremdet. Travestierende Anleihen machten bei der Tragödie schon die Dichter der Archaia, und mit Reminiszenzen an sie treibt noch Menander ein heiteres Spiel. Dem Vorbild ihrer früher vollendeten Schwestergattung verdankt die Komödie, dass sie zu formeller Einheit gelangte, und ohne zahlreiche motivische Anregungen von deren Seite wäre die thematische Vertiefung ihres Spiels nicht denkbar. Wie sich durch alle Verwandlungen hindurch die Hauptelemente der alten Komödienstruktur mit dem Liebesmotiv behaupteten, wäre in Einzeluntersuchungen darzulegen.

M. Handley : We can probably agree, in general, in finding several kinds of influence from Tragedy in New Comedy. Some elements, perhaps beginning from parody, seem so much at home in comedy by Menander's time that they can be thought of as part of the fabric. But the fifth-century tragedians continue to be influential in Menander's time, I take it, because the classics were still produced on the stage, read, and studied, and could give poets fresh inspiration. Thus tragedy itself gives one kind of continuity. An interesting set of illustrations of this process comes from what we could call " dramatic devices "—for instance, the formulae by which a chorus is introduced, and the similar sets of words which characters use when they " stand aside " to watch some new development (Fraenkel, *De med. et nov. com.* (Göttingen, 1912) 71 ; *Beobachtungen zu Aristophanes* (Rome, 1962) 24). None the less, the fact that the famous messenger speech in the *Orestes* was, by Menander's time, part of a dramatic tradition did not prevent him from making fresh use of it as background for his major speech in *Sikyonios.* As to discontinuity (still within the same field of tragic influence on comedy), it is perhaps worth reminding ourselves of the contrast between Aristophanes' recognition scene in the *Knights* (1232 ff.) and any of Menander's recognition scenes. The effect of an author's use of tragedy can be quite different even when the ingredients are similar ; and in a wider context too the gradation of difference within continuity is surely one of the fascinations of the study of motif.

Mlle Dedoussi : Paratragoedia, as we know it in Aristophanes, is not be found in Menander. The relation of tragedy to the comedy of Menander, and the use of tragedy by Menander are rather complicated. In the case of recognition scenes, like the one in the *Perikeiromene*, there is no *paratragoedia*. The subject of this scene comes from tragedy and with the subject comes the tragic vocabulary also. The scene is serious and the tone is elevated by the poetic vocabulary.

M. Wehrli: Welche Urbanität und Verinnerlichung der Ethopoie Menander in der *Samia* erreicht hat, lässt sich aufs schönste dem Monolog des Demeas ablesen. Die Worte, mit denen er seiner Reue Ausdruck gibt, haben in den erhaltenen Texten der neuen Komödie nicht ihresgleichen. Motivgeschichtlich gesehen, ist der Auftritt aus der Umgestaltung einer herkömmlichen Szene hervorgegangen, denn Demeas macht sich selber zum Vorwurf, was sonst der Alte von seinem Widersacher zu hören bekommt.

II

WALTHER LUDWIG

Die plautinische *Cistellaria* und das Verhältnis von Gott und Handlung bei Menander

DIE PLAUTINISCHE *CISTELLARIA* UND DAS VERHÄLTNIS VON GOTT UND HANDLUNG BEI MENANDER

Die Zufälle der handschriftlichen Überlieferung haben der *Cistellaria* des Plautus übel mitgespielt. Von der *Vidularia* abgesehen ist keine Komödie des sogenannten Varronischen Corpus in so schlechtem Zustand auf uns gekommen wie dieses Stück. Es hatte einst rund vier Quaternionen eines spätantiken Pergamentcodex gefüllt. Die beiden mittleren waren dann jedoch anscheinend herausgefallen, ein Verlust, den der Schreiber des Archetypus unserer mittelalterlichen Handschriften so wenig bemerkte, dass er an den letzten Vers des ersten Quaternio den ersten des vierten unmittelbar anschloss. Im *codex vetus Camerarii* (B) sind dann sogar Teile der beiden Verse zu einer einzigen Zeile verbunden. Der Umstand, dass Alcesimarchus, der jugendliche Liebhaber, in beiden Szenen auf der Bühne war, dürfte mitgeholfen haben, dass der Schreiber die Lücke übersah. Die Folge davon war, dass nicht nur in allen Handschriften der Palatinischen Rezension die 15 Verse des vorderen mit den 45 Versen des hinteren Szenenfragments verbunden sind, auch die Drucke der Renaissance übernahmen das Ergebnis dieser « Kuppelei » und Giovanni Battista Pio etablierte das künstliche Produkt als erste Szene des zweiten Aktes für alle Editionen der Folgezeit. Bis ins 19. Jahrhundert hat kein Philologe auch nur vermutet, dass diese « Szene » zwei Texte miteinander vereinte, die in Wirklichkeit ein grosser Handlungsabstand voneinander trennte. Über den textlichen Problemen der einzelnen Verszeilen hatte man die dramatischen und bühnenmässigen Zusammenhänge völlig aus dem Auge verloren. Dabei wurde man an sich durch eine nicht geringe Zahl indirekt überlieferter Fragmente, die sich in der überlieferten Fassung nicht fanden, geradezu mit der Nase darauf gestossen, dass mit der *Cistellaria* nicht alles in Ordnung sein konnte. Aber nachdem ein Scaliger erklärt hatte, diese Fragmente seien fälschlich für die *Cistellaria* bezeugt und einer anderen, unbekannten Komödie zuzuweisen, für die er den Titel *Clitellaria* in Vorschlag brachte, war dieser Stein des Anstosses beseitigt, die lästigen Fragmente fanden in den Ausgaben unter der Überschrift *Clitellaria* ihren Platz und die *Cistellaria* überdauerte als unerkannter Wechselbalg einer Komödie ohne Mittelstück.

Verwunderung erregte dann die Entdeckung des Ambrosianischen Palimpsestes durch Angelo Mai, der 1815 mitteilte, dass dieser Codex fünf Blätter aus der *Cistellaria* enthalte, deren Text sich in der gängigen Fassung nicht fände. Aber erst Theodor Ladewig, Gymnasialprofessor im mecklenburgischen Neu-Strelitz, gelang es, die Lücke im Archetypus der Palatini zwischen II, 1, 24 und II, 1, 25 (nach der Zählung der neueren Ausgaben) zu finden (*Rheinisches Museum* 3, 1845, S. 520 ff.). Unterdessen haben die Arbeiten von Studemund, Schöll und Süss sowohl den Umfang der Lücke — etwa 600 Verse — als auch die Stellen bestimmt, wo in dieser Lücke die Blätter des Ambrosianischen Palimpsestes mit insgesamt etwa 250 mehr oder weniger gut erhaltenen Versen zu plazieren sind. Der szenische Ablauf konnte wieder einigermassen rekonstruiert werden. Was zum Vorschein kam, war, was Duckworth als die menandrischste aller Plautuskomödien bezeichnet hat. Trotzdem ist sie vergleichsweise wenig beachtet geblieben. Auch die menandrische Flut im Gefolge der *Dyskolos*-Entdeckung hat daran kaum etwas geändert. Eine kommentierte Spezialausgabe existiert nicht, obwohl sie hier nötiger wäre als für viele andere römische Komödien, und die gängigen Ausgaben von Lindsay und Ernout versäumen es, zwischen den Textfragmenten den erschliessbaren Handlungsablauf kurz zu notieren, so dass dem Interessierten der Zugang zu diesem Schauspiel nicht leicht gemacht wird.

In meiner für einen weiteren Leserkreis bestimmten Neubearbeitung der Binder'schen Plautusübersetzung (erschienen im Winkler-Verlag, München 1966) habe ich deshalb die erhaltenen Fragmente durch Zwischentexte verbunden, die den Umfang der verbleibenden Lücken, die Abfolge der Szenen und den vermutlichen Fortschritt der Handlung angeben. Eine eingehendere Analyse des szenischen Aufbaus und der Struktur des dramatischen Vorgangs war dort nicht möglich. Beides versuche ich im ersten Teil meines Vortrags hier zu geben. Ein besseres Verständnis der *Cistellaria* und der ihr zugrunde liegenden *Synaristosai* kann aber auch einen Beitrag zu einem allgemeineren Problem liefern, das seit der Entdeckung des *Dyskolos* wiederholt erörtert wurde, ich meine die Frage nach der Funktion der Götter, nach dem Verhältnis von Gott und Handlung bei Menander. Dazu wurden in letzter Zeit teilweise meines Erachtens irrige Auffassungen geäussert, die sich in der Regel speziell auf die Verhältnisse in *Dyskolos* und in der *Aulularia* bezogen. Es scheint mir möglich zu sein, hier noch eine erhebliche Klärung zu erzielen, wenn die verschiedenen in dieser Hinsicht relevanten Menanderkomödien zusammen gesehen und die zum Teil unscharfen dramaturgischen Begriffe genauer bestimmt werden. Beides wird im weiteren Verlauf dieses Vortrags versucht.

I.

Ort der Handlung ist in der *Cistellaria* Sikyon, und die dortigen Dionysien spielen im Stück auch eine besondere Rolle. Wir kennen sie aus Pausanias als eine jährliche Nachtfeier, bei der die Bilder des Dionysos Bakcheios und des Lysios in einer Prozession unter Fackelglanz und Hymnengesang von einem « Kosmeterion » genannten Gebäude zum Dionysostempel getragen wurden. Bei einem solchen Dionysosfest hatte einst — 18 Jahre vor der fiktiven Handlung der Komödie (vgl. V. 755) — ein junger Kaufmann aus Lemnos, Demipho, die junge Phanostrata vergewaltigt *vinulentus*, *multa nocte*, *in via* (159). Als diese neun Monate danach ein Mädchen gebar, liess sie es durch ihren Sklaven aussetzen, da sie von dem wieder nach Lemnos geflüchteten Vater nichts mehr gehört hatte. Das Kind fiel einer Dirne in die Hände, die es an ihre kinderlose Freundin Melaenis weitergab, unter deren Obhut das nun Selenium genannte Mädchen heranwuchs, bestimmt zur künftigen Prostituierten, die aus ihren Einkünften auch ihre alt gewordene Pflegemutter ernähren sollte. Die letzten Dionysien wurden nun für die Herangewachsene so bedeutungsvoll wie jene vor 18 Jahren für ihre Mutter Phanostrata: Melaenis war mit Selenium ausgegangen, um die nächtliche Prozession anzusehen. Dabei bekam sie der junge Alcesimarchus zu Gesicht, der ihr bis nach Hause folgte und sich *blanditiis*, *muneribus*, *donis* ihre Gunst und die Zustimmung der Melaenis erwarb (90 ff.). Es begann eine Liebesbeziehung, Alcesimarchus zog mit Selenium in ein zu diesem Zweck gemietetes Haus und versprach seiner Konkubine sogar durch einen Eid die Ehe. Sein moralisches Verhalten steht in augenfälligem Kontrast zu dem damaligen leichtfertigen und verantwortungslosen Benehmen Demiphos gegenüber ihrer Mutter, was um so gravierender ist, als es sich bei Phanostrata um ein Mädchen aus dem Bürgerstand, bei Selenium aber scheinbar um die Tochter einer Hetäre handelt. Das Dionysosfest ist der identische Anlass und Rahmen der beiden schicksalhaften Begegnungen, die infolge des gegensätzlichen Verhaltens der Männer so verschiedene Folgen hatten.

Zu dem Ort der Handlung und der Bedeutung, die das dortige Dionysosfest in ihr spielt, würde es gut passen, wenn Menander das Original für die Aufführung im Theater in Sikyon, das neben dem Dionysostempel lag, verfasst hätte. Für eine Uraufführung in Athen blieben die Sikyoniaka des Stückes funktionslos (vgl. auch die Erwähnung des

Hippodroms in V. 549 ff.). Bei einer Aufführung in Sikyon könnte man sich jedoch vorstellen, dass die Begegnung von Alcesimarchus und Selenium bei der letzten bzw. letztjährigen Dionysosprozession stattgefunden hätte. Die Aufführung selbst war natürlich auch Teil eines Dionysosfestes. Es ist unbekannt, ob sie im Zusammenhang mit dem Fest der Dionysosprozession stattfand oder zu einer anderen Zeit des Jahres. Gleichviel, die Aufführung war sozusagen das dritte für Phanostrata und Selenium bedeutsame Dionysosfest in Sikyon : sie zeigt gewissermassen in einer Verschmelzung der fiktiven und realen Zeit den Tag der Wiedervereinigung von Mutter und Tochter und zugleich den Tag der endgültigen Vereinigung des Alcesimarchus mit Selenium.

Für die weiteren Betrachtungen wird es notwendig, kurz den überlieferten, bzw. rekonstruierbaren, szenischen Ablauf des Stückes zu vergegenwärtigen. (Die beiden auf. S. 50 und 51 folgenden Schemata geben die personellen Zusammenhänge — von der Bourgoisie bis zur Prostitution — sowie den Aufbau des menandrischen Originals und den Überlieferungszustand des plautinischen Stückes in übersichtlicher Kurzfassung wieder.)

Im exponierenden ersten Akt erscheinen in der ersten Szene Selenium, die Hetäre Gymnasium und deren Mutter, welche einst Selenium gefunden und Melaenis übergeben hatte, vor dem Haus, das Alcesimarchus für sich und Selenium gemietet hatte und in das während seiner Abwesenheit die beiden Freundinnen von Selenium zu einem *prandium* eingeladen worden waren. (Die Menandermosaike von Mytilene haben uns die griechischen Namen der Figuren bekannt gemacht ; Selenium hiess bei Menander « Plangon », Gymnasium « Pythias », ihre Mutter « Philainis ». Ich werde im folgenden der Einfachheit halber aber stets die vertrauten plautinischen Namen benützen, auch wenn es um die Handlung bei Menander geht, ausgenommen bei der in der

Personal der **Cistellaria (Synaristosai)**

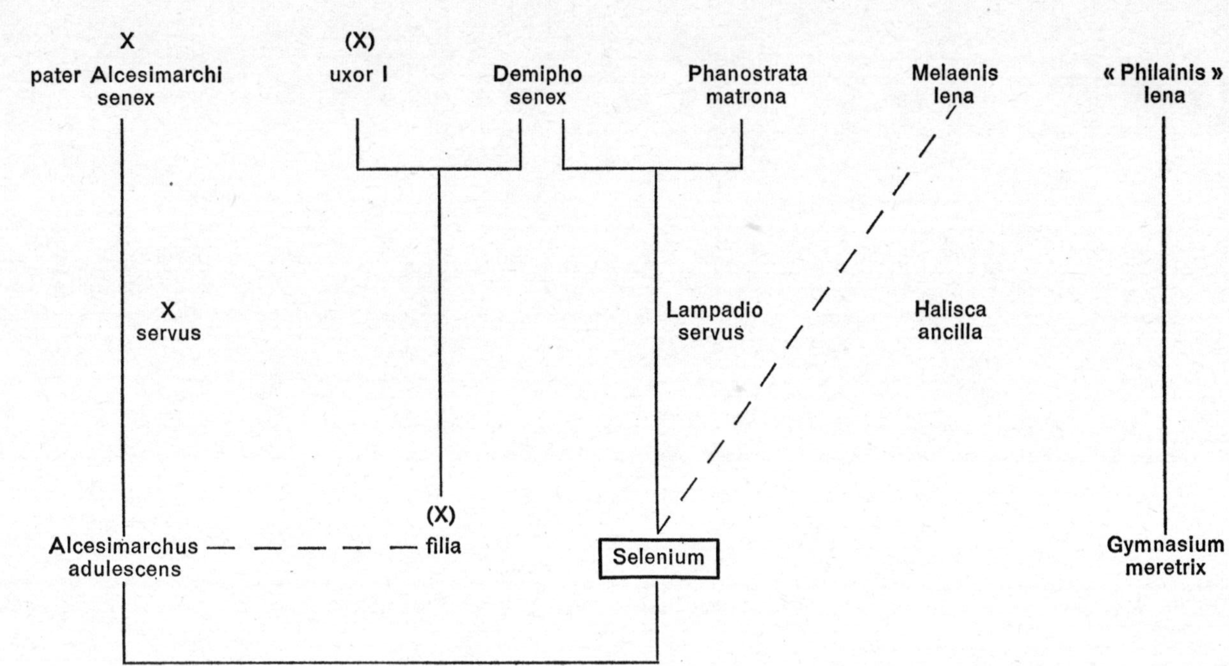

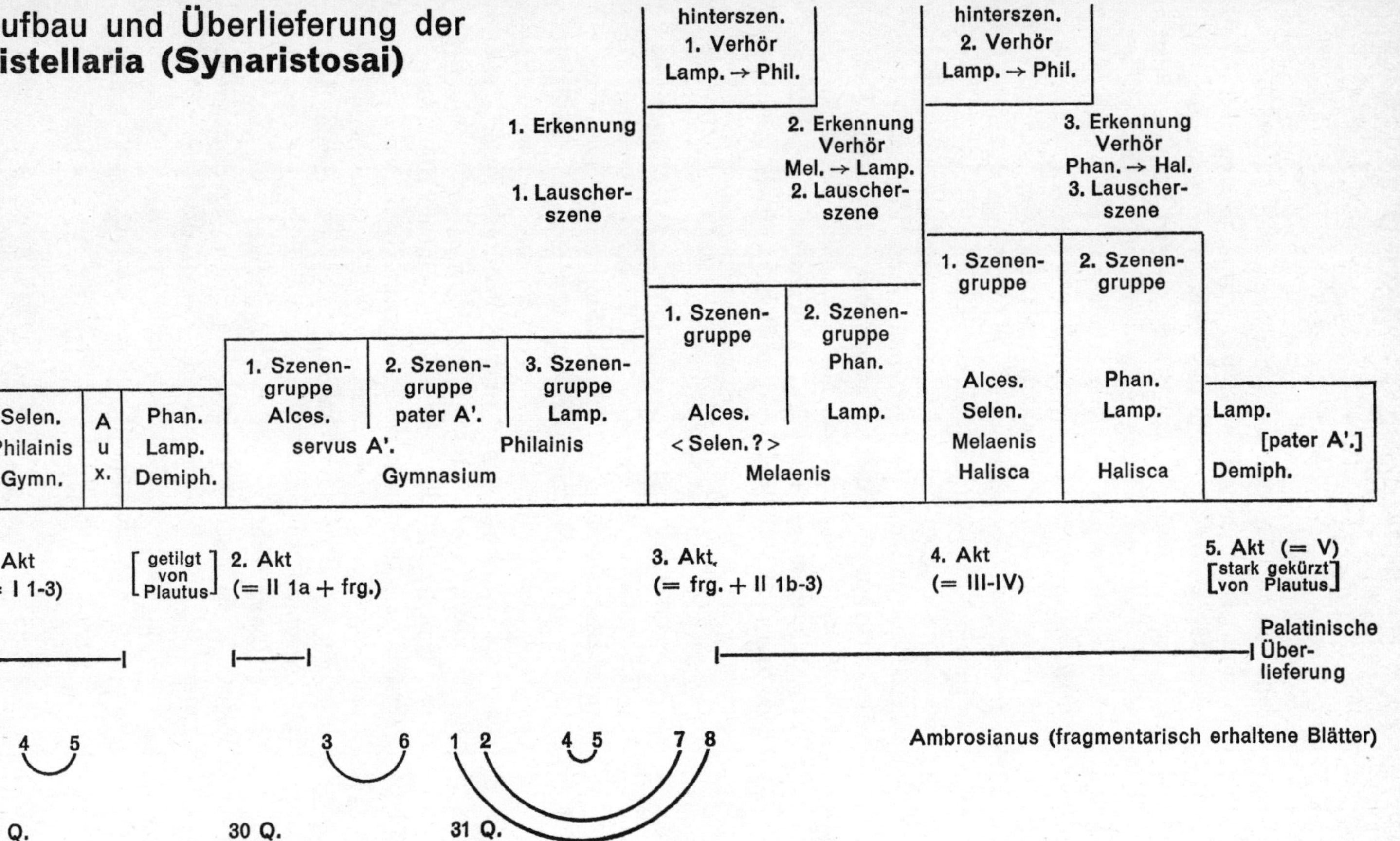

Aufbau und Überlieferung der
Cistellaria (Synaristosai)
hinterszen.
1. Verhör
Lamp. → Phil.
hinterszen.
2. Verhör
Lamp. → Phil.
1. Erkennung
1. Lauscher-
szene
2. Erkennung
Verhör
Mel. → Lamp.
2. Lauscher-
szene
3. Erkennung
Verhör
Phan. → Hal.
3. Lauscher-
szene
Selen.
Philainis
Gymn.
A
u
x.
Phan.
Lamp.
Demiph.
1. Szenen-
gruppe
Alces.
2. Szenen-
gruppe
pater A'.
3. Szenen-
gruppe
Lamp.
servus A'.
Philainis
Gymnasium
1. Szenen-
gruppe
Alces.
< Selen.? >
2. Szenen-
gruppe
Phan.
Lamp.
Melaenis
1. Szenen-
gruppe
Alces.
Selen.
Melaenis
Halisca
2. Szenen-
gruppe
Phan.
Lamp.
Halisca
Lamp.
[pater A'.]
Demiph.
1. Akt
(= I 1-3)
[getilgt von Plautus]
2. Akt
(= II 1a + frg.)
3. Akt
(= frg. + II 1b-3)
4. Akt
(= III-IV)
5. Akt (= V)
[stark gekürzt von Plautus]
Palatinische
Über-
lieferung
4 5
3 6
1 2 4 5 7 8
Ambrosianus (fragmentarisch erhaltene Blätter)
29 Q.
30 Q.
31 Q.

plautinischen Überlieferung nicht benannten Mutter Gymnasiums.) Selenium teilt nun in I, 1 ihren Gästen mit, dass sie auf Geheiss der Melaenis das Haus verlassen muss, nachdem der Plan einer Heirat des Alcesimarchus mit einem anderen Mädchen ruchbar geworden ist (sein Vater dringt auf eine standesgemässe Partie). Selenium bittet nach dem *prandium* ihre Freundin Gymnasium, das Haus zu betreuen, bis Alcesimarchus zurückkehrt. Die Heldin des Stückes, die am Ende, als *ingenua* erkannt, mit Alcesimarchus die Ehe eingehen wird, erscheint gleich zu Anfang in einem Gegensatz zu ihrer bedenklichen Umgebung. Die Vorstellung ihres Charakters und die Verdeutlichung ihres Verhältnisses zu Alcesimarchus sind die dramaturgisch wesentlichen Funktionen der Eröffnungsszene. Selenium hat sich nicht der Prostituiertenmoral angepasst, in deren Sinn sie *stulta* ist (60, 62, 76, 86). Sie liebt Alcesimarchus aufrichtig und hat sich nur ihm hingegeben (*nec pudicitiam imminuit meam mihi quisquam alius*, 86). Er seinerseits hat ihrer « Mutter » eidlich versichert, sie zu heiraten (96) und lebt mit ihr in einem eheähnlichen Verhältnis in einem Haus, über das sie sogar die Schlüsselgewalt hat (111). Die Bindung des reichen jungen Mannes an das Mädchen aus dem Hetärenmilieu ist damit enger und verbindlicher als in irgendeinem anderen bekannten Stück der Nea (es geht über die Verhältnisse in der *Andria* noch hinaus, wo Pamphilus die Glycerium auch *pro uxore* hält). Umgekehrt konnte auch der scheinbare Bruch seines Versprechens Selenium nicht gegen Alcesimarchus einnehmen (*utut erga me est meritus, in cordi est tamen*, 109), sie liebt ihn weiter und verlässt nur unter dem Zwang ihrer aufgebrachten Mutter das Haus — voll Trauer, so dass sie nicht einmal mehr auf ihr Äusseres achten mag (111 ff.). Nachdem sie nach rechts und Gymnasium ins Haus abgegangen ist, gibt Philainis, allein gelassen, die Herkunft der Selenium, soweit sie sie kennt, preis (ihr Abgangsmonolog ist in der Überlieferung als eigene Szene abgetrennt : I, 2).

Anschliessend teilt die Prolog-Gottheit Auxilium die verbleibenden, nur ihr bekannten expositionellen Zusammenhänge mit (= I, 3). Die Gottheit berichtet auch, dass Phanostrata den Mann aus Lemnos, der sie einst vergewaltigte, später geheiratet hat. Demipho ist nach dem Tod seiner ersten Frau, die ihm eine Tochter hinterliess, wieder nach Sikyon gekommen. Er und Phanostrata wohnen im zweiten Bühnenhaus. Auxilium informiert ferner darüber, dass die Suche nach der verschollenen Tochter durch Aussendung des Sklaven (Lampadio) in Gang gesetzt worden ist. Man hat wohl mit Recht vermutet, dass die plautinische Prolog-Gottheit auf eine menandrische « Boetheia » zurückgeht. Die Personifikation der göttlichen « Hilfe » scheint von Menander ad hoc erfunden zu sein. Er hat damit einen Aspekt des Göttlichen abstrahiert: βοήθειαν konnten die Götter allgemein den Menschen zuteil werden lassen (Pl. *Tim.* 77 *a*), insbesondere hatten Apollo und Artemis, die Dioskuren und Herakles, daneben später auch Tyche das Beiwort βοηθόος (Kall. *H.* 3, 21 ff., 153 f.; 4, 27; Theocr. 22, 23; Kaibel ep. 1039, 1040; vgl. auch Ov. *Met.* 15, 553 *deus opifer* von Aesculap, *CIL* XIV 3539 *Fortuna opifera*). Es fragt sich, was Menander zu seiner Namengebung verleitete, d.h. ob seine Boetheia im Stück irgendeine « helfende » Funktion hatte, die ihren Namen rechtfertigte und begründete.

Plautus konnte diesen Begriff ausser durch *auxilium* auch durch *ops* « übersetzen ». Was liess ihn dem Neutrum den Vorzug geben gegenüber *Ops*, welche bereits eine alte römische Kultgöttin war? Vielleicht wollte er gerade eine abstrakte, ad hoc erfundene Personifikation, wie die menandrische Boetheia es war (dass es ein Neutrum wurde, mochte ihm witzig erscheinen), und nicht eine seinen Hörern bekannte, mit individuellen Zügen ausgestattete und durch Feste und Heiligtümer verehrte Gottheit.

Auxilium führt sich zu Anfang seiner Prologrede als *deus* ein, der besser als die geschwätzige und trinkfreudige Alte die Exposition zu geben verstehe: *nam mihi Auxilio est nomen* (154). Als «Hilfe» verhilft sie dem Römer zum *argumentum*. Das ist die einzige — scherzhafte — Motivierung für ihr Auftreten bei Plautus, die einzige Hilfe, die sie bei ihm im Stück leistet. Von einer Hilfe, die sie etwa den Personen der Handlung erweisen wollte, ist nicht die Rede. *Auxilium* verabschiedet sich von den Hörern mit einem wortspielreichen Appell zum punischen Krieg, der auch die Aufforderung *augete auxilia* enthält (200). Dem *Auxilium* ist an den *auxilia* gelegen, womit es am Ende witzig gewissermassen zum Schutzpatron der römischen Hilfstruppen wird. Die beiden Anspielungen auf den Namen verknüpfen die Figur nur sehr lose mit dem Stück, in dem sie ausserhalb der expositionellen Information keine Funktion hat. Es wird sich später zeigen lassen, dass es hierin mit der Boetheia Menanders anders bestellt war.

Nach dem Götterprolog hat Webster einen Auftritt der Phanostrata, des Demipho und des Sklaven Lampadio für das Original erschlossen. Beweisend scheint mir dafür nicht so sehr seine Hypothese, dass einer Götterrede nicht unmittelbar ein Aktschluss folgen könne, als vielmehr die von ihm ausserdem angeführten Auftrittsverhältnisse: Demipho, der im letzten Akt *ex senatu* zurückkommt (776), und Lampadio, der im Verlauf des Stückes von seiner Suche zurückkehrt, sollten zunächst einmal ihr Haus auf der Bühne verlassen. Bei der Aussendung des alten Sklaven wird Phanostrata zugegen gewesen sein. Die Eheleute werden dabei auch von der Hochzeit der Tochter aus Demiphos erster Ehe, die mit Alcesimarchus geplant war, gesprochen haben, womit dem Zuschauer alle personellen Beziehungen schon im ersten Akt klar gemacht wurden. Selenium und Phanostrata, zu deren Wiedervereinigung das Stück führen sollte, traten so zu Anfang in zwei kontrastierenden Szenen in ihrem verschiedenartigen Milieu vor den beiden Bühnenhäusern auf. Plautus hat den ersten Akt wohl aus ähnlichen

Motiven verkürzt wie den analog strukturierten ersten Akt des Originals der *Aulularia*. Dort hatte er den Auftritt des Lyconides und seines Sklaven, der dem Götterprolog vorausging, gestrichen und nur die jenem folgende Szene mit Euclio und Staphyla beibehalten. Die Verkürzung der ursprünglich dreiteiligen Exposition bringt den Zuschauer rascher in den Genuss der Handlung, wobei Plautus in beiden Fällen die wirkungsvollere Szene (das Hetärenmahl und den Auftritt des Geizhalses) stehen liess. Anstelle der gestrichenen Expositionsszene der *Synaristosai* fügte Plautus V. 180-189 in den Götterprolog ein. Für die faktische Aufklärung genügte dies.

Am Anfang des zweiten Aktes tritt Alcesimarchus von links her auf (er kommt vom Land, wo er sechs Tage auf Befehl seines Vaters hatte zubringen müssen). Während seiner Monodie, in welcher er seine unwandelbare Liebe zu Selenium bekennt, bricht die palatinische Überlieferung ab. Es folgte eine Dialogszene des Alcesimarchus mit seinem Sklaven ; dann trat Gymnasium hinzu. Alcesimarchus erfuhr vom Weggang der Selenium, geriet in Verzweiflung, erklärte in den Heiratsplan seines Vaters nicht einzuwilligen und verliess schliesslich die Bühne, um, wie ihm Gymnasium geraten hatte, einen Bittgang zu Melaenis zu machen. — Die zweite Szenengruppe zeigte Gymnasium im Gespräch mit dem Vater des Alcesimarchus, der gekommen war, um mit Selenium zu sprechen, bei der er Widerstände gegen den Heiratsplan für seinen Sohn vermutete. Er glaubte in Gymnasium Selenium vor sich zu haben, und die listige Dirne machte das Spiel mit, bis er schliesslich selbst noch ihren Reizen verfiel, wodurch — nach Demipho — auch die moralische Position des zweiten Vaters geschwächt wird. Während des Gesprächs scheint Philainis dazugekommen zu sein, der Alte musste unverrichteter Dinge abziehen. Die Kupplerin will ihre Tochter abholen, nachdem Alcesimarchus wieder in der Stadt ist. — Eine dritte Szenengruppe setzte mit dem Auftritt des Lampadio ein, der von rechts auf die Bühne kam und in einem Monolog von seiner vergeblichen Suche nach der Tochter Phanostratas, bzw. nach jener Hetäre berichtete, die er einst beobachtete, wie sie das ausgesetzte Kind aufhob. Als er schon ins Haus des Demipho gehen will, erkennt er plötzlich in Philainis die lange Gesuchte. Er folgt den abgehenden Frauen, um sie auszuhorchen. Bei Menander schloss damit der zweite Akt.

Der dritte begann mit einem neuen Auftritt des Alcesimarchus, der mit Melaenis und, so wird gemeinhin angenommen, auch Selenium wieder auf die Bühne kam. Die äussere Motivierung des Zusammentreffens ist ungeklärt (vgl. dazu Süss, *Rh. Mus.* 1938, S. 131 f. und jetzt Prof. Sandbach unten, S. 97). Der junge Mann fleht, Selenium möge wieder zu ihm zurückkehren. Selenium traut ihm nicht und geht (vgl. dazu jedoch unten S. 59). Alcesimarchus beschwört Melaenis, ihm doch ihre Tochter wiederzugeben — die palatinische Überlieferung setzt nun wieder ein —, aber Melaenis weist ihn definitiv ab und Alcesimarchus verschwindet nach verzweifelten Drohungen und Verwünschungen in seinem Haus. — In einer zweiten Szenengruppe (= II, 2-3) belauscht die auf der Bühne verbliebene Melaenis zunächst ein Gespräch des Lampadio mit Phanostrata. Der Sklave berichtet von seiner Entdeckung. Er ist der alten Philainis gefolgt, die schliesslich gestand, dass sie einst das Mädchen aufgenommen hatte. Lampadio hielt natürlich zunächst Gymnasium für die verschollene Tochter, womit diese ein zweites Mal für Selenium gehalten wurde, die Alte beteuerte jedoch, sie habe das Kind an eine Freundin weitergegeben. Nur deren Namen hat sie noch nicht verraten. Lampadio will sie nun zu einem zweiten Verhör aufsuchen. Als Phanostrata in ihr Haus gegangen ist, tritt Melaenis hervor und spricht Lampadio an. Sie fragt nun ihrerseits Lampadio aus, der nicht ahnt, warum sie an der Sache so interessiert ist, und beschliesst nach seinem Abgang, da sie erkannt hat, dass Phanostrata Seleniums wirkliche Mutter ist, ihr Geheimnis selbst preiszugeben, um so der anscheinend unabwendbaren Entdeckung zuvorzukommen und sich wenigstens einigen Dank zu erwerben. Sie verlässt die Bühne, um Selenium zu holen.

Der vierte menandrische Akt entspricht Akt III und IV der konventionellen Einteilung. Melaenis kommt mit Selenium und ihrer Sklavin Halisca zurück. Letztere trägt das Kästchen mit den *crepundia*, anhand derer Selenium identifiziert werden soll. Die glückliche Lösung scheint unmittelbar bevorzustehen. Doch der dritte Auftritt des Alcesimarchus unterbricht den erwarteten Verlauf. Er eilt aus seinem Haus und will sich, verzweifelt über den Verlust seiner Geliebten, in sein eigenes Schwert stürzen. Der tragische Ton schlägt jedoch sogleich um. Selenium fällt ihm in den Arm, und er lässt sie nicht mehr los, sondern entführt sie alsbald in sein Haus. Melaenis folgt den beiden; Halisca verliert im Tumult das Kästchen. — Die zweite Szenengruppe (= IV, 1-2) setzt mit einem neuen Auftritt des Lampadio ein. Sein zweites Verhör der Philainis blieb ohne jeden Erfolg. Er ist weiter vom Ziel entfernt als im vorigen Akt. Da entdeckt er das Kästchen auf der Strasse und will es sich aneignen, ohne jedoch seine Bedeutung zu ahnen. Erst Phanostrata erkennt es wieder. Das Rätsel, wie es auf die Strasse gekommen ist, löst sich, als Halisca wieder erscheint, um danach zu suchen. Ihr Monolog wird von Phanostrata und Lampadio belauscht, das anschliessende Gespräch der drei führt zur Entdeckung der Identität Seleniums. Der Akt schliesst mit dem Abgang von Halisca und Phanostrata ins Haus des Alcesimarchus. Lampadio verliess im Original hier wohl die Bühne, um Demipho auf dem Markt zu suchen.

Im fünften Akt (= V, 1) kommt Demipho zu seinem Haus zurück und wird von Lampadio über das Vorgefallene unterrichtet, der ihn schliesslich auch in das Haus des Alcesimarchus schickt. Plautus hat diesen Akt derart verkürzt, dass er nur noch aus etwa einem Dutzend Versen besteht. Im Original trat vielleicht noch der Vater des Alcesimarchus auf, und die Komödie endete mit der offiziellen Verlobung der neugefundenen Tochter und dem obligaten Festmahl, das dann gewissermassen das konträre Pendant zu dem ἄριστον der Hetären am Anfang des Stückes gebildet hätte. Ein anderes Bindeglied zum ersten Akt bildet die Figur des Demipho, sofern dieser dort bei Menander sein Haus verlassen hat. Bei Plautus kommt er *ex senatu* zurück, ohne dass diese Senatssitzung für das Stück irgendeine Funktion hätte. Plautus benützt sie nur als eine scherzhafte, römisch kolorierte Motivierung für die Abwesenheit des Demipho, auf die er nicht weiter eingeht. Es ist denkbar, dass Menanders Demipho etwas anderes zu tun hatte. Am Anfang des Stückes steht die Heirat des Alcesimarchus mit Demiphos Tochter unmittelbar bevor (97); naheliegend ist es deshalb, dass Demipho im Original im ersten Akt sein Haus verliess, um auf dem Markt ein paar Einkäufe für das Festmahl der Verlobung zu tätigen. Als er damit zurückkehrt, kann er in der Tat die Verlobung einer Tochter feiern, aber es ist unterdessen nicht mehr diejenige, an die er zuerst gedacht hatte. Während er sich ahnungslos auf dem Markte aufhielt, haben die Ereignisse um Selenium einen immer schnelleren Verlauf genommen und die Situation entscheidend verändert. Die beiden anfangs auf verschiedene Töchter gerichteten Handlungslinien sind am Ende vereint. Die Konstellation erinnert sehr an die *Andria*, wo Pamphilus am Ende nicht die zuerst für ihn vorgesehene legitime Tochter des Chremes, sondern Glycerium zur Frau erhält, mit der er schon lange im Konkubinat gelebt hatte und die sich schliesslich als zweite Tochter des Chremes erwiesen hat. Die andere Tochter des Chremes ging in der menandrischen *Andria* (im Gegensatz zu Terenz!) ebenso leer aus wie die zweite Tochter des Demipho in den *Synaristosai*.

Schnitte dürfte Plautus übrigens auch in der ersten Szenengruppe des vierten Aktes (= III) durchgeführt haben. Sowohl der Auftritt der Melaenis mit Selenium und Halisca, als auch die Aiax-Attitude des Alcesimarchus und der Umschlag der Situation wirken epitomiert. Dagegen lässt der rekonstruierbare Umfang des zweiten Aktes bei Plautus eine erhebliche Erweiterung desselben gegenüber Menander vermuten. Die Verszahlen für die einzelnen Akte waren bei Plautus ca. 205 für den ersten, ca. 540 für den zweiten, ca. 160 für den dritten, 143 für den vierten und 14 Verse für den fünften Akt. Auch wenn man bei Menander keine gleich grossen Akte annehmen darf, diese Diskrepanz geht über das bei ihm Übliche sicher hinaus ; und Plautus, der den ersten, vierten und fünften Akt kürzte, dürfte dies am ehesten durch Zutaten im zweiten wettgemacht haben. Schon die Monodie des Alcesimarchus in II, 1 trägt Züge plautinischer Erweiterung. In den Dialogen der gewitzten Dirne Gymnasium mit Alcesimarchus und seinem Vater wird der römische Dichter dann ebenso in seinem Element gewesen sein wie bei der Erzählung Lampadios über seine Suche in allen Freudenhäusern der Stadt. Es entsprach seiner Art, wenn er die derbkomischen auf Kosten der sentimentalen Szenen verstärkte.

Es soll an dieser Stelle jedoch noch auf einen problematischen Punkt in dem entworfenen Bild des szenischen Ablaufs aufmerksam gemacht werden. Es ist der Auftritt der Selenium, die nach allgemeiner Annahme in V. 449-462/3 auf der Bühne sein soll. Dagegen erheben sich (worauf mich mein Frankfurter Kollege Wolf Steidle in einem Gespräch freundlicherweise hinwies) mehrere gewichtige Bedenken. In der Begegnung zwischen Alcesimarchus und Melaenis sucht dieser den Rat zu befolgen, den ihm Gymnasium in V. 301 ff. gegeben hatte : *ad matrem eius devenias domum, expurges, iures, ores blande per precem eamque exores, ne tibi suscenseat.* Selenium hat in dieser Bittszene keine vorbereitete oder irgendwie notwendige Funktion. Darüber hinaus stört ihr Verhalten in dieser Szene den Eindruck, den der erste Akt von ihr hinterlassen hatte. Ihr kühl und schnippisch abweisendes Wesen wird teils auf Verstellung, teils auf den Befehl der Mutter zurückgeführt. Aber ist es denn möglich, dass dieselbe Selenium, die Gymnasium einschärfte : *nolito acriter eum inclamare (utut erga me est meritus, in cordi est tamen), sed, amabo, tranquille : ne quid, quod illi doleat, dixeris* (109 ff.) und die vor Kummer nicht mehr fähig war, auch nur auf ihr Äusseres zu achten (111 ff.), jetzt, wo Alcesimarchus ihr gegenübersteht und sie mit flehentlichsten Worten bestürmt, zu ihm zurückzukehren, ja ihr sogar ein *supplicium*, eine widergutmachende Gabe nach ihrer Wahl, verspricht (vgl. Enk zu *Merc.* 991), keine anderen Worte für ihn findet als *valeas . . . nil moror*, dass sie auf sein Anerbieten patzig überhaupt nicht eingeht *(at mihi aps te accipere non lubet)* und sogar noch mitleidlos seinen Schmerz geniesst *(volup est neque tis misereri decet)* ? Ist das Mädchen, dessen edle *stultitia* die Anfangsszene eingeprägt hatte, überhaupt fähig, so « kalt und herzlos » zu sein, dass es einer Gymnasium alle Ehre machen würde ? Ja, darf sie als künftige bürgerliche Ehegattin sich überhaupt so verhalten ? Nicht die geringste Schwierigkeit schliesslich ergibt ihr Abgang. Sie soll nach V. 462/63 verschwinden, aber eine Motivierung wird nicht kenntlich und, was noch schlimmer ist, ihr Weggang macht auf Alcesimarchus so wenig Eindruck, dass er das Gespräch mit Melaenis weiterführt, als ob nichts geschehen sei, und auch diese nimmt in keiner Weise auf eine so deutliche Willensäusserung ihrer Tochter Bezug.

Diese Schwierigkeiten rechtfertigen gewiss die Frage, auf Grund welcher Textstellen man überhaupt zu der Annahme eines Auftritts der Selenium in V. 449 ff. gekommen ist. Da im *Ambrosianus* auf fol. 247r (V. 449-465) ihr Name selbst nicht auftaucht (eine Szenenüberschrift ist nicht überliefert), schienen in erster Linie wohl durch V. 451 f. drei

Personen, Alcesimarchus, Melaenis und Selenium, gefordert: *Germana mea sororcula! Repudio te fraterculum. / Tum tu igitur, mea matercula! Repudio te puerculum* (Leo, *fraterculum* A). / Beide Anreden lassen sich jedoch auch auf Melaenis beziehen. Zur Sitte solcher Anredeformen vgl. Hor. *ep.* I, 6, 54 f. *frater, pater adde; ut cuique est aetas, ita quemque facetus adopta* und Kiessling-Heinze zur Stelle. In der *Andria* 292 sagt die sterbende Chrysis, als sie Glycerium in die Obhut des Pamphilus gibt, zu ihm, zu welchem sie *nicht* in einem erotischen Verhältnis steht: *si te in germani fratris dilexi loco.* Umgekehrt kann *germana soror* als einschmeichelnde Anrede bei einer weiblichen Person wie Melaenis gelten. Gegenüber der geliebten Selenium wäre sie nicht einmal sehr passend. Alcesimarchus wählt das besonders vertrauliche Deminutiv, das in der abweisenden Aufnahme durch *fraterculum* ins Lächerliche gezogen wird. Er versucht es danach noch einmal im gleichen Stil auf noch ehrerbietigere Weise. War die erste Anrede schon an Melaenis gerichtet, würde er sich dann nicht an eine andere, sondern an die neu titulierte gleiche Person richten und erführe die entsprechende Abfuhr (*tum tu igitur* lässt allerdings zunächst an eine Hinwendung zu einer neuen Person denken). Das Spiel wirkt in seinem Witz plautinisch. Von den übrigen in V. 449 ff. überlieferten Worten her wäre man sicher nicht zu der Annahme gelangt, dass Selenium am Gespräch teilnimmt. Die Herausgeber selbst schwanken, ob 453 ff. Selenium oder Melaenis mit Alcesimarchus sprechen. V. 450 *aufer manum* lässt sich, von Melaenis gesprochen, als Abwehr einer Bittgeste auffassen. In V. 456 kann auch Melaenis die Annahme eines *supplicium* ablehnen (477 schlägt Alcesimarchus es abermals vor). (Übrigens ist in V. 454 vielleicht *satis sapimus tuis periuriis* zu lesen statt ... *sapit mihi* ...; PITMIKIA [!] wurde von Studemund mehr vermutet als gelesen.)

Der Gewinn, den eine Eliminierung der Selenium an dieser Stelle nach sich ziehen würde, ist beträchtlich. Nicht nur die vorher genannten Anstösse fielen weg. Die beiden verbleibenden Szenen, in denen Selenium im Stück auftritt, zeigen eine einheitliche Charakterlinie und stehen in einem durch den Wegfall des fraglichen Auftritts sogar noch deutlicheren Kontrastbezug. In der Anfangsszene verlässt Selenium blutenden Herzens das Haus des Alcesimarchus, ihn noch immer liebend, im äusserlich vernachlässigten Gewand einer Trauernden gleich. Im vierten Akt Menanders zeigt sie dieselbe Unmittelbarkeit des Gefühls. Als sie Alcesimarchus mit dem Schwert in der Hand sieht, ruft sie spontan : *mater mea, periimus ... Alcesimarchum non vides? ferrum tenet. amabo, accurrite, ne se interemat* (639 ff.). Und Alcesimarchus, die zu ihm eilende erblickend, erklärt : *O Salute mea salus salubrior, tu nunc, si ego volo seu nolo, sola me ut vivum facis.* Mit Melaenis, die auch eingreift *(hau voluisti istuc severum facere)* will er nichts mehr zu tun haben: *nil mecum tibi, mortuos tibi sum : hanc ut habeo certum est non amittere.* Die Szene wird dramatisch ungleich wirkungsvoller, wenn Alcesimarchus Selenium hier erstmals im Stück erblickt und von ihr nicht bereits dieselbe Abfuhr erlitten hat wie von Melaenis, von der er eben deshalb nichts mehr wissen will. Auch wirken im Vergleich zu der hier zum Ausdruck kommenden Wärme seines Gefühls die Worte, die er in V. 449 ff. angeblich an Selenium richtet, schwach, und es wird noch verwunderlicher, warum er beim Weggang der Selenium nicht darüber in Verzweiflung gerät, sondern weiterredet, als ob er gar nichts bemerkt hätte. Dem Verlassen des Hauses in I, 1 entspricht reziprok am Ende der Vorgang der Entführung in dasselbe. Der Trennung steht die Vereinigung gegenüber. Alcesimarchus bringt Selenium — nach seinem Willen für immer — in sein Haus zurück, und Süss (*Rh. Mus.* 1938, S. 138) machte mit Recht darauf aufmerksam, dass hier teilweise Formen des Hochzeitsrituals anklingen (vgl. die solenne Verriegelung der Türe der Brautkammer und den spezifisch römischen Brauch der über die Schwelle getragenen Braut).

Gegen die Beseitigung der Selenium in 449 ff. scheint allerdings der Umstand zu sprechen, dass sich im *Ambrosianus* zwischen 463 f. (Alc.: ... *neque te amittam hodie, nisi quae volo tecum loqui / das mihi operam*) und 465 (Mel.: *potin ut mihi molestus ne sis*) eine anscheinend leere Zeile befindet, wie sie normalerweise einen Szenenwechsel anzeigt. Eine solche Deutung ist hier freilich nicht gesichert, weil 463 f. und 465 im Redegang zusammengehören und ein Szenenwechsel an dieser Stelle deshalb ohnehin nicht vorstellbar ist (Leo schiebt ihn deshalb auch zurück nach 462). Es ist vielleicht auch zu berücksichtigen, dass Studemund sich über die Leerzeile nicht völlig bestimmt ausdrückt (*scriptura videtur vacare*, nicht *vacat*, wie sonst öfters). Die anscheinend leere Zeile könnte also auch eine andere Ursache haben.

Wenn sie aber tatsächlich im Sinne eines Szenenwechsels und damit eines Abgangs einer zuvor anwesenden Selenium zu deuten wäre, so halte ich die Annahme, dass der Seleniumauftritt eine erst plautinische Zutat ist, für das Wahrscheinlichste. Es ist zu beachten, dass V. 449-460 motivisch eine eigentümliche Dublette zu V. 465-484 darstellen : (1) *molestus es* (449) ~ *molestus ne sis* (465), der anschliessende Witz mit dem Namen '*molestus*' wirkt plautinisch. (2) *obsecro te* (453) ~ *obsecro* (468), jeweils mit folgender schroffer Abweisung. (3) Eid und Meineid in 454 und 470 ff. ; der Vergleich des *ius iurandum amantum* mit einem *ius confusicium* wieder plautinisch. (4) *supplicium volo polliceri* (455) ~ *supplicium* (477). Vgl. ausserdem *verba dare* (458) ~ *si mihi dedisses verba* (484) und *nil moror* in 453 und 482. Unabhängig von der Frage, ob Plautus in 449 ff. Selenium auftreten liess oder nicht, dürfte demnach eine starke Erweiterung der gesamten Szene durch ihn anzunehmen sein (vgl. auch den verballhornten Schwur in 512 ff.). Es schiene mir nicht ausgeschlossen, dass Plautus in diesem Zuzammenhang, um das Bild voll zu machen, auch Selenium neu auf die Bühne brachte. Dass die römischen Dichter manchmal ein figurenreicheres Bühnenbild bevorzugten, ist bekannt. Die gleichstimmige Ablehnung des Alcesimarchus durch Melaenis *und* Selenium könnte Plautus für ein wirksames Mittel gehalten haben, um die Situation des jungen Mannes noch hoffnungsloser zu machen. Der fragmentarische Zustand unserer Überlieferung, besonders das völlige Fehlen des Szenenanfangs vor V. 449 verhindert es, hier über Mutmassungen hinauszukommen. Die Schwierigkeiten, die sich aus einem Selenium-Auftritt in 449 ff. für die Gesamtstruktur der Komödie ergeben, sollten jedoch klar gesehen werden. Es scheint mir mit der menandrischen Kunst der Charakterdarstellung jedenfalls unvereinbar zu sein, dass bei Menander ein Auftritt Seleniums in der Art, wie er für V. 449 ff. bei Plautus bislang angenommen wird, vorgelegen hat.

Von dieser Frage abgesehen, dürften alle wichtigeren Daten des szenischen Ablaufs, wie wir ihn dargestellt haben, als geklärt gelten. Im Überblick lässt sich die Komposition des Dramas deshalb dergestalt beschreiben : Die eigentliche Handlung entwickelt sich im zweiten bis vierten Akt, vor und nach denen der exponierende erste und der das Finale bildende fünfte eine mehr statische Funktion haben. Tektonisch fällt die parallele Fügung des zweiten, dritten und vierten Aktes auf. Alle drei Akte enden mit einer Erkennungsszene. Am Ende des zweiten erkennt Lampadio in der alten Kupplerin die gesuchte Frau, am Ende des dritten erkennt Melaenis in Phanostrata die Mutter der Selenium, am Ende des vierten erkennt Phanostrata in Selenium ihre Tochter. Alle drei Erkennungen sind durch vorausgehende Lauscherszenen möglich geworden. Lampadio belauscht Philaenis und Gymnasium im zweiten, Melaenis belauscht Lampadio und Phanostrata im dritten, Phanostrata und Lampadio belauschen Halisca im vierten Akt. Lampadio ist als Exponent der auf die Anagnorisis gerichteten Handlungslinie jeweils im hinteren Teil der drei Akte auf der Bühne.

Umgekehrt tritt im vorderen Teil jeweils Alcesimarchus auf (beide Rollen dürften von ein und demselben Schauspieler übernommen worden sein). Zu Beginn des zweiten Aktes kommt der betrübte Verliebte vom Land zurück. Der Hörer erfährt von seinem Entschluss, trotz der Pläne seines Vaters nicht von Selenium zu lassen und erlebt seine ihn fast zu Wahnsinn und Gewalt treibende Verzweiflung über den Verlust seiner Geliebten (ein Gegenstück zu der Trostlosigkeit Seleniums in I, 1). Zu Beginn des dritten Aktes werden wir Zeuge seines Bittgangs zu Melaenis, dessen Vergeblichkeit im schliesslich sogar zu konkreten Gewaltdrohungen gegen Mutter und Tochter hinreisst (er ist völlig ausser sich). Seine Erregung entlädt sich zu Beginn des vierten Aktes in seinem Selbstmordentschluss, welcher eine überraschende Erfüllung des scherzhaften Rates seines Sklaven in V. 250 *suspendas te* und gewissermassen eine Umkehrung seiner Drohungen gegen Melaenis und Selenium in V. 524 ff. darstellt. Das Ende dieser Entwicklung bildet die gewaltsame Entführung der Selenium.

Die beiden Schwerpunkte der drei Akte, die stufenweise Anagnorisis und die Darstellung der Liebesbeziehung zwischen Alcesimarchus und Selenium weisen auf die innere Zweisträngigkeit der Cistellariahandlung. Den einen Strang bildet die Liebeshandlung. Alcesimarchus liebt und Selenium erwidert seine Liebe nicht auf Hetärenart. Ihr eheähnliches Verhältnis, dem der Schwur des Alcesimarchus sogar eine Legitimisierung in Aussicht stellte, droht durch die Pläne seines Vaters und die Reaktion der Melaenis zerrissen zu werden. Die Liebe der beiden jungen Menschen hält jedoch der Belastungsprobe stand: Selenium kann sich innerlich nicht von Alcesimarchus lösen, Alcesimarchus willigt nicht in die Pläne seines Vaters ein und will lieber sterben als von Selenium lassen. In diesem Augenblick rettet ihn die Begegnung mit Selenium, die ihm in den Arm stürzt und die er nun nicht mehr von sich lässt. Die Entführung tritt gewissermassen an die Stelle der verhinderten Hochzeit, an deren Ritual ihre Form teilweise erinnert. Soweit es an den Liebenden liegt, ist der Schwur des Alcesimarchus und der gleichsinnige Gegenschwur der Selenium (96, 241) erfüllt. Gegen die vom Vater des Alcesimarchus und von Melaenis ausgehenden, in den Konventionen begründeten Widerstände sind die beiden Liebenden zusammengekommen, freilich ohne die Legalisierung durch eine Ehe und ohne die Zustimmung der Angehörigen, so dass ihr Bund weiterhin gefährdert und provisorisch bleibt.

Damit die Verbindung durch eine recht- und standesgemässe Heirat zwischen Bürgern besiegelt werden kann, hat sich — getrennt und unabhängig von der Liebeshandlung — die Anagnorisishandlung entwickelt. Diese war aufgebaut auf zwei Voraussetzungen. Erstens hat Demipho Phanostrata in zweiter Ehe geheiratet, und beide haben beschlossen, die einst ausgesetzte Tochter zu suchen. Zweitens ist eine Suchaktion nicht aussichtslos, da Lampadio sah, wie eine Frau das Kind aufhob. Nachdem Lampadio ausgeschickt worden war, entwickelte sich die Anagnorisishandlung in drei Schritten. Erstens erkennt der Sklave in Philainis die gesuchte Frau wieder. Sein erstes Verhör spielt sich hinterszenisch zwischen dem Ende des zweiten und der zweiten Szenengruppe des dritten Aktes ab. Philainis rückt mit einem Teil der Wahrheit heraus, aber nennt noch nicht den Namen der Freundin, der sie das Kind gegeben haben will. Der zweite Schritt geschieht, als Melaenis zufällig den Bericht belauscht, den Lampadio seiner Herrin gibt, und den Sklaven anschliessend umgekehrt selbst verhört. Sie erkennt, dass Phanostrata die Mutter ihrer Pflegetochter ist, und entschliesst sich, die Wahrheit selbst preiszugeben, um einem Verrat der Philainis zuvorzukommen. (Vielleicht war bei Menander das moralische Verdienst, das sich die Hetäre für die bürgerliche Welt erwarb, stärker betont; vgl. die Figuren der Habrotonon in den *Epitrepontes* und der Chrysis im *Eunuchos*. Plautus könnte ein solches Motiv in V. 627 ff. aus fehlendem Interesse beschnitten haben.) Das zweite Verhör der Philainis durch Lampadio — es findet wieder hinterszenisch zwischen dem dritten Akt und der zweiten Szenengruppe des vierten statt — führt wider Erwarten nicht weiter, da Philainis nun alles ableugnet. Die Fortführung der Anagnorisishandlung ist damit von Lampadio auf Melaenis übergegangen. Der dritte Schritt setzt ein, als Melaenis sich mit Selenium und der die *cistella* tragenden Halisca zum Haus der Phanostrata begibt. Sie kann ihren Vorsatz, die Identität der Selenium zu enthüllen und durch die *crepundia* zu beweisen, jedoch nicht durchführen, da Alcesimarchus dazwischenkommt und Selenium enführt. Das Abhandenkommen der *cistella* bringt die Gefahr mit sich, dass ein rechtlich einwandfreier und unzweifelhafter Beweis der Identität Seleniums in Zukunft unmöglich sein wird.

Die Liebeshandlung und die Anagnorisishandlung haben sich genau in dem Augenblick zum ersten Mal gekreuzt, als Alcesimarchus Selenium, die auf dem Weg zu Phanostrata ist, entführt. Diese Tat, mit der sich Alcesimarchus ans Ziel seiner Wünsche zu bringen glaubt, hat zugleich die ungewollte Folge, dass die Erreichung der Anagnorisis und damit das letzte Ziel der Liebeshandlung, die Eheschliessung, aufs höchste gefährdet sind. Die innere Lösung ist erreicht, aber eben dadurch ist die äussere Lösung in Frage gestellt worden. Alcesimarchus, der sich innerlich richtig verhielt, wenn er sich nicht von Selenium trennen liess, hat äusserlich das Falsche getan.

Damit sein viel beredeter Schwur doch noch *voll* erfüllt wird, *muss* Selenium als Tochter der Phanostrata und des Demipho anerkannt werden. Für das Zustandekommen der Anagnorisis ist es nun entscheidend, dass gerade Lampadio und Phanostrata es sind, die die *cistella* finden und Halisca treffen. Die unheilvolle Auswirkung des Zusammentreffens der beiden Handlungsstränge wird durch den Zufall des Fundes wieder aufgehoben.

Die an der Handlung beteiligten Personen denken dabei an göttliche Hilfe. Als Phanostrata die *cistella* erblickt, ruft sie : *di, opsecro vostram fidem ... servate nos !* (663 f.). Als sie dem Sklaven erklärt hat, das seien die *crepundia* ihrer Tochter, fragt dieser : *unde haec gentium? aut quis deus obiecit hanc ante ostium nostrum, quasi dedita opera in tempore ipso?* Phanostrata betet: *Spes mihi sancta subveni* (668 ff.). Da tritt Halisca auf: *Nisi quid mi opis di dant, disperii, neque unde auxilium expetam, habeo* (671). Nur die *Spes* stammt hier als römische Kultgottheit von Plautus, im übrigen werden diese Worte dem griechischen Original entsprechen. Was bei Menander anstelle der *Spes* stand, lässt sich nicht sagen (*Epitr.* 587 Ζεῦ σῶτερ, εἴπερ ἐστὶ δυνατόν, σῷζέ με ist funktional vergleichbar) ; *ops* und *auxilium* aber gehen gewiss auf den Begriff βοήθεια zurück.

Von hier aus fällt meines Erachtens nun entscheidendes Licht auf die Funktion der Prologgottheit in den *Synaristosai.* Die göttliche Hilfe, die Phanostrata erfleht, von der Lampadio vermutet, dass sie am Werk gewesen sein könnte, und auf die Halisca ihre einzige Hoffnung setzt, war bei Menander mehr als nur eine Vorstellung der handelnden Personen. « Boetheia » war nicht nur exponierende Prologgottheit, sondern auch in der Handlung selbst engagiert. Die göttliche « Hilfe » versprach im Prolog, sich Seleniums anzunehmen. Das dürfte in ähnlicher Art geschehen sein wie in den entsprechenden Äusserungen im *Dyskolos* (34 ff.), in der *Aulularia* (23 ff.) oder in der *Perikeiromene* (42 ff.), wo Pan, Lar und Agnoia gegen Ende ihrer Prologrede ihr Interesse und ihre Fürsorge für das Mädchen erklären, um dessen Geschick es geht. In der *Cistellaria* fehlt auffälligerweise ein analoger Passus, obwohl er vom Namen der Prologgottheit her gesehen so nahe läge und diesen eigentlich erst rechtfertigen würde. Man vermisst die Erklärung nach

V. 196, nachdem Auxilium eben von der Liebesbeziehung und ihrer aktuellen Bedrohung gesprochen hatte. Danach fehlt sowohl ein Wort, dass Auxilium Selenium helfen wolle, als auch überhaupt jeder Ausblick auf die künftige Handlung, wie er in den drei vergleichbaren Fällen in irgendeiner Weise immer gegeben wird. Plautus scheint eine solche Stelle des Originals gestrichen und statt dessen seine römischen Verse 197b-202 ans Ende des Prologs gesetzt zu haben. Aus Menander könnte nur 197a *haec sic res gesta est* stammen (vgl. *Dysk.* 45). Am Ende der Rede der Boetheia stand vermutlich (vgl. *Aul.* 37 ff., *Dysk.* 47 ff.) die Auftrittsankündigung von Personen der folgenden Szene, die Plautus, wie vorher besprochen, ganz tilgte. Es ist nicht mehr sicher auszumachen, ob die Erklärung der Boetheia, dass sie Selenium helfen wolle, einfach aus technischen Gründen im Zusammenhang mit der Tilgung der folgenden Szene wegfiel (vielleicht war sie mit der Auftrittsankündigung zu eng verbunden), oder ob Plautus diese Stelle bewusst wegliess, um über die künftige Handlung nichts auszusagen. Das erstere halte ich für wahrscheinlicher, jedenfalls war es, wie die *Aulularia* zeigt, kein Prinzip des Plautus, Ankündigungen des Handlungszieles zu unterdrücken.

Die Konsequenz jener Streichung ist jedoch offenkundig. Erstens ist der Zuhörer nicht ausdrücklich darüber informiert worden, ob er annehmen darf, dass die Geschichte für Selenium und Alcesimarchus am Ende gut ausgeht (obwohl das für einen erfahrenen Theaterbesucher natürlich vom *argumentum* her als ausgemacht gelten konnte). Die Spannung des nicht distanziert reflektierenden Zuhörers wird durch dieses Nichtwissen zweifellos erhöht. Zweitens ist keinerlei Erwartung auf ein späteres Eingreifen des Gottes in die Handlung erregt worden. Die Gottheit wird dadurch völlig auf die Funktion, das *argumentum* zu exponieren, beschränkt und aus einer aktiven Verbindung mit der Handlung gelöst. Auxilium hilft nur noch dem Hörer. Wenn dieser dann später

V. 663-671 hört, hat er deshalb keinen Anlass, die von den Personen auf der Bühne ins Gespräch gebrachte göttliche Hilfe aus der Erinnerung an die Prologrede des Auxilium zu interpretieren.

Anders bei Menander, sofern es richtig ist, dass Boetheia sich zu ihrer Hilfe für Selenium bekannt hatte. Da ist es das von der göttlichen « Hilfe » oder, so liesse sich auch sagen, vom helfenden Göttlichen sanktionierte Ziel der Handlung, dass Selenium, die sich moralisch auch im Hetärenmilieu als *ingenua* bewährt hat, zu einer Heirat mit Alcesimarchus gelangt. Die beiden Teilhandlungen (Liebe und Anagnorisis) waren auf dem besten Weg gewesen. Das Ziel ist in greifbare Nähe gerückt, als Alcesimarchus es unwissend aufs äusserste gefährdet. In diesem entscheidenden Moment kommt alles wieder dadurch ins Lot, dass die richtigen Leute das verlorene Kästchen finden. Wenn angesichts dieses wundersamen Zufalls Lampadio fragt, ob denn ein Gott das Kästchen absichtlich zur rechten Zeit ihnen vor die Haustür gelegt hat, so wird der Zuhörer diese Frage in Kenntnis der Handlungszusammenhänge und in Erinnerung an den Fingerzeig, den Boetheia im Prolog gegeben hatte, positiv beantworten können : in der Tat hat da ein Gott die Hand im Spiel gehabt, nicht so konkret freilich, wie der Sklave es meint ; das scheinbar zufällige Zusammentreffen selbst geschah διὰ θεοῦ. Und wenn Halisca ausspricht, dass nur noch die Götter ihr *helfen* können, so weiss der Zuhörer, dass die göttliche *Hilfe* in einem weiteren Sinne und zu einem wichtigeren Zwecke bereits erfolgt ist.

Bei Menander sah der Zuschauer hinter die Ereignisse. Die Prologrede der Boetheia machte ihn fähig zu einer Deutung der Geschehenszusammenhänge und zu einem Urteil über die Aussagen der Personen in Hinsicht auf den Anteil des Göttlichen an der Handlung. Bei Plautus sieht der Zuschauer auf die Ereignisse. Es kommt darauf an, was, nicht warum etwas passiert. Die Handlung hat eine Tiefendimension verloren. Das dürfte damit zusammenhängen, dass der Zuschauer Menanders Personen auf der Bühne sieht, mit denen er sich identifizieren kann, da es Leute aus seiner Stadt sind und ihre Schicksale auch ihm begegnen können. Deshalb ist ihm auch an einem Begreifen und einer Deutung des Geschehens gelegen. Plautus dagegen schreibt für ein Publikum, das sich einmal ansehen will, was sich *Athenis Atticis* oder anderswo bei den tollen Griechen an Spannendem und Aufregendem begeben hat. Es ist — überspitzt ausgedrückt — nicht das Leben des Zuschauers, das sich hier spiegelt, sondern das Leben der anderen, das in buntem und unterhaltsamem Wechsel vor ihm vorüberzieht.

II.

Natürlich hat Plautus Elemente der Deutung nicht absichtlich beseitigt, sie konnten nur, da er auf sie nicht eigens achtete, bei ihm einmal unter den Tisch fallen. Weit mehr als in der *Cistellaria* sind sie im Prolog der *Aulularia* stehen geblieben. Ich habe das Verhältnis des Lar zur Handlung der *Aulularia* in einem früheren Aufsatz analysiert (*Philologus* 1961), möchte aber hier noch einmal auf dieses Problem zurückkommen, da unterdessen neben Stimmen der Zustimmung auch Einwände laut geworden sind, die, wie ich meine, die Verhältnisse unzutreffend beurteilen und zum Teil Grundsätzliches verfehlen.

Armin Schäfer hat sich in seinem wichtigen Buch über *Menanders Dyskolos* (1965) teilweise kritisch mit meiner Analyse auseinandergesetzt; ich bedauere, dass ich unsere Differenzen nicht mehr mit dem leider so früh Verstorbenen selbst diskutieren kann.

Meine Interpretation nahm ihren Ausgang von zwei « Vorverweisen » auf die künftige Handlung, die in der Rede des Lar enthalten sind : *eius honoris gratia feci thensaurum ut hic reperiret Euclio, quo illam facilius nuptum, si vellet, daret.* (25 ff.)

... *eam ego hodie faciam ut hic senex de proxumo sibi uxorem poscat. id ea faciam gratia, quo ille eam facilius ducat qui compresserat.* (31 ff.). Ein Missverständnis Schäfers lässt sich leicht bereinigen. S. 99, Anm. 2 erklärte er, es würden « nicht zwei Vorverweise wirklich existieren », der eine « Vorverweis » sei « im wirklichen Sinn ein Rückverweis », wovon « man sich leicht am Gebrauch der Tempora überzeugen » könne (« *faciam* in V. 31, aber *feci* in V. 26 »). Natürlich habe ich nicht den geschehenen Fund des Schatzes als Vorverweis bezeichnen wollen (das ist ein Rückverweis), sondern die in dem anschliessenden Finalsatz gegebene Perspektive.

Der wesentliche Einwand Schäfers geht jedoch gegen einen Teil meiner daran angeschlossenen Handlungsanalyse. Ich interpretierte (S. 53), dass der Gott den Schatz zur Mitgift für Phaedria bestimmt hat. Euclio durfte ihn finden, *quo illam facilius nuptum dare posset, si illam nuptum dare vellet* (so die Auflösung des brachylogischen Finalsatzes). Es wird sie leichter verheiraten können, weil er ihr nun eine Mitgift mitgeben kann. « Dass er das Gold für sich behalten könnte, daran ist hier nicht gedacht, da es ... eine nicht juristisch aber doch moralisch begründete Pflicht für ihn war, seine Tochter nach Vermögen auszusteuern » (eine *indotata* bekam dies in ihrer neuen Sippe zu spüren). Dagegen Schäfer (S. 98) : « Der Gott, der Euclio kennt, kann unmöglich erwartet haben, Euclio werde sich ohne Widerstreben in seine Pläne fügen, und wenn ihm eines sicher sein musste, dann dies, dass Euclio niemals den Schatz als Mitgift verwenden werde. Ein göttlicher Plan, der den Geiz des Euclio nicht in Rechnung gesetzt hätte, kann nie bestanden haben ». Schäfer spricht hier von Kenntnissen und Plänen des Gottes, wie er später sagt, in Anlehnung an meine angebliche Ausdrucksweise, da es nicht seine « wirkliche Absicht » sei, « dem Prologgott die Kenntnis des späteren Spielverlaufs zuzuschreiben und uns zu fragen, was er während des Spiels hinter den Kulissen treibt, da der Dichter von alledem nichts sagt». Er wolle allein den «Ablauf der *Aulularia* aus ihren eigenen Voraussetzungen, so wie sie der Gott angegeben hat», verstehen.

Das im letzten Satz erklärte Vorhaben teile ich völlig. Wir dürfen dem Gott keine Kenntnisse und Pläne zuschreiben, die er nicht äussert, bzw. durch seine Äusserungen impliziert. Deshalb muss die Interpretation des Prologs sich genau an die Aussagen des Lar halten und präzisieren, welche Erwartungen durch sie beim Hörer erweckt werden. Der Gott hat zuerst erklärt, Euclio sei *pariter moratum ut pater avosque huius fuit* (22). Dann kommt er in einem neuen Abschnitt seiner Rede auf die Tochter zu sprechen und rühmt die täglichen Spenden, die sie ihm darbringt. Ihr zu Ehren hat der Lar Euclio den Schatz finden lassen. Denn er sollte seine Tochter leichter verheiraten können, wenn er es wollte. Damit eröffnet der Gott eine ganz bestimmte Perspektive auf die künftige Handlung. Die Mitgift ist der Dank für das Wohlverhalten der Tochter gegenüber dem Lar. Es ist von der allgemeinen Lebenserfahrung her einsichtig, dass ein Vater seine Tocher leichter verheiraten kann, wenn er über eine Mitgift verfügt. Die Vorstellung bleibt ganz im allgemein Üblichen und berücksichtigt nicht die besonderen individuellen Verhältnisse bei Euclio und den Freiern der Phaedria. Aber es wäre völlig falsch zu argumentieren, dass der Gott doch wissen und berücksichtigen müsse, dass Euclio wegen seines Geizes nicht so handeln wird, wie jeder andere Vater handeln dürfte, und dass weder Megadorus noch Lyconides den Anreiz einer Mitgift überhaupt brauchen. Es geht nicht darum, was ein Gott, sofern er denn wirklich ein Gott ist, nach unserer Vorstellung wissen und erwarten muss, sondern um die Erwartungen, die er durch das, was er sagt, wirklich erweckt. Alles, was der Lar getan hat, bzw. in Hinsicht auf Megadorus noch tun will, dient dem Ziel, dass Phaedria Lyconides heiraten und den Schatz als Mitgift in die Ehe bringen wird. Aus der

Prologrede weiss der Hörer auch, dass Euclio *avido ingenio* ist. Es ist Schäfer zuzugeben, dass daraus die Spannung erregende Frage entsteht, ob Euclio gemäss der vom Lar gegebenen Aussicht mit dem Schatz verfahren wird. Das ändert jedoch nichts daran, dass er in der vom Lar hinsichtlich der Verheiratung erweckten Perspektive die natürliche und eigentlich normale Form der Handlungsentwicklung sehen wird. Der Lar hat eine Möglichkeit entworfen, die das Handeln Euclios erfüllen kann, bzw. an sich erfüllen müsste, sofern sein Geiz nicht auf irgendeine überraschende Weise interferiert.

In diesem Sinn habe ich davon gesprochen (S. 53), es lasse sich vorstellen, « wie das Stück aussehen müsste, wenn Euclio den Schatz sogleich seiner Bestimmung zuführen würde. Er würde dann seine Tochter an Megadorus mit der Mitgift verloben, nach dem Rücktritt des Megadorus käme die Mitgift an Lyconides, und das Ziel der Handlung wäre ohne Verzögerung erreicht ». Ich habe das selbstverständlich nicht, wie Schäfer mir unterstellt (S. 97), « für eine denkbare andere Variante der *Aulularia*» gehalten, «für eine Form, die ebenso hätte die ihre sein können ». Es ist auch nicht, wie Schäfer behauptet, « die Fabel eines ganz neuen Stückes ». Es ist überhaupt nicht die Fabel einer möglichen Komödie, da ihr glatter, spannungsloser Ablauf keine dramatischen Verwicklungen in sich birgt. Es ist gewissermassen die undramatische Lösung, von der sich die Entwicklung, die die *Aulularia* nimmt, differierend abhebt, die Normalerwartung, zu der die Handlung infolge von Euclios Charakter in Widerspruch tritt. Die Prologrede entlässt den Hörer mit zwei, getrennt gehaltenen, aber zueinander in einem etwas irritierenden Verhältnis stehenden Vorstellungen, mit der Kenntnis von Euclios individuellem Geiz und der Perspektive einer allgemein möglichen Handlungsentwicklung. Spannung und Reiz der *Aulularia* machen es unter anderem aus, zu sehen, wie diese beiden Dinge in der Spielhandlung miteinander in Konflikt geraten, wie Euclios Geiz die angepeilte glatte Lösung torpediert und wie am Ende doch noch das Ziel erreicht wird, das der Gott von Anfang an gesetzt hatte.

Das Stück läuft noch ganz in den Bahnen der allgemeinen Erwartung, als Megadorus sich in II, 1 zur Werbung entschliesst und sie in II, 2 ausspricht. « Dadurch dass Euclio Megadorus eine Mitgift verweigert (238), ist das Geschehen in eine andere Bahn gelenkt, auf der das ursprüngliche Ziel erst nach mannigfachen Verwicklungen erreicht werden wird » (S. 53). Schäfer opponierte : « Indem Euclio die Mitgift Megadorus verweigert, handelt er nicht gegen die Erwartung des Gottes, nicht gegen den ursprünglichen Plan des Spieles. Das Spiel nimmt hier nicht eine unerwartete Wendung » (S. 98). Aber die Kenntnis von Euclios Geiz ist im Prolog eben nicht in die Erwartung integriert worden, die der Gott über die von ihm erstrebte Handlungsentwicklung eröffnet hat. Schäfers Erwartungsbegriff ist zu wenig differenziert. Er vermengt die Handlungsperspektive nach V. 25 ff. mit der aus der Kenntnis von Euclios Geiz geborenen Frage, ob diese Handlungsperspektive sich auch so erfüllen wird. Die Verweigerung der Mitgift in V. 238 bedeutet einerseits auf jene Handlungsperspektive bezogen eine unerwartete Wendung des Stückes, andererseits eine erste Antwort auf die Frage nach dem Verhältnis des Geizes zu der in Aussicht genommenen Handlung ; eine pessimistische Erwartung in dieser Hinsicht kann sich bestätigt fühlen. Das bedeutet jedoch nicht, dass der Gott eine solche Entwicklung von Anfang an vorhergesehen und sich auf sie eingestellt haben müsste. Im Sinne dessen, was er gesagt hat, hat er Euclio eine bestimmte Handlung möglich gemacht. Dass dieser sie nicht ergreift, ist seine Entscheidung, die als solche nicht praedeterminiert war. Wie das Ziel des Gottes dennoch erreicht wird, darauf richtet sich nun die Spannung des Zuhörers.

Damit der Schatz, der seiner gottgewollten Bestimmung entzogen zu werden scheint, am Ende doch wieder eben dieser Bestimmung zugeführt werden kann, ist seine Entdeckung und Entwendung durch den Sklaven des Lyconides notwendig. Die scheinbar weiteste Entfremdung entpuppt sich in der Folge als Ursprung zur Lösung. Eine Analyse dieser Peripetie ergibt eine Reihe auffälliger Erscheinungen.

Erstens vertraut Euclio den Schatz der Fides (Pistis?) an. Er richtet an die Gottheit das Gebet, sie möge den Schatz für ihn behüten (608 ff.): *Tu modo cave quoiquam indicassis aurum meum esse istic, Fides ... vide, Fides, etiam atque etiam nunc, salvam ut aulam aps te auferam: tuae fide concredidi aurum, in tuo luco et fano est situm.* Aber es ist gerade das Gebet, das Euclio verrät. Die *fiducia* auf die Fides hat ihn getrogen. Der Sklave, der ihn belauscht hat, bittet dann seinerseits die Fides um ihren Beistand (618 ff.): *cave tu illi fidelis, quaeso, potius fueris quam mihi ... sed si repperero, o Fides, mulsi congialem plenam faciam tibi fideliam.* Euclio gelingt es zwar noch einmal sein Gold zu retten, aber sein Geheimnis ist bekannt geworden. — Zweitens hat der Sklave Euclio vom Altar Apollos aus belauscht. Dort sass er *sine omni suspicione* (606), völlig unverdächtig. Seinem Spionieren kam der Altar eben des Gottes zugute, den Euclio wenige Szenen vorher eigens um Hilfe angerufen hatte (394 ff.): *Apollo, subveni mi atque adiuva, confige sagittis fures thensaurarios.* — Drittens gelingt dem Sklaven der Diebstahl im Hain des Silvanus (Pan), dem Euclio schliesslich mehr vertraut hatte als der Fides (676): *certumst, Silvano potius credam quam Fide.* Der Sklave sieht sich von den Göttern beschenkt: *eugae, eugae, di me salvom et servatum volunt.* (677); *di immortales, quibus et quantis me donatis gaudiis!* (808). — Der Vorgang der Verbergung, der Entdeckung und des Diebstahls des Schatzes wird von den beiden beteiligten Personen in den Horizonten der Gewährung und Versagung göttlicher Hilfe gesehen.

Natürlich hat alles seine « profane » Erklärung, seine « natürliche » Motivation — ebenso wie der Fund des verlorenen Kästchens in der *Cistellaria*. Aber es sind wieder Umstände vorhanden, die einen vermuten lassen, dass Menander den Hörer zu einer bestimmten « religiösen » Interpretation des Vorgangs gelangen lassen wollte. Wenn es Euclio gelungen wäre, den Schatz im Heiligtum der Fides erfolgreich zu verbergen, hätte Lyconides Phaedria schliesslich ohne Mitgift heiraten müssen. Das Ziel der Ehe wäre erreicht worden, aber den Schatz hätte Euclio besessen, obwohl er ihn gar nicht für sich, sondern nur für seine Tochter hatte finden dürfen, und seine Tochter hätte arm und nach konventionellen Massstäben gering geschätzt die Ehe mit dem reichen jungen Mann geschlossen. Das Vorhaben des Prolog-Gottes wäre vereitelt, er selbst letzten Endes der Düpierte gewesen. Es war deshalb für das Handlungsziel wesentlich, dass es Euclio nicht gelang, den Schatz zu verbergen, und die Spannung des Hörers war vom Prolog her jetzt darauf gerichtet, wie die Handlung aus der in diesem Sinne verfahrenen Entwicklung befreit würde (dass es erreicht würde, war eigentlich zu erwarten : der Gott würde sich doch nicht von einem Euclio ausmanövrieren lassen !). Wenn sich nun die dafür entscheidenden Vorgänge dazu noch in Bezirken ereignen, die Göttern geweiht sind, und von den beteiligten Personen auch als göttliche Fügung interpretiert werden, und wenn berücksichtigt wird, dass man Schätze allgemein gerne göttlichem Schutz anvertraute und einen solchen Fund als Gottesgeschenk zu betrachten pflegte, dann drängt sich meines Erachtens der Eindruck auf, dass auch dem Zuschauer (gemeint ist : des menandrischen Originals) nahegelegt werden sollte, in dem Besitzerwechsel eine τύχη θεῶν zu erblicken. Freilich bezieht der Sklave fälschlich die Ereignisse allzusehr auf sich allein. Aber der Hörer kann aus der Überschau über das Ganze dessen egozentrischen Blickwinkel korrigieren.

Die Handlungsstruktur des euripideischen *Ion* bietet für uns eine ausserordentlich instruktive Parallele. Auch dort wird ein durch den Prolog bekannter göttlicher Plan durch menschliche Verfehlung durchkreuzt, worauf « Zufälle », die die *dea ex machina* Athena als μηχαναί Apollos erklärt, die Situation retten, so dass die Handlung zu ihrem gottgewollten Ende gelangen kann (vgl. dazu *Philologus* 1961, S. 54 f. und W. Steidle, *Stud. zum antiken Drama*, München 1968, S. 112 ff.). Durch das notwendige Fehlen des *deus ex machina* kann in der Komödie diese autoritative Bestätigung des göttlichen Eingreifens nicht erfolgen. Aber wer die Figur des Gottes und seine Aussagen im Prolog ernst nimmt und den Handlungsablauf mit dieser Aussage vergleicht, wird meines Erachtens nicht umhin können, ein solches als von Menander intendiert anzuerkennen.

Walther Kraus hat jedoch umgekehrt gerade dafür plädiert eine « gewisse Inkonzinnität » zwischen dem Götterprolog und der Handlung anzuerkennen (*Gnomon* 1968, S. 341 f.), die Götter spielten in der « Motivation des inneren Geschehens » keine Rolle, ebenso leugnet A. Theuerkauf « göttlichen Einfluss » in der *Aulularia* (*Menanders Dyskolos als Bühnenspiel und Dichtung*, Diss. Göttingen 1960, S. 70, Anm. 1) ; ähnlich C. Corbato : « la vicenda sia, malgrado l'iniziale apparizione divina, tutta umana nelle sue vicende e nelle sue motivazioni » (*Studi Menandrei*, Triest 1965, S. 107, Anm. 40). Ihre gemeinsame Grundanschauung lässt sich auf Friedrich Leo zurückführen : « *Aulularia* und *Rudens* haben gemein, dass ihre Einleitungsreden von göttlichen Wesen gesprochen werden, die der Dichter durch gefällige Erfindung äusserlich an die Handlung angeknüpft hat » (*Plautinische Forschungen*, 2. Aufl., Berlin 1912, S. 211). Während Schäfer und ich davon ausgingen, dass, was der Prologgott sagt, für das Stück belangvoll ist, wird von dieser diametral entgegengesetzten Auffassung her die Prologrede als blosse Information zur Exposition der Handlung betrachtet ; um sie einem Gott in den Mund legen zu können, hat man diesen durch einige unverbindliche, topische Motive mit der Handlung verbunden. In Wirklichkeit haben diese Motive keine Bedeutung für die Handlung, die ausschliesslich aus ihren menschlichen Motivationen und aus äusserlichen Zufälligkeiten zu verstehen ist. Dieser von ihren verschiedenen Anhängern nicht ganz einheitlich vertretenen Auffassung liegen meines Erachtens eine Reihe von Irrtümern und Missverständnissen zugrunde, die einzeln besprochen werden müssen.

Ein grundlegender Irrtum scheint mir die dabei involvierte Annahme zu sein, dass eine « natürlich » und eine « göttlich » motivierte Handlung einander ausschlössen. Der Umstand, dass alles seinen natürlichen Gang nimmt, dass die Handlung sich über innermenschliche Entscheidungen und über das unvorhergesehene Zuzammentreffen voneinander unabhängiger Kausalketten entwickelt, wird als Beweis dafür genommen, dass ein Gott hier nicht die Hand im Spiel haben könne. Anscheinend werden « übernatürliche » Wunder verlangt. Nur ein Gott, der die natürlichen Abläufe durchbricht, kann beanspruchen, als solcher anerkannt zu werden? Eine derartige Auffassung verkennt völlig die Vorstellungen, die unter Menanders Zeitgenossen populär waren. « Das Göttliche » offenbarte sich im und durch das Geschehen, nicht gegen und wider dasselbe. Im besonderen waren es unvorhergesehene und den Menschen unberechenbare (aber doch nach unserer Vorstellung « natürliche ») Ereignisse, die man als Wirkung des Göttlichen begriff. Der Hinweis auf die « natürlichen » Kausalzusammenhänge hätte hier zumeist als oberflächlich gegolten. Eine Trennung zwischen einer immanenten naturgesetzlich bedingten Ordnung des Geschehens und einem das Naturgesetz aufhebenden Eingriff eines transzendenten Göttlichen gab es ohnehin nicht. Wenn ein Mann plötzlich nichts ahnend einen Schatz fand, der drei Generationen begraben war, so war ein solches

« Wunder » ohne θεία τύχη nicht zu begreifen, und nicht weniger « wunderbar » und augenscheinlich gottgewollt war der Zufall, dass derselbe Mann seinen Schatz trotz aller Vorsicht kurz darauf wider verlor, nur weil ein Sklave, der aus einem ganz anderen Grund gekommen war, ihn beim Gebet belauschen konnte. Das Göttliche offenbarte sich aber nicht nur in solchen letztlich unbegreiflichen äusseren Begebenheiten, sondern unter Umständen auch in überraschenden Gedanken und Entschlüssen der Menschen selbst. Konsequenz ist dabei jedoch nicht zu erwarten. Eine Entscheidung konnte sowohl auf den Menschen, der sie traf, zurückgeführt werden, sie konnte unter einem anderen Aspekt aber auch, besonders wenn sie nicht mit seinem sonstigen Charakterbild harmonierte oder unvorhergesehen schwerwiegende Folgen hatte, durch den Impuls eines Gottes veranlasst scheinen. Der überraschende Entschluss des alten eingefleischten Junggesellen Megadorus, seine arme Nachbarstochter zu freien, welcher die Werbung des Lyconides auslöste, ist ein erheiterndes Komödienbeispiel für diese aus der Welt der Grossen und des Alltags bekannte Betrachtungsweise (vgl. dazu grundsätzlich A. Lesky, *Göttliche und menschliche Motivation im homerischen Epos*, Sitzber. Göttingen, 1961 ; eine Untersuchung der attischen Redner und hellenistischen Historiker in dieser Hinsicht wäre verdienstlich). Kurz : wenn ein Ablauf des Geschehens nach unseren Vorstellungen natürlich ist, schliesst dies nicht aus, dass er vielen Zeitgenossen Menanders erst durch den Hinweis auf göttliche Einflüsse in seiner tieferen Bedeutung, wir könnten auch sagen : in seiner Finalursache, erklärbar schien.

Ein anderer Irrtum ist es, wenn man die von dem Prologgott verheissene Fürsorge für das Mädchen als unverbindliches ad hoc-Motiv durch den Hinweis zu entkräften glaubt, dass dieser angeblich fürsorgliche Gott ja zunächst zuliess, dass das Mädchen ins Unglück geriet (so Theuerkauf). Natürlich war die Vergewaltigung eine Voraussetzung der späteren

Handlung und der Gott musste sie sozusagen bereits aus dramaturgischen Gründen zulassen. Seine später einsetzende Fürsorge wurde aber auch als solche nicht durch die fehlende frühere Fürsorge diskreditiert. Beides stiess sich für das religiöse Gefühl keineswegs. Es ist daran zu denken, wie tief eingewurzelt der Glaube an die gerechte göttliche Vergeltung bei den Griechen war: ἀλλὰ τῶν χρηστῶν ἔχει τιν' ἐπιμέλειαν καὶ θεός (Men. fr. 321 Koe.). Auch noch so zahlreiche Verstösse gegen die Gerechtigkeit auf Erden hatten es nicht bewirken können, dass man nicht die ausgleichende Hand der göttlichen Gerechtigkeit wahrzunehmen glaubte, wann immer es einem «Guten» gut oder einem «Bösen» schlimm ging, wann immer ein unschuldig Leidender gerettet oder ein Frevler gestürzt wurde. Dass die «fromme» Phaedria vergewaltigt wurde, war kein Beweis gegen die göttliche Fürsorge, aber es war ein Beweis für dieselbe, dass das arme und vergewaltigte Mädchen wie eine Tochter aus reichem Haus einen reichen jungen Mann heiraten durfte. Man unterschätzt die widerspruchsvollen Möglichkeiten des menschlichen Glaubens, wenn man daraus, dass kein Gott die Vergewaltigung verhinderte, ableiten will, dass auch ferner in der Handlung der *Aulularia* von keinem göttlichen Einfluss die Rede sein könne.

Ein dritter Irrtum liegt folgendem Gedankengang zugrunde: Megadorus und Lyconides wissen bei ihrer Werbung nichts von dem Schatz, Phaedria wäre auch ohne den Schatzfund Frau des Lyconides geworden. Der Lar sagt, er habe Euclio den Schatz finden lassen, damit er seine Tochter leichter verheiraten könne. Also ist diese Motivierung unsinnig und für das Stück irrelevant. Es ist eine Augenblickserfindung, die den Prolog in eine gewisse Verbindung mit der Handlung bringt, die aber für das folgende Stück keine Bedeutung hat und deshalb am besten alsbald vergessen wird. Prologrede und Handlung sind nicht völlig aufeinander abgestimmt. Hier geht man von der Vorstellung aus, dass

Ankündigungen des Prologgottes in bezug auf die folgende Handlung sich erfüllen müssen oder aber, wenn sie dies nicht tun, ohne Bedeutung für dieselbe sind. Es ist nicht zu vergessen, dass das Ziel der Handlung, das der Lar im Prolog steckt, sehr wohl erreicht wird (die Verwendung des Schatzes als Mitgift Phaedrias bei ihrer Heirat mit Lyconides) und dass der Gott eben dies und nicht weniger *eius honoris gratia* will. Natürlich wäre bereits die Heirat als solche für Phaedria ein grosses Glück gewesen, eine Heirat in dieser Form aber war zweifellos ein grösseres, und wir können dem Gott (oder Menander) nicht vorschreiben, wie er das Mädchen belohnt wissen wollte. Nur der Weg zum Ziel entspricht nicht ganz den Ankündigungen. Wer sich daran stösst, verkennt, dass der griechische Gott nicht alles vorauszuwissen braucht, sondern durch sein Wirken dem menschlichen Handeln gewisse Möglichkeiten öffnet, die der Mensch durch seine Entscheidung ergreifen kann, aber nicht muss (worauf es wieder bei der Gottheit steht, ob sie das Geschehen durch erneute Einwirkungen in die von ihr erstrebte Richtung lenken will), und er verkennt auch, dass es Menander gerade daran gelegen sein könnte, dem Zuschauer eine gewisse Handlungsperspektive zu geben, von der sich die aktuelle Handlung abheben wird, um ihr am Ende doch wieder zu entsprechen. Eine solche «Inkonzinnität» zwischen Prologrede und folgender Handlung beweist durchaus nicht, dass die Hinweise im Prolog belanglos wären, im Gegenteil eröffnet eben die Beachtung dieser « Inkonzinnität » das richtige Verständnis der Handlung.

W. Kraus, der sich durch die « Inkonzinnität » hingegen veranlasst sah, die Prologangaben teilweise nicht zu berücksichtigen, glaubte, dass seine Betrachtungsweise « den Weg freimacht zur Erkenntnis » des « eigentlichen Wesens » der *Aulularia*, « das nicht darin liegt, dass ein Hans seine Gretel bekommt, sondern dass an einem grossen, aber aus dem täglichen Leben gegriffenen Beispiel gezeigt wird, wie die durch das Leben erzeugte Verkrampfung einer Seele ihre Lösung findet». Hier haben sich wohl getrennt zu haltende Begriffe vermischt. Dass der «Hans» Lyconides seine «Gretel» Phaedria bekommt, ist tatsächlich nicht das «eigentliche Wesen» der Komödie, aber es ist das Ziel der Handlung. Damit dies erreicht werden kann, muss der Geiz des Euclio, wenigstens soweit er sich auf den Schatz bezieht, überwunden werden. Menander hat dargestellt, wie Geiz und Misstrauen das ganze Verhalten und Handeln des Euclio beherrschen; er zeigt, dass Euclio sich von sich aus unter keinen Umständen von seinem Schatz trennt. Und doch ist eben dies notwendig: Euclio *muss* ihn an Lyconides geben. Der Schock des Verlustes und die unerwartete Rückgabe bewirken dann eine Veränderung in dem Alten. Geheilt von seinem Misstrauen gegen die Menschen muss er schliesslich von seinem zähen Festhalten des Schatzes abgelassen haben. Die Opposition und ihre Überwindung ist von Menander so gestaltet worden, dass das ethische Interesse sich darauf konzentriert. Die Gestalt des Widersachers ist die wesentliche dichterische Leistung in diesem Stück und deshalb für uns wichtiger als das faktische Handlungsziel. Im Rahmen der Handlung und sozusagen *sub specie dei* aber ist die Wandlung des Euclio nicht Selbstzweck, sondern Voraussetzung für das glückliche Ende, und wir haben keine Veranlassung, den Hinweisen des Lar ihre Verbindlichkeit abzusprechen, weil der Gott die Heilung Euclios von seiner Besessenheit nicht zu seinem Ziel erhebt.

Schliesslich sehe ich auch keinen Grund, die Hinweise des Gottes, die ihn mit der Handlung verknüpfen, deshalb nicht ernst zu nehmen, weil der Prologgott sich in mehreren Komödien eine Einwirkung auf die Handlung zuschreibt. Man hat dies einen Topos genannt, der den Auftritt des Gottes motiviere, im übrigen unverbindlich sei. Unverbindlich wäre er nur, wenn die Hinweise funktionslos blieben. Dass sie dies in der *Aulularia* nicht sind, glaube ich gezeigt zu haben. Dann aber wird man in dem Umstand, dass ähnliche Hinweise sich auch in anderen Komödien finden, besser ein noch nicht genügend berücksichtigtes Element der Eigenart dieser Komödien sehen, als dass man ihn als unbeachtlich beiseite schiebt.

III.

Wir haben Menander bisher fast ausschliesslich durch den plautinischen Filter betrachtet. Ein Blick auf den *Dyskolos* kann unsere Beobachtungen bestätigen und ergänzen. Für dieses Stück setzte die Debatte über den Einfluss des Pan auf die Handlung bereits im Jahr der Editio princeps ein. Photiades, Cantarella, Corbato, Kraus, Turner, Theuerkauf, J. Martin, Pastorino, Schäfer, Stössl, daneben ich und andere haben sich an der Diskussion beteiligt. Mit dem Standardkommentar von E. W. Handley (1965) hat sich eine besonnene Auffassung durchgesetzt: « Pan, like the Lar, sets in motion a chain of events which will lead to the girl's marriage, and at the same time to the discomfiture of her disagreable father ; and in this he has the Nymphs as allies. The gods are thus a factor in the course of the action, and they are recalled to the audience by the presence of their shrine, and by the character's references to them ; they add ' atmosphere ' to the play and coherence to its structure, but they do not, except in a very limited sense, make it into a religious play, or one dominated by the divine » (S. 135 zu V. 37 ff.). Ich stimme damit im ganzen überein und möchte Einzelnes nur noch einmal der Übersicht halber herausgreifen und seine Implikationen verdeutlichen.

Pan hat seine und der Nymphen Beteiligung an der Handlung im Prolog klar ausgesprochen : τάς δὲ συντρόφους ἐμοὶ Νύμφας κολακεύουσ' ἐπιμελῶς τιμῶσά τε πέπεικεν αὐτῆς ἐπιμέλειαν σχεῖν τινα ἡμᾶς (36 ff.). Es ist eine Generalankündigung der göttlichen Fürsorge, die der Hörer für alles folgende im Gedächtnis zu halten hat (ἐπιμελῶς τιμῶσα und ἐπιμέλειαν σχεῖν führen auf die griechischen Begriffe, die in *Aul.* 17 *mihi honorem haberet*, 19 *curare minusque me impertire honoribus*, 25 *eius honoris gratia*, zugrunde liegen). Schäfer hat gezeigt, dass der Prolog hier letzten Endes nur durch und für diese Erklärung notwendig ist, da er keine anderen den beteiligten Personen unbekannten expositionellen Angaben enthält. Göttliche Fürsorge für ein frommes und verhältnismässig armes Mädchen besteht selbstverständlich darin, dass ihm zu einer Heirat mit einem reichen, es liebenden jungen Mann verholfen wird. Wenn Pan deshalb noch präzisierend sagt: νεανίσκον τε καὶ μάλ' εὐπόρου πατρός ... κατὰ τύχην παραβαλόντ' εἰς τὸν τόπον αὐτῆς ἔχειν πῶς ἐνθεαστικῶς ποῶ; (39 ff.), so entnimmt der Hörer daraus auch, dass es das Ziel des Gottes ist, dass Sostratos das Mädchen heiratet (anders würde seine Liebe mehr schaden als nützen!), und ist auf mögliche andere Hilfsmassnahmen vorbereitet. Es kann nicht verlangt werden, dass Pan solche schon im einzelnen ankündigen müsste, damit sie später wirklich als von ihm herrührend aufgefasst werden.

Die erste Dialogszene knüpft unmittelbar an die eben besprochenen Verse an. Es wird nicht nur anschaulich, wie das Mädchen die Nymphen verehrt (es bekränzt sie!), es ist auch bezeichnend, dass Sostratos gerade in diesem Augenblick von der Liebe getroffen wurde: die Gottheiten erweisen ihren Dank. Kraus hat natürlich recht, wenn er schreibt: « Um einen Jungen verliebt zu machen, ist sonst kein Gott nötig, und von seinem Eingreifen ist auch natürlich nichts zu merken » (Ausgabe 1960, S. 18), aber das trifft überhaupt nicht die Sache, um die es geht. Das Verliebtwerden konnte als innermenschlicher Vorgang aufgefasst werden, ebensogut aber auch als Eingriff einer Gottheit. Nach der Erklärung Pans sollen wir es hier so verstehen, und der Vorgang spielte sich auch ebenso ab, wie man sich eine Liebe unter göttlichem Einfluss vorstellte: der begüterte junge Städter, der zur Jagd aufs Land gekommen war, verliebt sich blitzartig und mit Haut und Haaren in das ihm bislang unbekannte, arme, schlichte Landmädchen, mit dem er noch kein einziges Wort gesprochen hat. Beide Personen entstammen völlig verschiedenen Lebenssphären, so dass die Liebe des Sostratos alles andere als ein gewöhnlicher Vorgang ist. Dass Pan hier sozusagen die Funktion des Eros übernimmt, ist im übrigen nicht anstössig. Erstens sind er und die Nymphen allgemein zuständig für alles, was sich im Bereich ihres Heiligtums ereignet, zweitens findet Pan sich öfters in erotischer Gesellschaft (vgl. die *RE*, Suppl. VIII, Sp. 1000 ff. genannten Vasenbilder mit Aphrodite und den Eroten), und auf die Bedeutung der Nymphen als Hochzeitsgöttinnen hat Pastorino eigens hingewiesen (*Menandrea* 1960, S. 87).

An die Beziehungen dieser Gottheiten zur Handlung wird der Hörer das nächstemal in der Szene erinnert, wenn das Mädchen erstmals auf die Bühne kommt und — nun zum zweitenmal — Sostratos begegnet, der sie jetzt anspricht. Ihr Gruss ὦ φίλταται Νύμφαι (197) zeugt wieder für das Nahverhältnis des Mädchens zu ihren göttlichen Beschützerinnen. V. 203 τίς ἄν με σώσαι δ̣[αιμό]νων; ist in der Sprecherzuweisung umstritten: gleichviel ob Sostratos oder das Mädchen es sagen, der Hörer bemerkt die Ironie und denkt daran, dass Pan für einen guten Ausgang sorgen wird. Ähnliche Ironien bergen z.B. 225 f., 309 ff., 346 f., 444 f., 543 ff., 557 f., 570 ff., 601 f., 639 ff., 666 ff., 736, 861 ff., 876 ff. Nur die Kenntnis der Prologrede gibt diesen Äusserungen Hintergrund und lässt sie zu dem Sprecher nicht kenntlichen Hinweisen auf das göttliche Engagement an dem Spiel werden, das auf diese Weise nie aus dem Auge verloren wird.

Aus dem Dialog zwischen Sikon und Getas (400 ff.) wird dann deutlich, dass Pan den Anstoss zu einer zweiten Handlungslinie gegeben hat. Den Traum der Mutter des Sostratos nimmt der Hörer als echten Wahrtraum, weil er weiss, dass die im Traum teils symbolisch, teils direkt prophezeiten Ereignisse tatsächlich eingetreten sind. Die Symbolik der Fesseln ist für ihn durchsichtig. Darüber hinaus erkennt er, dass auch die Hackarbeit von Pan gewollt ist. Sie ist es erstens als Folge der von Pan erzeugten Verliebtheit, zweitens, da erst durch die Opferhandlung äusserlich Raum für sie geschaffen wurde. Sostratos hatte Getas als Heiratsvermittler schicken wollen; da er den bereits von seiner Mutter für das Opfer in Anspruch genommenen Sklaven nicht zu Hause vorfand (es ist die erste Überkreuzung der beiden Handlungslinien!), war er selbst zurückgekommen, um mit Knemon zu sprechen. Nur dadurch aber wurde die Begegnung zwischen ihm und Gorgias möglich, die zu seinem Entschluss, mit aufs Feld zu gehen, führte. Eine andere Folge der Opferhandlung ist, dass umgekehrt Knemon nicht, wie erwartet, aufs Feld geht, wodurch die Absicht, die Sostratos mit der Hackarbeit verband, scheitert. Sein Einsatz scheint umsonst, wird aber später seinen Lohn finden und sich damit als sinnvoller Teil des göttlichen Plans entpuppen.

Als Sostratos unverrichteter Dinge wieder zurückkommt (vgl. 543 ff.!), findet er das Opfer auf eine gewisse Weise οὐκ ἄκαιρος (558); es ist es in einem tieferen Sinn, ebenso wie er mehr, als er ahnt, recht hat mit seinem makabren Scherz, er habe noch nie einen Menschen εὐκαιρότερον beinahe ersticken sehen (666 ff.). Der Koch hat den Brunnensturz bereits als Beweis für die vergeltende Gerechtigkeit der Götter interpretiert (639 ff.): die Nymphen hätten seine Missachtung gerächt. Natürlich ist sein egozentrischer Blickwinkel wieder einseitig, aber der Hörer kann den Fingerzeig richtig interpretieren. Der Brunnensturz des Knemon war in Hinsicht auf das Ziel des Pan notwendig, da nur so seine abweisende Haltung durchbrochen werden konnte. Der « Zufall » hat selbstverständlich seine « natürlichen » Ursachen, das morsche Seil, etc. Aber man verkennt wieder den Charakter der θεία τύχη, wenn man aus diesem Grund eine solche leugnet. Der Brunnensturz ist θεία τύχη, weil er gerade jetzt passiert und derartige Folgen hat.

Die Beurteilung des Geschehens durch Sostratos, in der dieser sich unter Verwendung gängiger Sentenzen das Verdienst zuschreibt, ἐπιμέλειᾳ καὶ πόνῳ die Heirat erreicht zu haben (860 ff.), erinnert den Hörer daran, wie gering im Grunde sein « Verdienst » an der Sache ist und wieviel auf das Konto der ἐπιμέλεια der Götter zu gehen hat. Ohne θεία τύχη wäre Sostratos nicht nur nicht zu seinem Ziel gekommen, auch das Ziel selbst hatte ein Gott erst gesteckt. Die durch den Traum veranlasste Opferhandlung ist eine sekundäre Handlungslinie, die durch ihre mehrfachen Überschneidungen mit der Sostratos- und der Knemonlinie dazu beigetragen hat, das Ziel der Haupthandlung zu erreichen, mit welcher sie sich am Ende auch vereinigt.

Aber trotz allem: ein « frommes Lehrstück » ist der *Dyskolos* so wenig geworden wie die *Synaristosai* oder das Original der *Aulularia*. Worin liegt dann die Bedeutung des religiösen Aspekts dieser Dramen? In welchem Verhältnis steht er zu den Schwerpunkten des Interesses? Und welche Schlüsse lassen sich aus der Handlungsstruktur auf die Religiosität Menanders ziehen?

Dramaturgisch gesehen gibt die Gottheit der Handlung Einheit und Zusammenhang, auf der Bühne wird sie zu Beginn für den Zuschauer sichtbar (realistischerweise nicht für die Bühnenperson ; nur den Heroen des Mythos erscheint der *deus ex machina*). In einem gewissen Sinn sind die Komödien Illustrationen der Vorstellung, dass Gott die Tugend belohnt und für den Frommen sorgt. Die Gottheit setzt der Handlung das Ziel und hilft, wenn sie aus der « richtigen » Richtung geraten ist, die Widerstände zu überwinden. Sie greift in den äusseren und inneren Geschehensablauf ein. Überraschende Zufälle, ein Fund, ein Verlust, ein Unfall, können ebenso ihr Werk sein wie unerwartete Emotionen und Entschlüsse. (Nur einmal — in der Traumerscheinung des Pan — wird dabei das, was wir die « natürliche » Kausalität des Geschehens nennen würden, durchbrochen ; aber für Menander und seine Zeitgenossen gehörten Erscheinungen eines Gottes im Traum eben auch zur Wirklichkeit der Welt und waren nicht wunderbarer als ein Schatzfund). Es sind, wie Handley richtig empfindend feststellte, dennoch keine « religiösen Spiele » im vollen Sinn des Begriffs. Sie sind es schon deswegen nicht, weil es in den Stücken nicht so sehr um die Götter oder die Beziehungen der Menschen zu den Göttern, als vielmehr um die Menschen geht. Die Götter bleiben im allgemeinen hinter den Kulissen, auch bestimmen sie die Handlung nicht völlig, sondern geben ihr nur gewisse Anstösse, lassen aber dann den Raum für menschliche Entscheidungen frei. Sie sind weder allmächtig noch allwissend und haben auf die menschlichen Aktionen ebenso erst zu reagieren wie umgekehrt die Menschen auf die göttlichen. Es geht nicht ohne den helfenden Gott, aber es geht ebensowenig ohne den Menschen, der die Gelegenheit ergreift und sie durch seine Entscheidung und Tat zu seiner eigenen macht. Dazu kommt, dass der religiöse Aspekt, den wir durch eine isolierende Analyse hervorhoben, in der Realität der Stücke keineswegs dominierend wirkt. Die herauspräparierte religiöse Grundlage wird nicht aufdringlich betont, nicht lehrhaft eingeschärft, sie wird dem Publikum nicht als eine erstaunliche Entdeckung vorgeführt, für die es erst gewonnen werden müsste, sondern wirkt mehr wie eine von Autor und Publikum geteilte Voraussetzung. Dass sich Geschehen grundsätzlich auf solche Weise vollzieht, scheint als ausgemacht zu gelten. Wie es sich im besonderen Fall abspielt, interessiert. Das beschriebene Verhältnis des Göttlichen zur Handlung ist der allgemeine und als anerkannt hintergenommene Rahmen, für die Realität des Dramas aber ist seine Füllung wichtiger. Ähnlich ist auch das Handlungsziel, die Heirat des Mädchens, ein stereotypes Element des allgemeinen Formcharakters dieser Stücke. Die Spannung des Kenners richtet sich nicht so sehr darauf, ob, sondern wie dieses Ziel erreicht wird. Für die Würdigung der dichterischen Leistung ist das Spezifische ausschlaggebend. Im Mittelpunkt des Interesses stehen deshalb in den Widersacherkomödien *Aulularia* und *Dyskolos* die Gestalten des Euclio und Knemon, sowie die Methoden, wie ihre Widerstände überwunden und wie sie in die Gesellschaft der Menschen zurückgeführt werden, in der Anagnorisiskomödie der *Synaristosai* entsprechend die Entwicklung von Gefühl und Verhalten der beiden Liebenden und der verschlungene Weg zur Entdeckung. Der Blick auf den göttlichen Hintergrund deutet das Geschehen, aber das Geschehen wird nicht nur um seiner Deutung willen dem Zuschauer vor Augen geführt.

Für die Religiosität Menanders sagen die Stücke nur indirekt etwas aus. Es ist zu scheiden zwischen dem allgemeinen Charakter des Geschehensablaufes, jenem Wechselspiel von Gott und Mensch, und der Frage, wie oft nun das Göttliche in der Tat den « Guten » belohnt. Das erstere wird als der grundsätzliche Rahmen, innerhalb dessen sich die Handlung ereignet, begriffen und dürfte wohl dem Weltverständnis Menanders und eines guten Teils seines Publikums entsprechen. Aber man täuschte sich natürlich nicht darüber, dass es an der göttlichen Belohnung der Tugend oft haperte. Tyche musste sich ihr blindes Walten vorwerfen lassen. Das beseitigte jedoch nicht den Wunschglauben an die göttliche Gerechtigkeit und man freute sich, wenn Menander in der Komödie einen Fall darstellte, wo jene sich bewährte. Man darf den Sieg der göttlichen Gerechtigkeit da nicht schlechthin abwerten und ausschliesslich für eine Sache der dramaturgischen Konvention erklären. Es wäre unkritisch, wenn man nur die kritischen Äusserungen in den Komödien als Menanders eigene Stimme, nur den Erfolg skrupelloser Parasiten als Symbol für sein Weltbild gelten liesse. Menanders pessimistische Lebensauffassung im Konflikt mit dem erzwungenen Optimismus der poetischen Gerechtigkeit ist zwar eine attraktive Vorstellung, die gut in das allgemeine Bild passt, das man sich von der « aufgeklärten » oder « zerrissenen » Religiosität seiner Zeit zu machen pflegt, aber es spricht einiges gegen sie. Es ist eine schlechte Propaganda für kritische Äusserungen über die göttliche Gerechtigkeit, wenn diese durch den Verlauf des Stückes selbst widerlegt werden. Noch wichtiger ist : Menander war nicht gezwungen, die poetische Gerechtigkeit mit Hilfe der göttlichen durchzusetzen. Er hätte auf die Prologrede des Pan verzichten können (die expositionellen Daten wären in den folgenden Szenen unterzubringen gewesen), und dem Geschehen wäre sein « metaphysischer » Hintergrund entzogen gewesen, ohne dass der Zuschauer auf das befriedigende Ende hätte verzichten müssen. Menander hat auch nicht in allen Komödien die Götter an der Handlung beteiligt (für den Δὶς ἐξαπατῶν ist ein Götterprolog unwahrscheinlich ; von der *Samia* wissen wir jetzt, dass sie keinen hatte). Dass er es in einer anscheinend beträchtlichen Anzahl von Stücken tat, ist meines Erachtens nicht als dramaturgischer Zwang zu erklären. Es scheint mir ein indirektes Bekenntnis, eine nicht erzwungene Zustimmung zur Idee einer vergeltenden göttlichen Gerechtigkeit darin zu liegen, womit er kaum — ich vertraue da auf eine gewisse Aufrichtigkeit des Autors ! — seinen Zuhörern nur nach dem Munde reden wollte. Nur dass sich aus den Stükken natürlich nicht entnehmen lässt, wie häufig oder wie selten Menander diese Gerechtigkeit in der Wirklichkeit erfüllt sah. Die Komödie hatte die positiven Fälle darzustellen, die nicht dadurch als Möglichkeiten unglaubwürdig wurden, dass es in der Wirklichkeit auch negative gab.

IV.

Die Aufschlüsse der behandelten Komödien bieten auch Interpretationshilfen für die übrigen mehr oder minder fragmentarisch überlieferten Stücke, denen hier noch einige kurze Bemerkungen gelten sollen.

In der *Perikeiromene* wirkt der für die Prolog-Gottheit gewählte Name Agnoia verwunderlich. Wie kann die personifizierte « Unwissenheit » den Menschen zum Wissen verhelfen ? Wie kann die wissende Gottheit « Unwissenheit » heissen ? Die beteiligten Personen befinden sich anfangs zum Teil in Unwissenheit über die Identität der Geschwister. Die Unwissenheit des Moschion lässt ihn Glykera lieben, und Polemon gerät aus Unwissenheit angesichts der missverstandenen Kussszene in einen jähen Zorn, der den Ursprung für die ganze zur Anagnorisis führende Handlung bildet. Die Unwissenheit ist so in gewissem Sinn Ursache des Wissens, indem aus ihr eine zum Wissen führende Entwicklung hervorging. Menander beschreibt letztlich nichts anderes als die wirkliche Situation, eigentümlich ist nur die Interpretation, die er gibt. Die Unwissenheit, die die Menschen beherrscht, ist eine reale Macht und — τὸ κρατοῦν γὰρ πᾶν νομίζεται θεός (Men. fr. 223 Koe.) — damit ein Gott oder, so verstehen wir das Gemeinte besser, ein Aspekt des Göttlichen. Polemon handelt unter der Einwirkung der ὀργή, die ihn erfasst hat, ganz anders als sonst, anders als es seiner natürlichen Wesensart (φύσις) entspricht ; die ὀργή ist deshalb ein Werk der Gottheit, und da sie durch seine Unwissenheit hervorgerufen ist, also ein Werk der göttlichen Macht, die hinter seiner Unwissenheit steht. Da von der ὀργή eine Kausalkette zur μήνυσις führt, erscheint die göttliche « Unwissenheit » letztlich als Urheberin für das Wissen. Der « böse » Zorn mit seinen schlimmen Folgen hat ein « Gutes » bewirkt, wodurch das Üble sich als Glied eines göttlichen Planes erweist: διὰ γὰρ θεοῦ καὶ τὸ κακὸν εἰς ἀγαθὸν ῥέπει γινόμενον (49 f.). Nach der Anagnorisis beginnen Glykera und Polemon diese Zusammenhänge zu entdecken: νῦν μὲν γὰρ ἡμῶν γέγονεν ἀρχὴ [πραγμάτων] ἀγαθῶν τὸ σὸν πάροινον· — ὀρθῶ[ς γὰρ λέγεις] (443 f.). Der Papyrus bricht mit dem Ausruf ὦ Γῆ ab; es ist möglich, dass hier die Teilnahme des « Göttlichen » an der Handlung bewusst wurde. Für die Hörer bedeutete V. 443 f. einen bestätigenden Rückverweis auf die Aussagen der Prolog-Gottheit. Das ist die gleiche Art der Interpretation des menschlichen Geschehens, wie sie in den anderen Komödien vorlag. Der Name Agnoia sollte auch für das menandrische Publikum paradox wirken. Die Freiheit der Namengebung zeugt für die letztliche Beliebigkeit der Namen, nicht für die Unwirklichkeit des gemeinten Göttlichen. Für den Prologgott schieden die unpersönlichen und unbestimmten Bezeichnungen, die man an sich für die Benennung des « Göttlichen » bevorzugte (θεός, θεοί, δαιμόνιον) aus. So griff Menander entweder zu lokalen Gottheiten, mit denen das Stück in Beziehung stand, oder hypostasierte Aspekte des Göttlichen, die zugleich Aspekte seiner Wirklichkeit waren.

In den *Epitrepontes* hat Wilamowitz für die zweite Szene einen Götterauftritt erschlossen, da nur ein Gott darüber informieren konnte, « dass Pamphile von Charisios geschwängert war und ihr Kind in dem nahen Wald hatte aussetzen lassen » (Ausg. S. 50). Es ist zu vermuten, dass die Gottheit dort auch ihre aktive Beteiligung an der Handlung erklärte mit dem Ziel, dass die Ehe der armen anständigen Pamphile glücklich wiederhergestellt werde. Darauf führen spätere Hinweise auf göttliches Wirken, die erst von einer solchen Ankündigung her ironisches Profil erhalten. Die zahlreichen analogen Fälle, z.B. im *Dyskolos*, scheinen mir eine solche Vermutung zu rechtfertigen. V. 535 ruft Pamphile verzweifelt: τίς ἂν θεῶν τάλαιναν ἐλεήσειέ με; Sie weiss nicht, dass Habrotonon soeben mit ihrem Kind auf die Bühne gekommen ist und die Anagnorisis unmittelbar bevorsteht. Am Ende der Szene sagt Habrotonon sozusagen respondierend μακαρία γύναι, θεῶν τις ὑμᾶς ἠλέησε (553 f.). Diese die entscheidende Erkennungsszene rahmenden Hinweise auf ein göttliches Erbarmen würden ein zusätzliches Gewicht erhalten, wenn der Hörer vom Prologgott her wüsste dass ein Gott sich tatsächlich Pamphiles erbarmt und ihr aus ἔλεος geholfen hat. In der übernächsten Szene, in der reziprok Charisios zur Erkennung gebracht wird, dass er und Pamphile die Eltern des Kindes sind, tritt dieser zunächst gleichfalls verzweifelt auf die Bühne. Er gesteht: εὖ μοι κέχρηται καὶ προσηκόντως πάνυ τὸ δαιμόνιον und deutet das, was ihm passiert ist, als göttliche Lehre (591 ff.). Der durch den Prologgott vorbereitete Hörer sieht darin keine subjektive Interpretation des Geschehens, sondern weiss, dass die Gottheit ihn tatsächlich zum Zweck von Pamphiles Glück einen solchen Weg des Lernens hat gehen lassen. Schliesslich fällt auch auf die berühmte Reflexion des Onesimos über die Götter (727 ff.) von einem solchen Götterprolog her ein besonderes Licht. Die Frage οἴει τοσαύτην τοὺς θεοὺς ἄγειν σχολήν, ὥστε τὸ κακὸν καὶ τἀγαθὸν καθ' ἡμέραν νέμειν ἑκάστῳ; weckt beim Hörer den Gedanken daran, dass die Götter im vorliegenden Fall wirklich für das Geschick der Menschen gesorgt haben, er weiss, dass hinter dem ταὐτόματον, das nach des Onesimos Meinung Smikrines vor einer schlechten Tat bewahrte, göttlicher Wille steckte (vgl. die ähnlich ironische Verwendung des αὐτόματον in *Dysk.* 545). Die « philosophierende » Erörterung über die Zusammenhänge zwischen den θεοί, dem τρόπος jedes Menschen und dessen Wohlergehen sind ein Versuch, das alte Problem der Beziehung von Verdienst und Schicksal zu lösen. Der Sklave hat die Verhältnisse aber nur teilweise zutreffend erfasst. Er entwickelt die alte Erkenntnis, dass der Charakter dem Menschen ein sein Geschick bestimmender Daimon ist, in etwas aufwendiger und anspruchsvoller

Redseligkeit wie eine eigene Entdeckung. Der Hörer könnte ihn im Sinn Menanders darauf aufmerksam machen, dass manche Menschen auch gegen ihren τρόπος ein κακόν tun oder leiden und dass die Götter dennoch dabei ihre fürsorgende Hand im Spiel haben können.

Auch die Funktion mancher isolierter Fragmente, in denen über die Götter oder das Walten der Tyche reflektiert wird, kann von der Technik des menandrischen Götterprologs her besser verstanden werden. Äusserungen wie die in den *Koneiazomenai*, V. 13-20 Koe., passen zum Ende der Komödie und verlangen nach einer Prolog-Gottheit, deren Erklärungen den Hörer schon lange wissen liessen, was der junge Mann erst jetzt erkennt. (Zur Tyche in der eben bekannt gewordenen *Aspis*, vgl. unten M. Turner S. 102 f.).

Ähnlich lassen Ter. *Eun.* 875 ff. *quod si hoc quispiam voluit deus? — equidem pol in eam partem accipioque et volo* und 1031 ff. *o populares, ecquis me hodie vivit fortunatior? nemo hercle quisquam; nam in me plane di potestatem suam omnem ostendere quoi tam subito tot congruerint commoda* vermuten, dass bei Menander ein Gott sich im Prolog auch für die Handlung engagierte. Die konsequente Beseitigung des Götterprologs durch Terenz bedeutete mithin auch sozusagen eine Profanierung der Komödien Menanders.

Es war für die spätere, neuzeitliche Entwicklung des Lustspiels bedeutungsvoll, dass weder Plautus noch Terenz bei ihren Bearbeitungen auf den spezifischen religiösen Sinngehalt der menandrischen Komödien Wert legten und dem Abendland eine Komödie überlieferten, in der die Menschen mehr oder weniger unter sich sind und ihre Äusserungen in Hinsicht auf die Götter nur ihre subjektiven häufig redensartlich geprägten Auffassungen wiedergeben, die vom Hörer nicht allzu ernst genommen und vor allem nicht aus einem Wissen über einen tatsächlichen Anteil einer Gottheit an der Entwicklung der Handlung beurteilt werden. Das in der Tradition des Plautus und Terenz stehende Lustspiel hat immer einen profanen Charakter behalten. Die Komödien Menanders waren noch in andere Zusammenhänge eingebettet. Sein dionysisches Festspiel war wie in mancher anderen Beziehung auch hier Erbe der Tragödie. Webster hat auf die Möglichkeit hingewiesen, dass es Menander selbst war, der von Euripides die Idee eines Götterprologs übernahm, der das Publikum befähigen sollte, die Ironie bestimmter Situationen im Lauf des Stückes voll zu erfassen (*Stud. Men.* S. 186). Der aufs Dramaturgische beschränkte Gesichtspunkt lässt sich erweitern. Der Götterprolog schuf zugleich die Möglichkeit, dem Hörer einen Blick in eine Handlungsebene hinter oder über der menschlichen zu verschaffen und das Geschehen aus einem göttlich-menschlichen Wechselspiel zu verstehen. Menander hat damit eine für die Tragödie wesentliche Perspektive auch für seine im «bürgerlichen» Milieu spielenden Komödien gewonnen und in einer ihnen und ihrer Zeit gemässen Form bewahrt.

DISCUSSION

M. Sandbach : I have listened with great pleasure to Herr Ludwig and for the most part found him quite convincing. There are two points I should like to raise, one concerning *Cistellaria*, the other *Aulularia.*

I agree that there cannot have been a part in the Greek play like that of Selenium at 449 ff. Of Herr Ludwig's alternative explanations, the second, that ca. 449-464 are a Plautine addition, seems the most attractive. One may perhaps find some support for the view that Selenium did not in the original accompany her " mother " here by asking what is the reason for Melainis' presence, why she has come from her house which is somewhere else in the town. One can only guess, but a probable answer is that she has come to tell Alcesimarchus that his affair with Selenium is at an end, his conduct makes its continuance impossible. If this is so, she would not bring Selenium with her. In fact she would come to him rather than wait for him to visit her, just in order to avoid the presence of the girl, who does not wish to break with him.

On *Aulularia* Herr Ludwig's answer to Schäfer and Kraus satisfies me entirely. Nevertheless the Lar does not in Plautus, whatever may have been the case with the corresponding Greek divinity, appear to affect the action after the play has begun. In this point he is in contrast with Pan of *Dyskolos,* who is constantly mentioned and whose influence is kept in the audience's mind. So far as this goes *Dyskolos* seems to me the better play. There are also in *Aulularia* two features which strike me as dramatic weaknesses. I may be wrong and should be glad to be put right. But these three things cause me to have some scruples about accepting *Aulularia* with complete confidence as Menandrean.

The dramatic weaknesses are these. Lyconides is inadequately motivated. He knows who the girl is whom he has ravished, but for nine months he has made no attempt to see her or make himself known. Only the news that Megadorus is about to marry her suddenly causes him to want her himself. He is not in the position of many young men, who cannot marry a poor girl without their father's consent; his father is dead, and he could at any time have offered to marry Euclio's daughter, if he had wanted. His sudden change of attitude needs more explanation.

The other weakness, as it appears to me, is the similarity between the two scenes (IV ii and IV vi) in which Lyconides' slave overhears Euclio saying out aloud to himself where he intends to hide the treasure. That this should happen once may be credible; that it should happen twice streches belief, and perhaps argues some lack of inventiveness on the part of the dramatist.

In both instances, the Greek original may have done more than Plautus to achieve likelihood. But not knowing that it did, I do not feel absolutely convinced that it was by Menander.

Of course Menandrean prologue gods may not always have played a discernible part in the following play. I think that Τύχη probably did in *Aspis*—although Τύχη is so wide-ranging that there may be few plays where she could not be seen to be at work. But it is harder to see a continuing influence of Ἄγνοια in *Perikeiromene* after the initial impulse she gives through the ignorance of Polemon and Moschion that Glykera is the latter's brother.

M. Ludwig: Ich freue mich sehr über Ihre Zustimmung zu meinen Zweifeln an einem Auftritt der Selenium bei Menander an der V. 449 ff. entsprechenden Stelle.

Mit einem Zweifel an der menandrischen Herkunft des Originals der *Aulularia* kann ich mich allerdings nicht befreunden. Zu der mangelnden Motivierung des Lyconides bitte ich *Philologus* 1961, S. 49 f. und 70 f., zu der wiederholten Lauscherszene ebda. S. 65 zu vergleichen.

M. Handley: I do very much welcome what Professor Ludwig has said about the rôle of Pan and the Nymphs in the *Dyskolos*.

But perhaps it would be right to ask if this play is in some sense a special case, because the prologue speaker and his companions in the shrine are so intimately related to the country setting of the play, and some of the references to them, whatever other function they may have, have one function in helping to give the atmosphere of the setting.

M. Reverdin: Permettez-moi de glisser une remarque au sujet du rôle de Pan dans le *Dyskolos*. Ce rôle — M. Ludwig l'a bien marqué — est actif. Pan et les Nymphes sont présents. Non seulement en leur qualité de dieux du nymphéion, mais, psychologiquement, dans les sentiments de plusieurs des personnages. Cela ne serait-il pas dû au fait que la pièce date d'une époque où le culte de Pan et des Nymphes, divinités familières, était en train de prendre une place fort importante dans la religiosité attique? Il suffit, pour s'en convaincre — mieux : pour le sentir —, de se laisser pénétrer par l'atmosphère qui se dégage des autels, des reliefs, des statues, des ex-voto que l'on a groupés au Musée national d'Athènes dans un vestibule auquel on a cherché à conférer l'atmosphère d'un ὕπαιθρον, ou encore de hanter en Attique les grottes de Pan, que ce soit celle de Phylé, ou celle de Vari, décorée par l'architecte Archidemos de Théra qui se proclame νυμφόληπτος (IG I^2, 788 ; comp. Plat. *Phaedr.* 238 *d*).

En respectant la vraisemblance et la vie, qu'il imitait, Ménandre pouvait faire intervenir Pan non seulement comme θεὸς προλογίζων, mais comme divinité participant réellement à l'action. Les grands dieux du panthéon civique ni les abstractions divinisées n'eussent été aptes à tenir un tel rôle, à occuper une telle place. Le cas de Pan dans le *Dyskolos* doit donc, à mon avis, être considéré comme un cas particulier, et traité comme tel.

M. Handley: Rudens, as another play with a remote and romantic setting, is in some ways comparable to *Dyskolos*. The presence of Arcturus as prologue-speaker, as well as the shrine of Venus which figures in the setting and in the action, is also a parallel for the distinction which Professor Ludwig would like to make between prologue-speaker and shrine in the *Aulularia*. Plays with special shrines like these (one thinks also of *Curculio*, set at Epidaurus) possibly give different opportunities for references to the gods from plays with no special shrine, and with a personified abstract as prologue-speaker rather than a known divinity.

On the repetition of motif in *Aul.*, I think we may have to remember the two scenes of borrowing in *Dysk.* (464 ff., 499 ff.) and their reprise in the ragging of Knemon at the end of the play, and to allow that there are ways in which Menander can repeat a motif.

One very general point which inclines me to favour the view that *Aul.* is from a Menandrean original is that it seems to have so many elements in common with *Dysk.*, and also to use them in a contrasting composition, much in the way I should expect if the same author designed two plays on a similar theme, and was conscious of the contrast. May I try to develop this? Something of the likeness in conception of the two plays—I do not speak of detail—can be recalled if we set out a number of statements which seem to be true of both. Thus the central figure, about whom each play is built, is an old man with an obsession of an antisocial character. He lives alone, with a daughter of marriageable age, and a single old slave woman who was the girl's nurse. The divinity who speaks the prologue, and provides the moving force of the action has been treated with grudging respect by the old man; his daughter has performed her religious observances with a simple, attentive piety. The course of the plot brings a mounting series of misfortunes for him, from which at last he learns the error of his ways; for her, there is the reward of a desirable marriage with a young man of superior social class. This all comes about through two converging lines of action. The one begins from the young man in love with the girl, and traces the progress of his attempt to win her; the other is initiated by the young man's mother, from motives of her own, and only the audience knows that the chain of events which follows will ultimately prove to be relevant. The marriage is an issue from the start, not merely a contrived ending; the young man becomes acceptable to the girl's father in the course of helping to deliver him from the consequences of his misguided behaviour; he also has to win approval within his own family; and he has to cope, in the course of all this, with the deficiencies of his own helper or helpers.

In the same general terms, we can state some basic differences between the two plots. In the *Dyskolos*, the girl has a youthful half-brother, who plays a prominent part in the action, and provides an immediate contrast of character for the young lover. In the *Aulularia*, a correspondingly prominent part is played by a second *old* man, the brother of the young man's mother; he provides a character contrast with the elderly hero. The plays are alike, however, in that a main ingredient of the contrast is the antithesis between wealth and poverty, or rather the mental attitudes attendant on those states. To resume, in the *Dyskolos*, the young daughter is given a part to play, although a small one, whereas in the *Aulularia*, for necessary reasons, she is no more than a cry off stage; in the *Dyskolos* the mother remains in the background (whether or not we give her a few lines to speak), while in the *Aulularia* she takes part in person both in the complication of the action and in its resolution. The most striking fact of this kind is of course the treatment of the comic hero himself, who in the *Dyskolos* is on the stage for about a quarter of the time the play would take to act, while in the incomplete *Aulularia*, so far as one can judge, he will have been there for about three-quarters of the time: the actual fraction is of the order of five-eighths. There is therefore a major difference of emphasis on the two age-groups, and it is reflected in the order of events. In the *Dyskolos* the action begins with, and develops from, the affairs of the young lover; in the *Aulularia* it begins with and develops from those of the older people; the lover himself, long though we expect his presence, does not in fact appear in Plautus' play until a very late stage, line 681 of the text.

I do not wish to dispute the idea that he may appear earlier in Menander's version, but merely to underline the difference of emphasis, as it seems to me, from the *Dyskolos*.

Certainly these resemblances and differences can be explained in more than one way. But I would argue that both, and not merely the likenesses, are worth taking into account in a discussion of authorship.

M. Turner : I understand that the audience may have thought a god such as Pan or Apollo (present in the person of his statue : μὰ τὸν 'Απόλλω τουτονί), influenced human action or events. It is more difficult to imagine how they might have accepted an abstraction such as ῎Αγνοια, Βοήθεια, ῎Ελεγχος (Koe. fr. 717) as doing so. *Abstracta* may easily be personified and deified if they are aims of human ambition (so Jocasta warns against Φιλοτιμία, Eur. *Phoen.* 532, ἄδικος ἡ θεός ; the Athenians warn the Melians against ἐλπίς, which should perhaps have a capital letter, *Thuc.* V, 103).

Τύχη is easier to accept than most of these figures. In the prologue to *Aspis*, she speaks of herself as goddess and seems to promise help (97 ff.). She announces that Kleostratos is not dead, but a captive and " will survive directly ". The influence on human events of Τύχη (the prologue goddess or mere " coincidence ") is recognized at vv. 18, 58 (reading ἐκ τύχης for εὐτυχῶς), 248 ; and the " goddess " herself is ironically apostrophised by Daos at 213. We may wonder what is her relationship to ταὐτόματον ? In other plays, too (*Misoumenos*, see below ; *Dysk.* 584 ; *Sik.* 352) events or even a person's physical characteristics are mentioned as arising ἀπὸ τύχης. It may be deliberate artistry that has kept ταὐτόματον out of the *Aspis* (it has not figured in the fragments published to date).

Whatever the relation of ἀπὸ τύχης and ταὐτόματον, either concept is convenient to a playwright constructing his action, and not necessarily a naive device. Reasonable men as well as ordinary men could allow that coincidence plays a part in human affairs. Aristotle, *Physics* 199 *b* (a passage recently adduced by M. Gigante, *Boll. Comitato, Acad. naz. dei Lincei* 1966, pp. 13 sqq.) recognized that a final cause (τὸ οὗ ἕνεκα) and the means to realize it (ὃ τούτου ἕνεκεν) might in certain circumstances arise ἀπὸ τύχης. Aristotle refers to the incident of the man on the way to the Olympic games who put in at Aegina, found Plato there bound as a slave and ransomed him. His commentators (especially Simplicius) apply the phrase ἀπὸ τύχης to Demeas' arrival in the *Misoumenos*. " A useful end resulted from his arrival in order to pay a ransom, even though the person arriving did not come for that purpose."

Prologue divinities allow themselves to make moral comments on the characters in the play. Pan says of Knemon that he is ἀπάνθρωπός τις ἄνθρωπος σφόδρα (*Dysk.* 6). Τύχη speaks of Smikrines with out and out condemnation: πονηρίᾳ δὲ πάντας ἀνθρώπους ὅλως ὑπερπέπαικεν (*Aspis* 116-117). These are the persons due to be fought down. They are not enemies of gods, as Hippolytus is Aphrodite's enemy. The prologue deity enlists the audience's sympathy against them on moral grounds.

M. Wehrli: Dass Menander sich auf einen noch lebendigen Glauben beziehen konnte, wenn er das Bühnengeschehen in *Dyskolos*, *Aulularia* oder *Cistellaria* durch eine Prolog-Gottheit zum glücklichen Ende steuern liess, hat Herr Ludwig überzeugend dargelegt. Während jedoch das wunderbare Walten der Gottheit für Euripides häufig selbständiges Thema ist, wird man bei Menander nur mit Vorbehalten auf seinen persönlichen Glauben schliessen dürfen. Der ausgeklügelte Charakter seiner Theaterschicksale ist für ein religiöses Bekenntnis allzu profan. Ausserdem verlieren sie durch die einleitende Exposition den Charakter des Verblüffenden, der z.B. den aretalogischen Geschichten eigen ist, und schliesslich scheint Menander mit der Wahl seiner Prologsprecher, zu denen auch Abstracta gehören, mehr dichterische als glaubensmässige Absichten zu verfolgen. Mit ihrer konventionellen Topik, zu der u.a. der Anagnorismos gehört, kann die

Handlung in ihrer reinen Gegenständlichkeit nicht das eigentliche Anliegen des Dichters sein. In vielen Fällen ist es offensichtlich, dass bei ihm Kunstgriffe nur der poetischen Gerechtigkeit dienen, dem liebenden Mädchen sein verdientes Glück zu verschaffen. Wie viel dramatisches Leben aus ihnen für die einzelnen Szenen erwächst, ist trotzdem ohne weiteres eindeutig.

M. Ludwig: Die Warnung ist berechtigt, dass die Bedeutung des religiösen Hintergrundes des Geschehens nicht überbetont werden darf. Eine Analyse, die die Aufmerksamkeit speziell auf diese Erscheinungen richtet, gerät leicht in Gefahr, diesen Eindruck zu erwecken. Die religiöse Perspektive, wenn ich diesen vagen Ausdruck einmal benützen darf, kann in einem Stück Menanders mehr oder weniger deutlich sein, aber auch ganz fehlen.

Eine Singularität dürfte der *Dyskolos* in dieser Hinsicht meines Erachtens aber nicht dargestellt haben. Ihr widerspricht einerseits die geringe Zahl der Menanderstücke, die uns hinlänglich bekannt sind, andererseits die relativ grosse Zahl der bekannten Stücke, in denen eine irgendwie geartete Beteiligung einer Gottheit an der Handlung sichtbar wird. Dass im *Dyskolos* der göttliche Anteil dem Hörer öfter, als wir es sonst kennen, ins Gedächtnis gerufen wird, gebe ich gerne zu.

Die Wahl Pans ist durch die Szenerie motiviert, aber die Szenerie hat nicht die Handlungsstruktur als solche (die Beteiligung eines Gottes an der Handlung) hervorgerufen. Letztere war für Menander grundsätzlich eine dramaturgische Möglichkeit. Die Szenerie war nur von Bedeutung dafür, *welchen* Gott Menander hier den Prolog sprechen liess.

Für die Frage, warum bisher keiner der grossen Götter in der Komödie als Prologgott auftrat, möchte ich zweierlei anführen. Erstens wurden in Hellenistischer Zeit die grossen Götter der Staatskulte kaum für die Lenkung der privaten Geschicke in Anspruch genommen (vgl. Nilsson, *Gesch. d. griech. Rel.* II, S. 187), niederere Gottheiten wie Pan und Asklepios standen den Menschen näher. Oder man sprach unbestimmt von θεός, θεοί, δαιμόνιον. Als Prologgott war ein solches Göttliches nicht zu gebrauchen. Die Personifikationen von Abstracta kamen hier zu Hilfe. Ein Aspekt des Göttlichen konnte mit einer allegorischen Figur angesprochen werden. Natürlich existierte eine *Boetheia* nicht für das religiöse Gefühl als eigenständige Gottheit. Aber sie konnte vielleicht als dichterisches Symbol für das manchmal so merkwürdig in das menschliche Leben eingreifende Göttliche gelten. Zum anderen passten die Olympier nicht zur niederen Gattung der Komödie (abgesehen von der Mythentravestie). Sie hatten ihren Platz im Mythos, wo sie mit den Heroen verkehrten, und damit auch in der Tragödie. Auch in der hellenistischen Tragödie werden sie noch aufgetreten sein, als Teil einer Konvention, die auch im Epos beibehalten wurde.

Der Unterschied zwischen Menander und Euripides in Hinsicht auf die Bedeutung der Beteiligung der Götter an der Handlung ist sicher beträchtlich. Trotzdem könnte Menander—wie so oft—gerade an Euripides angeknüpft haben, wenn er auf seine Weise die Mitwirkung göttlicher Kräfte am menschlichen Geschick darstellte (vgl. bes. *Ion*).

Menander kann den Begriff ταὐτόματον bewusst ironisch gebrauchen, vgl. *Dysk.* 543 ff. und Handley S. 225 f. Was Sostratos ein Zufall scheint, entspricht, wie der Hörer weiss, letztlich dem Willen Pans.

M. Handley : There is one class of references to ' fortune ' and the like which seems to me to have the special function of limiting the audience's curiosity, in that it invites them to accept a fact as given, and not to look for further explanation. I should, I think, agree with Professor Turner in taking some of the instances he gives in this way, and should certainly include his excellent ἐκ τύχης at *Aspis* 58 : for the purposes of the incident being narrated, a hill is required, and ἐκ τύχης δέ τι / λοφίδιον ἦν ἐνταῦθ' ὀχυρόν. At *Dysk.* 584, the discovery of the loss of the mattock is made because Knemon ἀπὸ τύχης intended to shift some dung. It could have been expected that the hard-working Knemon, prevented from having his day in the fields (442 f.) would want to do something at home: it is 'given' that he chooses, for no reason which need be defined, something which suits the structure the playwright has in mind. Naturally, as Professor Ludwig rightly stresses, it can be that an event which is seen by a character as pure chance appears very differently to the superior knowledge of the audience, and they can be given that knowledge to create the effect of dramatic irony. Accordingly context, in a very wide sense, is likely to be important when we enquire into the meaning and function of these expressions.

M. Questa: Sono perfettamente d'accordo con il collega Ludwig per quanto concerne la 'Profanisierung', ossia 'laicizzazione', dello spettacolo comico in Plauto e Terenzio (circa Menandro la questione è diversa, ed il collega ha fatto bene a discutere a fondo quella che era un po' la *communis opinio* vulgata, ma si tengano presente anche le acute considerazioni di Wehrli). Vorrei porre al collega due domande: (*a*) la completa assenza di prologo divino in Terenzio dipende in prevalenza da motivi letterari, nel senso che Terenzio abolisce il prologo espositivo di origine euripidea per sostituirvi sistematicamente un prologo 'polemico' o 'letterario' (che avrà enorme fortuna nei secoli)? oppure in Terenzio la scomparsa del θεὸς προλογίζων è anche la conseguenza di una concezione dello spettacolo ancora più 'profana' e 'laica' di quella di Plauto, favorita dall'ambiente sociale raffinato, filosoficamente colto in cui il poeta è stato educato? (*b*) crede il collega che le conclusioni da lui tratte per Menandro siano estensibili anche ad altri poeti della νέα? Come giudica Difilo, il quale scrive quasi una 'teodicea' seria nella *Rudens* e d'altra parte i Κληρούμενοι-*Casina*, cioè una commedia completamente priva di quei risvolti seri che vediamo nella *Rudens*? E, infine, come avrà accolto il pubblico romano l'apparizione in scena di astrazioni o allegorie come *Auxilium* o *Luxuria*?

M. Ludwig: Es ist immer schwierig, von einem sichtbaren Resultat auf die Motive des Dichters zu schliessen, die zu ihm geführt haben. Ich würde auch in der Einführung des literarischen Prologs einen Anstoss zur Eliminierung des Götterprologs sehen, der eine zweite lange Monologrede gebracht hätte. Dass damit ein Gott von der Bühne verschwand, könnte eine nicht unerwünschte Folge gewesen sein, die Terenz aber möglicherweise sogar schon von Anfang an intendierte. Im Ergebnis hat Terenz jedenfalls das, was bei Plautus nur nebenbei in Wegfall geraten konnte, prinzipiell beseitigt.

Göttliches Engagement an der Handlung war sicher nicht nur bei Menander zu finden. Auch ohne den *Rudens* müssten wir dies vermuten. Der Hinweis von Prof. Questa auf den Kontrast zwischen *Rudens* und *Casina* scheint mir wichtig, um die Spannweite anzudeuten, die auf der komischen Bühne Athens und im Werk ein und desselben Dichters möglich war (bei Menander sind die Extreme etwa mit *Dyskolos* und Δὶς ἐξαπατῶν bezeichnet).

Die Frage nach der Wirkung der Erscheinung von Personifikationen auf das römische Publikum ist schwierig und interessant. Grundlegend immer noch Deubner und Stössl in Roscher und *RE* s.v. Man wird differenzieren und jeden Fall gesondert betrachten müssen. Personifikationen spielten zur Zeit des Plautus im Kult eine beträchtliche Rolle (Anspielungen darauf auch in seinen Komödien). *Auxilium* dagegen war als *deus* schon wegen seines grammatisch neutralen Geschlechts für das Publikum wohl ein Witz, *Luxuria* als allegorische Figur ein Spiel der dichterischen Phantasie (dasselbe gilt von ihrer Vorgängerin bei Philemon).

Mme *Kahil:* Chez Euripide déjà, la responsabilité divine perd de son importance et la responsabilité humaine devient prépondérante (qu'on songe, par exemple, au dialogue entre Hécube et Hélène dans les *Troyennes* vv. 983 ss.). En fait la coupure est sensible à Athènes vers la fin de la guerre du Péloponnèse. C'est à cette époque que les grands dieux olympiens voient les hommes se tourner de préférence vers les divinités plus accessibles (dieux sauveurs, dieux guérisseurs, dieux ou déesses des religions à mystères ; à l'époque hellénistique il faut y ajouter la religion isiaque). D'autre part, c'est vers la même époque que les allégories commencent à se répandre. L'art reflète cette évolution spirituelle. Voyez le groupe de Céphisodote représentant Eirènè portant Ploutos, dont l'influence a été considérable et qui inaugure réellement un courant nouveau. A partir de ce moment, le nombre des allégories ira croissant : c'est ainsi que Tychè jouera dans tous les domaines un rôle qu'elle n'avait point auparavant.

Chez Ménandre cette tendance est manifeste comme on vient de le démontrer : à côté de divinités locales comme le Pan de Phylé rappelons que la *Théophoroumènè* nous montre les adeptes du culte de Cybèle (dont l'expansion est post-classique). Parmi les grands dieux c'est Apollon qui chez Ménandre joue le rôle le plus important (cf. par exemple la *Leucadia* dont les fragments sont si peu nombreux, malheureusement, mais auxquels s'ajoute maintenant la mosaïque de Mytilène).

Mlle Dedoussi : I should be interested to hear what Professor Ludwig does think about Menander's own religious attitude. Is there any religious aspect expressed in his comedies? The traditional popular religion had, of course, an important part in the life of people during Menander's time, and provided him with much material for his comedies.

M. Ludwig : Man ist heute vorsichtig geworden, aus einem Werk auf die persönliche Auffassung des Dichters zu schliessen. Die Frage nach der dramaturgischen Funktion der Götter ist eine literaturwissenschaftliche, die nach Menanders persönlichen Glauben eine religionsgeschichtliche, wobei die erste durch Analyse der Stücke, soweit sie hinreichend überliefert sind, klar beantwortet werden kann, die zweite dagegen nur vermutungsweise. Offensichtlich war Menander an Erscheinungen des religiösen Lebens seiner Zeit interessiert, da er solche öfters zur Darstellung bringt, aber das ist nur ein Teil seines allgemeinen Interesses am menschlichen Verhalten im gesellschaftlichen Zusammenleben.

Etwas anderes ist die Deutung des Geschehens, die aus der Analyse des gott-menschlichen Wechselspiels in einigen seiner Komödien erhellt. Hier handelt es sich nicht um subjektive (und vielleicht kritisch betrachtete) religiöse Vorstellungen der Personen auf der Bühne, sondern um die objektive Geschehensstruktur dieser Komödien, wobei sich anschliessend nur wieder die Frage stellt, wie weit diese der subjektiven Auffassung Menanders vom Lauf des menschlichen Lebens entspricht und wie weit sie *nur* eine dramaturgische Konvention darstellt, für die Menander in der Wirklichkeit kein Korrelat sah, obwohl einige seiner Zuhörer sie sicher « ernst » nahmen. Diese Frage nach der subjektiven Auffassung Menanders wird sich nie zwingend beantworten lassen. Ich persönlich sehe zur Zeit keinen Anlass, warum Menander hier öfters aus freier Wahl dramaturgischen Konventionen folgte (obwohl er ihnen erwiesenermassen nicht folgen musste), wenn er nicht der Meinung war, dass diese Beteiligung einer Gottheit an der dramaturgischen Handlung auch in der Wirklichkeit gewisse Entsprechungen hatte. Andere mögen ihn für skeptischer halten und ihm zutrauen, dass er uns da sozusagen nur etwas vorspielen will. Zu widerlegen ist eine solche Einschätzung nicht. Aber ich möchte im Interesse der Klarheit noch einmal unterstreichen, dass es auch nach meiner Meinung Menander nicht darum geht, eine bestimmte religiöse Anschauung zu propagieren, sondern dass sein dichterisches Interesse dem menschlichen Leben zugewandt ist, bei dessen Darstellung dann fallweise auch der ihm gegenwärtige göttliche Hintergrund in dichterischer Symbolisierung einbezogen werden konnte. Eine gewisse subjektive Akzentuierung ist hier, wie gesagt, leider unvermeidlich und so muss dieser Teil meiner Antwort einen hypothetischen Charakter haben.

M. Sandbach: It is certainly impossible to *know* the dramatist's personal religious views. But some probable guesses may be made. Dodds in *The Greeks and the Irrational* pp. 107 ff. called attention to a type of dream common in the ancient world, in which a revered figure, dead parent or divinity, appeared and gave advice. This was often accepted and acted upon even by educated persons—we may remember that Plato represents Socrates as doing so, *Phaedo* 60 *e*—from which it may be supposed that there was a general belief that such dreams gave a real communication from outside the human world. Thus, although the dream sent by Pan in *Dyskolos* is fictional, there is no reason for supposing, in the absence of any evidence to the contrary, that the poet rejected the current belief that dreams of that kind were supernaturally inspired.

M. Questa: Nei vv. 42-43 dell'*Amphitruo* sono menzionati, tra altri θεοὶ προλογίζοντες della tragedia, *Victoria* e *Virtus.* C'era quindi un punto di contatto tra commedia e tragedia, almeno nell'uso di certe allegorie? (seppure il passo del prologo non è scherzoso e non mescola divinità veramente apparse nella scena ad altre immaginate da Plauto).

M. Ludwig: Die Frage nach der Herkunft der allegorischen Prologfiguren in der römischen Tragödie, deren Vorkommen *Amph.* 42 f. beweisen, ist sehr schwierig. O. Skutsch, der zuletzt diese Frage behandelte (*Harv.-Stud.* 1967, S. 125 ff.), nahm an, dass die *Praetexta* und die *Nea/Palliata* darauf Einfluss gehabt hatten, dass die Römer auch bei griechischen Tragödien solche Prologgötter neu eingeführt hätten. Vielleicht benützten aber auch schon griechische Tragödien der hellenistischen Zeit solche Figuren.

III

F. H. SANDBACH

Menander's Manipulation of Language for dramatic Purposes

MENANDER'S MANIPULATION OF LANGUAGE FOR DRAMATIC PURPOSES

This subject may have been suggested in order to give me as free a hand as possible, for it is one to which almost anything could be relevant. Trimeters and tetrameters cannot be written without the manipulation of language, and Menander wrote his for the stage, that is, for dramatic purposes. This paper cannot do more than begin the discussion of some arbitrarily selected topics.

A familiar passage of Plutarch may provide a start. In the extract preserved from his *Comparison of Aristophanes and Menander* he complains that Aristophanes for all his varied vocabulary cannot give a king dignity, an orator eloquence and so on, but " assigns his characters any words that come handy, as if by lot ; and you couldn't tell whether his speaker is a son or a father, a rustic, a god, an old woman or a hero. But Menander's diction is so polished, and has so coalesced by being mixed to a consistency (συμπέπνευκε κεκραμένη πρὸς ἑαυτήν), that while it passes through many emotions and types of character and is adapted to all kinds of personage, it appears to have unity and preserves its uniformity (ὁμοιότητα) as it employs common, familiar words in ordinary use ... no workman ever made the same shoe for man and for woman, for youth and for old man and for family slave, nor the same mask or outer garment, but Menander so blended (ἔμειξε Herwerden: ἔδειξε) his diction that it fitted every nature, disposition, and time of life."

What exactly was Plutarch's meaning is, as often with him, not easy to determine. The final comparison may suggest that Menander had in some miraculous way compounded a style which was identical for all characters, so that one could not tell from the words and expressions used who the speaker was, but which was yet appropriate for everybody. On the other hand the contrast with Aristophanes might imply that Plutarch believed Menander to differ from him in that Menandrean sons and fathers, gods and old women, were distinguishable in their vocabulary. This is not however a necessary interpretation. Plutarch's contrast may be merely this: Aristophanes had a huge vocabulary, from which he ought to have been able to find suitable differing styles, but did not; Menander, with his restricted vocabulary, found a single style that suited all characters.

I must confess that I find it easier to support the view that Menander distinguished his speakers by their language than to find clear evidence for a single style. Yet it is perhaps true that his various characters have a good deal in common in their talk, and are distinguished by excrescences from a common central territory; and that since he was a delicate artist, who avoided exaggeration, the range of difference is limited. 'Avoided exaggeration' is possibly not strong enough; rather he may not have fully reflected the range of differences that must have existed between the speech of individuals at Athens. Above all, it is scarcely credible that foreign slaves all spoke Greek as well as do those of the plays. The representation of life for which Menander was praised cannot then be a simple realism in language any more than in incident. It is a procedure that selects from life and modifies what it selects, but with a tact that leaves a result that seems lifelike.

Now can we recognise any features that are common to all his characters or nearly all? And that may constitute this single style of which Plutarch speaks? I hope it is a correct guess that they talk prose such as might have been heard in the streets of Athens. The fitting of this into metre, in particular iambics, is achieved with remarkably little violence to the natural order of words, which is departed from mainly to indicate emotion or confusion; and even this departure is, as Wilamowitz noticed (*Schiedsgericht* p. 156), true to life. But this prose is not *all* that could be heard in the streets. Obviously indecent language is nearly excluded, and never admitted for its own sake; at *Perikeiromene* 234 it characterises one whom we know to have had too much to drink, and at *Dyskolos* 892 one of whom we may suspect it; less striking words are used by angry men at *Sikyonios* 266 and *Dyskolos* 462. Similarly there is little that can be called slang; what may be termed literary decency is preserved. At the other end of the scale elevated or poetical vocabulary is sometimes used by some characters, in strict moderation and always for a purpose, but more readily, one may suspect, than it was used in real life. Of this more later.

But within this similarity of style there are marked differences between individual characters, of a kind that I do not see reproduced by Terence in his adaptations, although Professor Arnott has kindly shown me an article soon to be published in *Greece and Rome* in which he makes it clear that such differentiation is by no means completely absent. In Menander an extreme example is the pretended Doric doctor of *Aspis*. Apart from his dialectical forms—and whether his inconsistencies are deliberate or the work of copyists I see no way of deciding—his vocabulary is full of unusual words. Ἀναφρίζω, is known by LSJ only from Phrynichus; the compound ἀνερεύγομαι first occurs here, and the simple verb, for which the Attic form was ἐρυγγάνω, only in poetic and Hippocratic authors; for θάλπω, ' give false comfort ', cf. S. *El.* 888 and also A. *P.V.* 684. Φρενῖτις is a medical technical term for inflammation of the diaphragm (not of the ' brain ' as LSJ have it). Βιώσιμος 'likely to live' is known from Theophrastus *H.P.* ix.12.1 and several passages of Arrian, e.g. *Anab.* ii.4.8, ' the doctors did not think him βιώσιμος.' Πάμπαν, although a favourite word of Aristotle, is not found in comedy or the orators. But this man is an exceptional case, valuable only to show that Menander was prepared to give a character a distinctive mode of speech.

The two young men in *Dyskolos* are clearly distinguished. Sostratos' speech is easy and flexible; one can rarely guess what is coming next, so that it seems to take shape as it is uttered. Gorgias talks like a book; his thought takes the antithetical form familiar in the orators, so that his sentences are determined before they begin. Almost as soon as he enters we have the symmetrical sentence (250 ff.)

τοῦτον οὔθ' ὅτῳ τρόπῳ
ἀναγκάσαι τις εἰς τὸ βέλτιον ῥέπειν
οὔτ' ἂν μεταπείσαι νουθετῶν οἶδ' οὐδὲ εἷς,
ἀλλ' ἐμποδὼν τῷ μὲν βιάσασθαι τὸν νόμον
ἔχει μεθ' αὑτοῦ, τῷ δὲ πεῖσαι τὸν τρόπον.

The details of the text are uncertain (I use that of Lloyd-Jones and Jacques) but the general structure is clear. The passage contains an example of a construction surprisingly rare in Menander, οὔτε ... οὔτε used to join not words but clauses. Gorgias does this again at 823-826, again in combination with a μέν ... δέ opposition:

ἐγώ σε Σώστρατ' εἶναι μὲν φίλον
ὑπολαμβάνω σπουδαῖον ἀγαπῶ τ' ἐκτόπως,
μείζω δ' ἐμαυτοῦ πράγματ' οὔτε βούλομαι
οὔτ' ἂν δυναίμην μὰ Δία βουληθεὶς φέρειν.

Similarly he uses μήτε ... μήτε, each with its imperative clause, at 284-286. These three instances are half of the whole number we yet have in Menander: the others are frag. 335, a moralising and perhaps slightly ridiculous speech by a slave, *Dysk.* 743-745, intentionally impressive lines by Knemon, and almost certainly *Sik.* 176, the opening of the messenger's speech, modelled on Euripides' *Orestes* 866 ff. Menander must have felt that this construction belongs to formal thought-out speech, not to normal conversation. Gorgias, I said, talks like a book. His hard life will have given him little practice in the art of talk, but plenty of time to acquire the habit of arranging his thoughts in antithetical form. Analysis of 271-287 would demonstrate at least seven antitheses, but I confine myself to noticing the wide separation of μέν (274) and δέ (280). This is unusual, and the only parallel for six intervening lines is in Moschion's speech at the beginning of *Samia* Act V. Here he tells the audience that he has quite lost control of himself, ἐξέστηκα νῦν τελέως ἐμαυτοῦ. It is an indication that this is nothing but the striking of an attitude that he immediately explains his position in a sentence ten lines long, organised round this μέν and δέ.

If a sort of footnote may here be allowed, there is a passage of *Sikyonios* where a μέν, probably followed by a δέ, shows how it is to be taken. Theron has been coaching an old man in a story he is to tell to impersonate Kichesias; he does not know that the old man *is* Kichesias. At 361 Dromon suddenly speaks:

ἡ μὲν τροφίμη 'στὶν ἀσφαλῶς τηρουμένη,

then some lines are lost. The question is whether Dromon has been present listening to the conversation unseen, as Kassel and Barigazzi believed, and here makes himself known, or whether he enters with these words. I do not believe that a loyal slave, seeing his master for the first time for at least ten years, would be calm enough to address him with such a μέν-clause, presumably with a δέ in mind. But a character entering the stage not infrequently uses μέν and δέ, appropriately, for he may be supposed to have been reflecting and to have arranged and organised his thoughts. Examples are *Aspis* 97, 164, *Dysk.* 259, 394, *Samia* 399, 616, *Perik.* 77. Similarly here Dromon, who was last heard of as he accompanied Philumene to her place of refuge with the priestess, comes back ; and it may be guessed that he said to himself or to the audience, without immediately seeing the others ; ' my young mistress is in safe keeping, but now her father must be found.'

To return to Gorgias, another feature that distinguishes him from all other major characters in the play is that he uses no oaths but the plain, trite νὴ Δία and μὰ Δία (each twice). There is one exception : at 777 he exclaims, of the approaching Kallippides, Πόσειδον, ὀξυπείνως πως ἔχει . αὐτίκ' αὐτῶι ταῦτ' ἐροῦμεν, or so B. But was Foss perhaps right in assigning thə first clause to Sostratos, not so much because of the impropriety he saw if Gorgias remarked on the appetite of his new friend's father, but because of the exclamation Πόσειδον. I also think that ' shall *we* tell him ? ' is more likely in the mouth of Sostratos, who is always anxious to associate Gorgias in what is going on, than in that of Gorgias, who will in a moment suggest that Sostratos should talk to his father alone : λάλει τῶι πατρὶ κατὰ μόνας (781). But we are here entering a field where observations on the use of language may breed suspicions rather than dictate any departure from the tradition.

It is worth remark that Gorgias uses the word ἐθέλω, twice in the aorist (269, 767) and once in the future (854). These are the only instances in Menander of ἐθέλω (as opposed to θέλω), and they have no parallel in the fragments of Middle or New Comedy, except that ἠθέλησα occurs in paratragic surroundings in fragment 3 of Kriton, whom Pollux counts among οἱ νεώτεροι. The evidence of inscriptions shows that θέλω replaced ἐθέλω in Attica, but the word is not of very common occurrence and Meisterhans-Schwyzer quote nothing between about 300 B.C., their latest ἐθέλω, and 250 B.C., their earliest θέλω. Comedy suggests that ἐθέλω was obsolescent in the later 4th century. For that matter Menander had no liking for θέλω. In his plays it occurs only in the formula ἂν θεὸς θέλῃι (*Georgos* 45, fr. 39) and in a quotation from Aeschylus. In the fragments there are three occurrences (45, 97, 499), none quite beyond doubt, but this is not the place for discussing them. The solid fact is that, apart from a possibly paratragic instance, Gorgias is in our remains of Middle and New Comedy the only person to use ἐθέλω. What is the reason for this? It is possible that in 317 B.C. Menander was himself still using the form ἐθέλω, although on the point of giving it up. There might be a parallel in the fact that seven times in *Dyskolos* he attaches πως to an adverb, e.g. πως ἐνθεαστικῶς, πως φυλακτικῶς: elsewhere he does this only once (fr. 153). If we possessed Ὀργή and Μέθη we might find more instances of ἐθέλω. But I should prefer to think, guess though it may be, that Gorgias uses ἐθέλω because it was an old-fashioned form that Menander felt to be appropriate to this youth who lived tucked away in the country remote from the modern fashions of the town.

Another pair of characters distinguished by their way of talk are Getas and Sikon. Getas' vocabulary and phraseology is almost entirely conventional. He uses half-a-dozen words not recorded elsewhere in Middle or New Comedy, but none of it is ' fine language '. Sikon's speech is picturesque, as was noted by Giannini (*Acme* xiii, 1960, 190) ; he deploys otherwise unknown metaphors, νεωλκῶν 399, βεβωλοκόπηκεν 515, σφαιρομαχοῦσι 518, and gives the proverbial expression ἐν φρέατι κυνὶ μάχεσθαι a literal turn. He is full of oaths, one every seven lines (Dohm, *Mageiros* 229), to varied gods (six besides Zeus). His peculiar vocabulary, unlike that of Getas, consists mainly of words found elsewhere in authors with some claims to style. The list is ἀδιήγητος, ἀθῷιος, ἀνάπηρος, ἀνιέναι τὰς ὀφρῦς, ἀποιμώζω, ἐπικωλύω, θαλλός, ἱεροπρεπής, κολακικός, χυτρόγαυλος. I omit the metaphors already mentioned. All this prepares the way for his climax in the last act, as he describes the scene of revelry in the cave, using poetic language and a simile that has caused editors a lot of trouble (*perobscurum* says Lloyd-Jones). Handley rightly remarks that similar scenes are elsewhere reported in elevated language. It may be added that Menander has prepared for Sikon's poetic style here by earlier representing him as imaginative and unusual in his wording.

The distinction between Sikon and Getas may be relevant to the textual problem at 550. The metaphor ὄνος ἄγειν δοκῶ μοι τὴν ἑορτήν ascribed by many editors to Getas does not fit his usual down-to-earth style, which knows abuse and sarcasm, but not metaphor. This reinforces the other objections to the proposal of Barrett and others to read ὄνος for ολος, namely that confusion of λ and ν is not paralleled in B, and that Getas had already made a reference to donkeys at his entrance, τεττάρων γὰρ φορτίον ὄνων συνέδησαν αἱ κάκιστ' ἀπολούμεναι φέρειν γυναῖκές μοι. The reference is more appropriate there because a donkey is a proverbial beast of burden, as Getas then was, and not, what he here complains of being, a factotum. Ἄγω δοκῶ μοι τὴν ἑορτήν is sarcasm, typical of Getas : ' I'm keeping the holiday, I believe '. The association of ἑορτή with the idea of 'not working' is well illustrated in LSJ s.v. 2 and 3. ολος should be ὅλως, but whether to be taken with ἄγω τὴν ἑορτήν or with the preceding words is scarcely to be determined.

Nikeratos in *Samia* is a man of short sentences, often in asyndeton ; if he manages to keep going for two whole lines, the sentence may be composed of small units, as 401-402. His style is well illustrated by 410-420 :

> ἤκουσα καὐτὸς τῶν γυναικῶν, ὅτι τρέφεις
> ἀνελομένη παιδάριον. ἐμβροντησία.
> ἀλλ' ἔστ' ἐκεῖνος ἡδύς. οὐκ ὠργίζετο
> εὐθύς ; διαλιπὼν δ' ; ἀρτίως ;

I follow the division of speeches on which B and C are agreed. Then Chrysis answers in a contrasted sentence of three lines, after which Nikeratos goes on with his brevities, Δημέας χολᾶι, κτλ. There is one passage which provides a striking exception to this style, the great sentence 507-513 in which he declares what *he* would have done to a son or mistress who had treated him so. I believe this is deliberate. It is a measure of the strength of his indignation that it lends him an unusual power of sustained speech.

With some hesitation I now mention an idea that has not yet commended itself to any of my friends who have heard it. I should not suggest it at all if I were not one of those who believe Ritchie to have been right to give Sostratos' mother a speaking part. My suggestion is less bold.

When Demeas and Nikeratos first appear at 96, the former opens : ' Don't you already feel the change of place, and what a difference there is between things here and your troubles there ? ' Then there follow $3^1/_2$ lines of disconnected phrases, that jump from one thing to another and are certainly intended to be comic.

> Πόντος· παχεῖς γέροντες, ἰχθῦς ἄφθονοι,
> ἀηδία τις πραγμάτων. Βυζάντιον·
> ἀψίνθιον, πικρὰ πάντ'. Ἄπολλον. ταῦτα δὲ
> καθαρὰ πενήτων ἀγαθά.

This is in Nikeratos' style, not that of Demeas, who proceeds to the serious prayer, 'Αθῆναι φίλταται and so on. Apart from language, is it likely that the wealthy Demeas should recommend Athens as a place where poor men enjoy unadulterated good things? How does he know? It is of course true that some rich men will tell the poor how lucky they are, but it is a tasteless proceeding. Certainly by modern feelings it is better that Nikeratos should congratulate himself than that Demeas should tell him that Athens is a fine place for the poor.

It is a characteristic of many persons in real life that they have favourite tricks of speech, expressions of which they are fond. Sometimes these may be significant of something in their character, but often enough it would be difficult to deduce anything about the person from them, any more than from the shape of his nose. Such favourite expressions, however, like the shape of his nose, form part of that complex which we recognise as an *individual* human being. To guard against misapprehension let me say that there may be some truth in physiognomy, but it is an uncertain art; similarly turns of speech may be significant of character, but they are difficult to interpret with certainty.

These individualising touches are to be found in some of Menander's personages. Thus it has been noticed that the vituperative vocative ἀνόσιε is used three times by Knemon (108, 469, 595) and never by anyone else. That does not mean that in the next play discovered there will not be some person who uses the word. A snub nose is not peculiar to Socrates, but it is part of what makes the individual Socrates. The phrase εἰπέ μοι is quite widely used in various plays, but no one is as fond of it as Demeas in *Samia*. Of 7 instances one is in the mouth of Moschion (677) and another (453) probably is, but at least 5 belong to Demeas: 482, 589, 690, and 692 are indubitable; 170 is not assigned by Austin to any speaker, but surely there can be no doubt. Demeas has undertaken to persuade Nikeratos to hurry on the marriage of his daughter to Moschion. The two old men meet at 169, as is shown by χαῖρε πολλὰ σύ. Then someone says μνημονεύεις, εἰπέ μοι, [ ]ν ἐθέμεθα ἡμέραν. 'Εγώ is the reply. In the next line we have τὴν τήμερον, and then a series of questions and objections: ποῦ; πότε; τρόπῳ τίνι; ἀλλ' ἔστ' ἀδύνατον. πρὶν εἰπεῖν τοῖς φίλοις; It is clear that Nikeratos is very naturally surprised and taken aback at the proposal to marry his daughter that very day, and so it will have been Demeas who introduced the subject by some such words as μνημονεύεις, εἰπέ μοι, [ὡς οὐχὶ πρότερο]ν ἐθέμεθ' ἡμέραν, 'you remember that we did not previously fix a day?' In this εἰπέ μοι is otiose; there is no reason to press for an answer. Demeas uses the phrase because he has the habit. One may contrast the state of affairs in *Dyskolos*, where six instances are shared between five persons.

There are some other characters in whom such tricks of speech may be observed, but they are not many, and Menander did not sow with the sack for his effects. Accordingly the question may be asked whether in observing such things we are observing something that is there certainly, but is there by accident, so that it does not deserve attention? Is it not possible that these peculiarities in the language of individuals are due solely to chance? Now put in that simple way, this may not be a very useful question. Plays are written, not by chance, but by human beings; human beings have a tendency to repeat words at a short distance unwittingly, often indeed to their own annoyance when they observe what they have done. Hence the useful question is whether the repetition of locutions is any more frequent than what would arise by the mechanical working of the human brain. But brains differ: we are concerned with the working of Menander's brain. And here we seem to meet an impenetrable wall, for we have no evidence, except in the plays themselves, of how his brain worked. I see no way past this difficulty, and what follows has no claim to be anything more than guesswork.

A single repetition of a word at a short distance seems most naturally explicable as the result of the tendency for a word once used to be used again; it seems to be readily available to the mind. Thus when at *Epitrepontes* 247 Onesimos says ἐπιεικῶς πυκνά and at 253 (probably) ἐπιεικῶς μέγα, or at *Aspis* 24 Daos says ἐπιεικῶς μάχαις πολλαῖς and at 35 ἐπιεικῶς συχνά it would be rash to see any significance, although the word is not repeated elsewhere in what we have of either play. But when the repetitions of a word or phrase by a single character are more numerous and well spaced out, it is harder to put them down to a mere mechanical trick of the mind. It seems more likely that the playwright's mind associated the word and the character. This association may, it is true, have been an unconscious one. Menander may have made a character repeat a word without realising what he was doing. But that does not imply that we should necessarily refuse to notice the repetition. Writers are not always aware of the processes of composition. Housman recorded that stanzas often came suddenly and fully formed into his head (*The Name and Nature of Poetry*, 49) ; we should not be justified in saying that the lines must have rhymed by accident. Unfortunately we do not know how far Menander was conscious of the details of his writing. Sophocles is reported to have said of Aeschylus καὶ γὰρ εἰ τὰ δέοντα ποιεῖ, ἀλλ' οὐκ εἰδώς γε. Perhaps the same could have been said of Menander. Whether he knew what he was doing or not, these tricks of speech are there and make their small contribution to the lifelikeness of their users.

I now turn to another subject, and shall discuss Menander's use of elevated or poetic language.

There are two possible extreme views. The first is that he used such diction seriously, because he wished to stir other emotions than that of amusement. According to this view the recognition scene in *Perikeiromene* is in stichomuthia to help the spectator to experience the pathos and the drama of what is going on. The other extreme is that poetic diction in domestic drama always has some element of absurdity. My own belief is that no generalisation will apply correctly to all the facts.

Let us start with a very simple case, the treatment of a syllable as long when it contains a short vowel preceding a mute and liquid. This means that the division between syllables was made to fall between the two consonants and not before them both, as regularly in comedy. Such scansion, that is such a way of pronouncing, was used in tragedy. Whether it was ever used in Attic households in moments of emotion, how can we tell? But I think it not erroneous to call it tragic scansion.

Now when at *Misoumenos* 214 Demeas embraces his lost daughter with the words ἔχω σε, τέκνον, using this scansion, it is a sign of his emotion, and there can be no question but that the audience is to share that emotion without reservation or complication. But when at *Samia* 516 Nikeratos exclaims ἀλλ' ἐγὼ πρὸς τοῖσιν ἄλλοις τὴν τὰ δείν' εἰργασμένην εἰσεδεξάμην μελάθροις τοῖς ἐμοῖς, it is equally clear that the audience may observe, but will not share, his emotion. It is absurd that the poor Nikeratos should denote his house by the poetic word μέλαθρα, usually applied to the palaces of kings. Is not the absurdity heightened by the scansion of μελάθροις as a bacchiac? Even in tragedy the word is often scanned with a short second syllable. The long syllable, like the long form τοῖσιν in the previous line, is intended to indicate Nikeratos' emotion, but that is an emotion at which the audience will smile, knowing it to be based on ignorance of the facts. An intermediate case is *Epitrepontes* 148, where Syros imagines that the foundling when grown up will undertake θηρᾶν λέοντας, ὅπλα βαστάζειν, τρέχειν ἐν ἀγῶσι. Βαστάζειν is a verb as absent from Attic prose as lions from fourth-century Greece. Syros is striking out a rhetorical phrase, which must appear slightly comic in the mouth of a slave, and the unusual scansion ὅπλα adds to the comic flavour. Is there also perhaps an anti-climax achieved by starting with lion-hunting and ending with running at a sports-meeting, as is suggested by De Falco? At the same time Syros is not, like Nikeratos, a figure of fun. He may exaggerate his points, he may use figures of rhetoric that would be more at home in a court of law, where they are expected, than at an impromptu arbitration, where they stand out as rhetorical; but his case is basically a sound one and his arguments essentially right. So that although the hearer may smile at the form of expression, he is not hostile to what is said; he can therefore simultaneously be amused and moved by the language. It is a mistake to suppose that an audience's reaction must always be *either* one thing *or* another. Just as they are not expected, above all by Menander, to find all characters *either* good *or* bad, or every action or mode of conduct either completely right or completely wrong; or as they are at once present at the happenings on the stage, so that the man in the play may address them, take them into his confidence, perhaps even ask their help, and yet not present, for they cannot interfere in any way with the progress of events; even so they can at the same moment find a character ridiculous and sympathetic, so that they can both laugh at him and still to some extent share his emotions.

These remarks may be thought both obvious and erected on an insufficient base, consisting of a handful of scansional oddities. But unusual diction is to be found in other fields besides that of scansion, and the principle that it can meet with what may be called a " multiple response " is one widely applicable and not to be lost sight of. But that said, one may still maintain that some passages require one predominant response, and others another.

The longest piece of poetic diction that survives is the recognition-scene of *Perikeiromene*, conducted in the artificial form of stichomuthia and composed according to the metrical rules of tragedy. It is therefore sharply contrasted with the style of the rest of the play, and has been felt by some critics to damage its unity. Yet this scene is not simply a tragic foreign body. To see it as such is to forget the presence of Moschion as an eaves-dropper, a figure who prevents one from taking it absolutely seriously. One may compare the scene in *Samia* where the attempts of the cook to interfere in Demeas' expulsion of Chrysis prevent that episode from being one of unrelieved seriousness, passion and pathos. In *Perikeiromene* the stichomuthia begins in abrupt contrast to the very plain language of Moschion that immediately precedes. Again there is disharmony between it and Moschion's conversational line 357

τουτὶ μὲν ἕν μοι τῶν ἐμοὶ ζητουμένων

or again his colloquial ποῦ ποτ' εἰμὶ γῆς at 363. These are reminders that the dialogue is being conducted in artificial language and according to an artificial formula, and must, I think, prevent the spectators from taking it with unalloyed seriousness. When they hear the question

πῶς οὖν ἐχωρίσθητ' ἀπ' ἀλλήλων δίχα;

and recall the famous passage of Euripides on the separation of heaven and earth, ἐπεὶ δ' ἐχωρίσθησαν ἀλλήλων δίχα, they must smile at the impudence of transferring this phrase from cosmology to the separation of a pair of children. It is not to my mind improper to see in this scene an element of tragic parody or to find an intentional touch of absurdity in 355

μόνη δ' ἔκεισο; τοῦτο γάρ σήμαινέ μοι.

or in Glykera's interruption at 375

τί γίνεταί ποθ'; ὡς τρέμω τάλαι[ν' ἐγώ.

When an early critic wrote ' the style rises in dignity to the level of tragedy, to correspond with the importance of the subject ' (T. W. Lumb, *New Chapters in Greek Literature* i. 82) or a recent one says ' il tono stilistico . . . denuncia e accentua il clima patetico e drammatico della vicenda ' (D. del Corno, *Menandro* : *Le Commedie*, 305), these judgements give only a half-truth. No doubt the dramatist wished to indicate the emotion and excitement of Pataikos and Glykera, but at the same time he was not writing a tragedy, but a comedy : he wanted his audience to feel amusement at the characters' language as well as sympathy with their emotions. The capacity of the human being for a complicated multiple reponse makes this a feasible aim. Nevertheless I wonder whether Menander does not here demand rather a lot. To take a convention at its face value, for the purpose for which it was devised, and at the same time to know that fun is being made of it, is a difficult feat, and perhaps he was expecting a tour-de-force by his actors if they were to enable the audience to achieve it.

A ' parody of tragic style ' has also been seen in some damaged lines from the recognition scene of *Sikyonios*, published by Jouguet in 1906. When that phrase was written it was not known that much more of the play was composed in a style nearer that of serious poetry than had been met before in Menander. Having only mutilated lines from a mutilated play, it is dangerous to hazard an opinion ; but I doubt whether what remains of this passage is so far above the general level that we have adequate reason to speak of parody : it may rather be imitation, a piece of fine writing for a crucial incident in the plot.

There is, however, another passage in this play which at first sight at least appears to be tragic parody. At 169 the wrangle between Smikrines and the person I shall call 'the democrat' is abruptly terminated. Someone cries ὦ γεραιέ, μεῖνον ἐν παραστά[σιν and Smikrines replies μένω· τίνος δὲ τοῦτο θωύ[σσεις χάριν; (the supplement is certain). This reply is in language unknown to comedy and typical of tragedy, and it makes not unlikely the supplement of the previous line by the poetical word δόμων. Γεραιός is also found mainly in tragedy, where it is scanned, as here, as a tribrach in Sophocles, *O.C.* 200 and Euripides, *H.F.* 446. Unfortunately what follows is badly damaged, but the remains of the next three lines suggest that the elevated style may not have been maintained. 172 βουλόμεθ' ἀκοῦσαι τὰ περί τ[is prosaic enough, and 174 might be e.g. εἰδώς γ' ἃ πυν[θάνει λέγοιμ' ἂν ταῦτ' ἐγώ. Neither πύνδαξ nor ἀπυνδάκωτος seem likely alternatives. If this is right, Smikrines' tragic language in 170 may be used because he wishes to make fun of the elevated diction of the other speaker. But what then is the reason for that diction? Here we are up against our imperfect understanding of the plot. Is the speaker someone who has no part to play except to report the events at the propylaea? Is he one who passes across the stage like a meteor in the manner of a messenger in tragedy? He seems to take it for granted that Smikrines will be interested in his tale, even before he has been encouraged to tell it: and he departs without waiting for comment or thanks, of which he receives no word. Perhaps Menander has here taken over the practice of serious drama and used it for his comedy. Then the tragic language of the messenger's entrance at 169 must be regarded as a signal of what is afoot. 'Here is a messenger, such as you know in tragedy.'

But if there is any element of parody here it is a very small one. The tale starts with a clear reference to the messenger's speech in Euripides' *Orestes*; but the phrases used are perfectly appropriate to their new position; there is no attempt to make fun of Euripides. Nor in all that follows is there any sign of parody of tragic language. The story is a serious one seriously told. But the language is not particularly poetic. One may notice ὠρεχθήσαμεν (196), the phrases κατεσβέσθη ἦχος (198) and perhaps εὔνοιαν εἵλκυσε (244), and the absence of articles in μητρὸς διαθήκας καὶ γένους γνωρίσματα (248). There are one or two unusual but prosaic words: μοιχώδης, ὑπόλειος and ἀντιτάττομαι. But the seriousness of the speech is marked not so much by its vocabulary as by the comparative strictness of its rhythms. For example, of 28 lines from 236 to 263 only six fail to satisfy the metrical rules of tragedy, or nine if one disallows the ending with a fourth paeon, uncommon in tragedy.

Before leaving this may I say that it does not appear quite certain that a new speaker enters at 169? If the democrat departs at 168, the scene between him and Smikrines is a strange fragment that seems to lead nowhere. But if we had the whole play it might be more intelligible. More serious, Smikrines seems to assume that the speaker of 169 will be able to inform him of what has passed in some particular circumstances, but there is nothing said to give rise to such a belief. If, however, the speaker of 169 is the democrat, as is maintained by A. Barigazzi, *SIFC* XXXVII (1965), 18, the audience may guess that Smikrines and he had been talking about these circumstances before they entered at 150.

I began by quoting from Plutarch, but omitted a sentence, because I do not understand it. However he says that when Menander has occasion for indulging in sounding language he quickly and convincingly closes down and restores his speech to the proper style.

What I am now concerned with is what Plutarch calls the convincing restoration of ordinary speech. It is, I believe, illustrated in *Perikeiromene*. The quasi-tragic stichomuthia starts abruptly, but at the end, from 380 onward, the level of speech subsides slowly to the normal. As far as can be seen from a mutilated text the metre remains tragic for a dozen lines, so far as caesura, Porson's Law, and resolved feet are concerned; but the vocabulary and phraseology become those of ordinary life. At the same time the lines are broken by change of speaker at varying points, in the style of comedy. At 392 the line probably ended with the untragic διαφανές τε χλανίδιον, certainly with a diminutive of some sort. Hence χρυσῆ τε μίτρα in 393 is suspicious; there seems to be no case for elevated speech or emotion at the end of this prosaic catalogue that begins at 390 with πορφυρ[ᾶ ζώνη τις ἦν. Herwerden's transposition μίτρα τε χρυσῆ should at least be in the apparatus criticus here.

I should also think it likely, although it can be no more than a guess, that 397 does *not* open with a tragic synizesis of ὦ θεοί, but that we have the first line of a scene in trochaic tetrameters, making a lively contrast with the one that has preceded. Unlike his sister, Moschion is not a figure to be taken seriously.

The exclamation ὦ θεοί is not used by Menander at random. Of five instances in all, no fewer than three are in the mouth of Habrotonon in a single scene of *Epitrepontes* (303,313,372). In the first two places she uses it almost casually, to emphasise an adjective, εὐπρεπής τις, ὦ θεοί, λεπτόν, ὦ θεοί, ταραντῖνον, and in all three it is parenthetic. I think it must be intended as a characteristic of her talk, but we do not know whether at the end of the fourth century this use would suggest any particular sort of character or milieu. The other two instances are in this scene of *Perikeiromene*, where the phrase is both times used initially, to indicate surprise or dismay. The first (377) is in the mouth of Glykera. Recent editors give the second (397) to Pataikos, but are they right? The fact that the other four uses are all by women may give a slight initial probability to Körte's original view that it is Glykera who cries ὦ θεοί, τίς ἐστιν οὗτος;. The emotional reaction to Moschion's intervention may suit her better than her father, who elsewhere seems to maintain a high degree of calm. Of course she knows Moschion and he may not; but they are both equally surprised by the voice that interrupts their embrace, so that she can exclaim 'Who is this?' as well as he can.

To return to the question of adjusting an elevated or poetic passage to the normal level, there seems to be no example of the sort of thing Plutarch had in mind apart from the passage of *Perikeiromene* just discussed. *Sik.* 171 ff. is too uncertain for analysis. But there is a passage in *Samia* where the relation of poetic and ordinary language has some interest. I have already spoken of the absurdity of

Nikeratos' εἰσεδεξάμην μελάθροις (517). His elevated language begins at 495, ὦ τὰ Τηρέως λέχη Οἰδίπου τε καὶ Θυέστου. The poetic word λέχη may be thought not unnatural in these mythological surroundings; but he is set off on his poetic course: he reinforces τοῦτ' ἐτολμήσας with τοῦτ' ἔτλης, a verb little used in prose; then ὀργὴν λαβεῖν probably has tragic colour (Eur., *Suppl.*, 1050). But with εἶτ' ἐγώ σοι δῶ γυναῖκα τὴν ἐμαυτοῦ θυγατέρα; we are back to the simplest everyday words. At 506 he calls Demeas an ἀνδράποδον for putting up with an injury (cf. Pl., *Gorg.* 483*a*); the word is purely prosaic, but the following sentence returns to tragedy with ᾔσχυνε λέκτρον and ἡ συγκλιθεῖσα (Eur., *Alc.* 1090). Next the barbers' shops in which people will sit and chatter from dawn bring us back to earth, from which we rebound with the description of Moschion's crime as a 'murder'. The passage provides a series of sudden alternations between the poetic and the colloquial, certainly intended to be comic; and there will shortly be yet another when Nikeratos rushes out of his house with the sounding couplet

> οἷον εἰσιδὼν θέαμα διὰ θυρῶν ἐπείγομαι
> ἐμμανὴς ἀπροσδοκήτωι καρδίαν πληγεὶς ἄχει.

but follows that up with

> τὴν θυγατέρα < > τὴν ἐμὴν τῶι παιδίωι
> τιτθίον διδοῦσαν ἔνδον κατέλαβον.

Nikeratos' poetic language is not blended into his ordinary style, but set in stark contrast with it, and so made to be primarily funny.

A related topic is the use of quotations from tragedy. Once again, no one explanation will suit them all. When Demeas at *Samia* 325 quotes ὦ πόλισμα Κεκροπίας χθονός, ὦ ταναὸς αἰθήρ, words assigned by B to Euripides' *Oedipus*, that is probably true to life. He cannot find words to express his seething indignation and has recourse to a phrase that has stuck in his memory from a play. But when the messenger in *Sikyonios* opens his speech in a way that recalls the messenger's speech in Euripides' *Orestes*, and even quotes an almost complete line from it, one need not suppose that he is conscious of what he is doing, or that more than a minority of the audience knew; that minority would take pleasure in recognising the origin of the passage, but it has no dramatic significance. The same speech of *Orestes* provides a line for Charisios in *Epitrepontes* 590: ἀκέραιος, ἀνεπίπληκτον ἠσκηκὼς βίον comes out as ἀκέραιος, ἀνεπίπληκτος αὐτὸς τῶι βίωι. Here quotation is pointless and I imagine that Menander did not himself remember from where these words came into his mind.

There are two surviving plays in which quotations from tragedy are made as being applicable to the situation. In both places they are used by a slave, who knows that they will puzzle an old man. The more remarkable is *Aspis* 407 ff., where Daos cites Aeschylus, Chairemon, Karkinos, and Euripides, and all by name. (Handley's brilliant recognition of Χ̣α̣ι̣ρημ̣ο̣ν̣ος at the end of 427 enables one to say that.) This is a literary feat of which probably few slaves were capable, but Menander has made it a plausible one by representing Daos as once a *paidagogos*: he will have accompanied his young master to school, and have had the opportunity of picking up crumbs from his literary education. Moreover Daos has already hinted some acquaintance with tragedy, so that his ability to quote should occasion no surprise. His opening speech, with which the play begins, comes very close to the tragic style. Of 17 lines none lacks the penthemimeral or hepthemimeral caesura, and only one infringes Porson's Law; nowhere is an iambus replaced by an anapaest. There are 11 resolved feet, but passages of tragedy show a higher proportion, e.g. 10 in 9¹/₂ lines of Eur. *I.A.* 1214 ff. The vocabulary, although it contains nothing that is specifically tragic, includes very little that is not found in tragedy: παραπλήσιος, παραλόγως and διαλογίζομαι are perhaps all words that tragedy would eschew; the absence from the tragedians of ἀνάπαυσις (found in Mimnermus and Pindar) is probably an accident. But his ability to speak in an elevated style once established in a passage where his emotion makes it appropriate, Daos uses a straightforward workaday vocabulary for his account of the disaster in Lykia; and, although he tells the story well, there is little in the way of figures of speech, except the asyndeton of ἀκούω θόρυβον οἰμωγὴν δρόμον ὀδυρμόν and ἐπιρρεῖν ἱππεῖς, ὑπασπισταί, στρατιῶται. The other place where a slave quotes from tragedy is *Epitrepontes* 765. Here a line and a half is quoted from Euripides' *Auge*, and a threat is made to recite the whole speech. I have argued (*Proceedings of the Cambridge Philological Society*, 1967, 44) that the speaker is not the old nurse Sophrone but the domestic slave Onesimos, and shall assume that to be true. Onesimos has not shown any familiarity with tragedy, but he has displayed a certain knowledge of out-of-the-way words, which makes it more credible that he should know such a speech by heart. His opening monologue in Act III uses μηνυμάτων in the sense 'informations laid', cited by LSJ only from Thucydides. Then he has three rare nouns in -μός: βιασμός (277), 'rape', a sense found in Satyrus, *Life of Euripides* fr. 39 vii; βρυχηθμός (573), 'roaring' (not 'gnashing of teeth', as LSJ), not known in any earlier author; and τιλμός (ibid.), which had been used by Aeschylus (*Suppl.* 839). A fourth, ἀναγνωρισμός (763), is not quite so rare: it occurs once in Aristotle, and Durham found five examples in the Christian era. He also has four adjectives in -τικός: τοπαστικός is a hapax (381), προνοητικός (385) comes a number of times in Xenophon, ταρακτικός (402) first outside Menander in Mnesitheos, a doctor of the third century B.C. The fourth, λογιστικός, is fairly common, but mainly in philosophical authors.

That these nouns in -μός and verbal adjectives in -τικός are unusual appears from a comparison with the language of other persons in the plays. Onesimos has four nouns in -μός; all other characters put together have five, of which one is the well-established word λογισμός (*Sam.* 620). Daos in *Aspis* uses ὀδυρμός (51), a word found 4 times in Euripides, and also in Plato; the same character has πνιγμός (423), an unremarkable word, occurring in Anaxandrides and at least 4 times in Aristotle. Syr(isk)os in *Epitr.* has μερισμός (285) and Knemon has ἐπηρεασμός (178) for the usual ἐπήρεια. Hence at *Sik.* 277 βάδιζ' εἰς ἐξέτα[σιν is much more likely than ἐξετα[σμόν. I should add that συγκλυσμός is found in frag. 656 and that grammarians cite with distaste the words ὀψωνιασμός (Pollux calls this παμπόνηρον, vi. 38) νουθετησμός and τηγανισμός, without comment κιγκλισμός and μυκτηρισμός, with approval ἀγαπησμός. Adjectives in -τικός are as rare. Counting their adverbs, four occur in *Dyskolos*: πρακτικός is used by Sostratos of Chaireas at 56, and by Chaireas himself in the comparative at 128, φυλακτικῶς by Pyrrhias at 95, ἐνθεαστικῶς by Pan at 44. Otherwise there is nothing but two or three instances in fragments: εὑρετικός (34), θεραπευτικός (333), πειστικός (407). Against this set Onesimos' four instances. He stands alone among Menander's persons in this tendency to use nouns in -μός and adjectives in -τικός. But it is typical of Menander that he does not overdo the tendency, he does not exaggerate it to the point of caricature. The listener is given the feeling, of which he may not even be consciously aware, that Onesimos is not quite in the ordinary run in his language. That makes a knowledge of tragedy more appropriate, more credible, when it comes. Incidentally I now note that in line 772, which I give to him, not to Sophrone, whom I believe to be a persona muta, the word εὐτύχημα was noted by Wilamowitz to be not at all common in the fourth century. The only other Menandrean instance is *Samia* 618, a speech by Moschion which contains several other pieces of elevated or unusual diction.

Whether it is right or not to give Onesimos the quotation from Euripides, the investigation of his suitability does at least show him to be another of those characters to whom Menander has given individuality by some particular mode of speech. This is a field in which one may guess there are more observations to be made. But scope for them is limited by the mutilated state of several of those plays of which there are considerable remains. Not only is it desirable to have the whole of an actor's part to examine for its vocabulary, but it would also seem that discovery of what is significant is aided by finding contrasts between one character and another. Just as this is a method for elucidating their psychology, so it may illuminate their language. But the method of contrast must be insecure so long as we cannot compare a whole with a whole. In particular any conclusion that depends on noticing what a person does not say must be provisional until we possess the whole of his part. The discovery of a new scene may upset a negative generalisation. Nevertheless, handicapped as we are in this way and also, let us never forget, by our imperfect knowledge of the Greek spoken in fourth-century Athens, we may hope for further progress and an increased appreciation of Menander's plays.

DISCUSSION

M. Handley: Among many things to welcome in Mr. Sandbach's paper, I am much impressed by the ways in which he has extended his study of Menander's style beyond that of rare or poetic words to uses of common words and of sentence structure. Perhaps an example to mention in support would be Sostratos' speech at *Dysk.* 666-690, where I have myself thought that the speaker's mood—perhaps even something of his character—is reflected in the repetition of common qualifying phrases and in the informal structure (*Dyskolos of Menander* on 683 f.). In contrast, Gorgias' speech at 271-287 seems to give a good example of the stilted formality which Professor Sandbach finds characteristic of him; it is a further point, perhaps, that he opens with a *gnome* which he tries to work out (rustics are especially γνωμοτύποι according to Aristotle, *Rhet.* 1395 *a* 6), and that the working out brings what Post has called " a gorgeously incoherent attempt at logic " (AJP 1959, at p. 410). It seems that when we try to describe the language of Menander's characters, we are often drawn into considering what they say as well as how they say it.

M. Ludwig: Darf ich an die ausserordentlich aufschlussreichen und anregenden Beobachtungen von Herrn Sandbach eine Frage anschliessen, die sich mir aus seinem Vortrag ergeben hat: Für die Bestimmung der stilistischen Physiognomie eines Textes sind die Satzstrukturen ebenso wichtig wie der Wortschatz. M. Sandbach hat auch in dieser Hinsicht einige ausgezeichnete Beispiele gegeben. Freilich waren, so weit ich sehe, seine Beobachtungen zum menandrischen Wortschatz erheblich zahlreicher als die zur Syntax. Das ist nicht verwunderlich, da es leichter ist, einigermassen sichere Aussagen über die Atmosphäre eines Wortes zu machen. Wie könnte man in der Erfassung der « poetischen

Syntax» Menanders weiterkommen? Auf welche syntaktischen Bereiche sollte man zunächst die Aufmerksamkeit richten?

M. Sandbach : This is a very interesting, and I fear very difficult question. Subjects that might repay attention are

1. the use or absence of connective particles in continuous discourse ;
2. the construction of sentences in prologues and in other narrative passages (are subordinate or coordinate clauses predominant ?) ;
3. hyperbaton. This last is so usual in verse that it may pass unnoticed in Menander and be more frequent than I have supposed.

These are merely first thoughts, and there may easily be more profitable subjects for enquiry.

M. Handley : One wonders how far metrical and rhythmic effects contribute to those of sentence structure. Naturally something can be done by analysis when the metre is unusually strict, and the elevated tone is also given by language. But in Menander's normal or less formal style it is much harder to be clear about the effect of his handling of the metrical pattern, and it would perhaps be good if more work could be done here.

The alternation of emotion seems to be well reflected in the changes of tone and verse rhythm in Demeas' speech in *Samia* 325 ff.

M. Turner : M. Sandbach's suggestion that *Samia* 98-101 Austin should be given to Nikeratos, though it is against the indications in the Bodmer papyrus, seems to me to carry conviction. It is a welcome example of what [Demetrius] Περὶ ἑρμηνείας calls διαλελυμένη λέξις being used to distinguish between a pair of characters. Demetrius lays stress on the suitability to the stage and inherently dramatic character of this " disjointed style ". Asyndetic triplets (especially verbs) such as Demeas' ἠγνόησ', ἥμαρτον, ἐμάνην (*Samia* 703 Austin) are emphatic and evoke a crescendo to a climax : κινεῖ γὰρ ὑπόκρισιν ἡ λύσις. No wonder actors loved Menander, and left Philemon to be read in the study. But this very recognition of the fact that Menander knew how to write for actors may be one of the reasons for the ὁμοιότης of which Plutarch speaks. Certainly asyndetic cola are used by characters of varied social standing, and in moments of different emotional tension. It might be interesting to examine further examples. A case that immediately comes to mind is *Samia* 673-674 Austin, where the slave Parmenon's excitement in wishing to tell Moschion (what he thinks the latter does not know) that the marriage is on is given vent in asyndeta that are also contaminated by the high style :

ποοῦσι γάρ σοι τοὺς γάμους· κεράννυται,
θυμιᾶτ', ἐνῆρκτ', ἀνῆπται θύμαθ' Ἡφαίστου φλογί.

M. Wehrli : Es war ein glücklicher Gedanke, für die Behandlung der Sprache Menanders von der plutarchischen Feststellung auszugehen, dass jener im Gegensatz zu Aristophanes seine Sprache trotz der Einschränkung ihrer Scala doch den wechselnden Stimmungen und Personen anzupassen wusste. Und dass ihn die Kunst der Ethopoiie auch gegenüber seinem römischen Bearbeiter Terenz auszeichnet, ist in der Diskussion mit Recht in Erinnerung gerufen worden. Das Urteil des Plutarch steht mit der herrschenden stilkritischen Würdigung in Einklang, welche Menander in der Antike genoss. Wenn z.B. Quintilian (X 1, 69) seine Lebensnähe rühmt, so meint er die unaufdringliche, auf jede Rolle abgestimmte Differenzierung einer umgangssprachlichen Atthis. Mit dieser nimmt Menander offenbar auch unter seinen Zeitgenossen eine Sonderstellung ein. Wenn nämlich im Anschluss an Plutarchs Vergleich zwischen Aristophanes und Menander von einer Gesamtentwicklung der komischen Bühnensprache gesprochen werden darf, so führte diese durch den

Abbau poetischer Ausdrucksmittel zunächst bloss zu einem der gehobenen Alltagsprosa nahen Stil einförmigen Gepräges. Wie ausschliesslich die hier wirksamen Stiltendenzen auch für die Uniformität der terenzianischen Verse mit ihrem Ideal der Sprachreinheit (*Heautont.*, Prolog 46) massgebend gewesen seien, soll hier nicht zur Diskussion gestellt werden.

Einen Vorgang, welcher der Veränderung des komischen Sprechverses gleicht, stellt Aristoteles (*Rhet.* 1404 *b* 25) unter Hinweis auf Euripides für die Tragödie fest. Dass dieser die Tonhöhe derselben herabgestimmt habe, ist vor allem angesichts des aischyleischen Stiles evident, aber von der Umgangssprache bleibt der euripideische Sprechvers in seiner kunstvollen Gewähltheit doch weit entfernt, und der Mangel an Flexibilität macht ihn für ethopoetische Nuancierungen ungeeignet. Es zeigt sich damit, dass Menanders Sprachkunst auch von hier aus gesehen etwas Neues ist. Euripides hat die Tragödie zwar durch zahlreiche aus dem Alltag gewonnene Motive bereichert und damit den komischen Dichter angeregt, dafür aber den passenden Sprachstil zu schaffen blieb diesem vorbehalten.

M. Turner: Professor Sandbach has said that there is little in Menander which can be called " slang ". A word which may represent popular idiom and is still alive today is κατέδομαι, *Dysk.* 124, 468 (and perhaps *Phasma*). Patrick Leigh Fermor, *Roumeli* (London, 1966), p. 131 recalls how after the German conquest of Crete in 1942 « some greybeard would say ' Never fear, my child, with Christ and the Virgin's help we'll eat them!' »

M. Ludwig: Der Stil eines Textes resultiert nicht nur aus dem Vorkommen gewisser sprachlicher Erscheinungen, sondern auch aus der relativen Häufigkeit derselben. Der Vergleich der relativen Frequenzen einer sprachlichen Erscheinung in verschiedenen Texten Menanders einerseits und in menandrischen und nichtmenandrischen Texten andererseits dürfte zu einem wesentlich deutlicheren Bild führen. Welche Möglichkeiten sehen Sie für solche Untersuchungen oder halten Sie diese augenblicklich noch für verfrüht?

M. Sandbach: I am inclined to think that such New Comedy texts as are certainly non-Menandrean are too short to make a comparison with Menander fruitful. To compare different Menandrean plays might bring some useful results, although it may be that we still have too few plays to allow of certain conclusions. If one was very lucky one might find evidence for the dating of plays. But I have a suspicion that different plays may have different levels of vocabulary to accord with their atmosphere. Thus the frequency of terms of vulgar abuse may be a sign not of date but of what sort of play is being written.

M. Handley: It seems hard in Menander to find much sign of "poetic" or other abnormal syntax. One small illustration might be given from his use of the definite article, where, outside set phases like ἐξ ἀγροῦ, or with names for members of the family (including τροφίμη, κεκτημένη and so on), one has a few instances of omission of the article in 'paratragic' or elevated style, as ἕρπ' ἀπ' οἴκων τῶνδε, fr. 679 *Koe.*, or ἀνῆπται θύμαθ', *Sam.* 674.

M. Turner: Certain words, which may be of traditional type, help to enlist the involvement of the audience in what is going on. Μοι δοκεῖ and its variants fulfil this function, and evoke a response "I think—don't you?" We should not restrict the audience's involvement to verses in which they are directly addressed.

Mme Kahil: Il est un type de recherche où l'étude de la langue devrait s'allier à celle des monuments, et que l'on pourrait peut-être envisager maintenant, à la lumière des nouveaux textes et des nouveaux documents figurés qui ont permis l'attribution de masques aux divers personnages des comédies de Ménandre (je songe en particulier aux études de T. B. L. Webster). Il s'agirait de rechercher si à tel ou tel caractère de comédie, qui porte un masque déterminé, correspond un langage plus ou moins défini (par exemple langage de la pseudokorè, de la vieille entremetteuse, de tel ou tel jeune homme, de tel ou tel vieillard, etc.). Cela pourrait donner des résultats intéressants.

M. Turner: Menander writes occasionally a strong ' exit ' line for an actor. One thinks of Knemon's ἐπηρεασμὸς τὸ κακὸν εἶναί μοι δοκεῖ, *Dysk.* 178 f., on which he disappears indoors. Analogous are the preparatory lines preceding the entry of a new actor, e.g. Sostratos' at *Dysk.* 151-152: δέδοικα... αὐτόν· τί γὰρ ἄν τις μὴ οὐχὶ τἀληθῆ λέγοι; Recently Professor T. B. L. Webster has called attention to the unsatisfactory nature of *Misoumenos, POxy* 2656, 269, if the line is divided between Thrasonides and Getas, and suggested (on the analogy of *Dysk.* 152) that in spite of the manuscript all 269 should be spoken by Thrasonides (without punctuation after πῶς). ' How should I wonder at the new situation? '

M. Questa: M. Sandbach ha mostrato la raffinatezza dei mezzi stilistici del poeta, che sa esprimere nel modo più adatto ogni situazione scenica.

Confrontato con Menandro, Terenzio può sembrare e probabilmente è (pur nell'abbondanza di πάθος che distingue ogni testo latino rispetto a quello greco da cui è ' tradotto ') meno vario nell'uso dei mezzi linguistici (la presenza di stilemi comici tradizionali o ' plautini ' in *Eunuchus* e *Phormio* non muta granchè il quadro).

Io vorrei chiedere a M. Wehrli e a M. Ludwig se essi credono deliberata e voluta questa maggiore uniformità di Terenzio (mi riferisco anche all'annunciato articolo di Arnott), oppure se essa dipende dalle possibilità insite nel ' codice ' del latino e in particolare del latino dell'ambiente di Terenzio (per certi lati è la cultura latina a non avere certi ' mezzi espressivi ': per es. Menandro può scrivere trimetri di stile tragico anche nella tecnica metrica e trarne effetti singolari, come alla fine della ἀναγνώρισις della *Perikeiromene*, giusta quanto ha osservato Sandbach ; Terenzio *non* può farlo, perchè senario tragico e senario comico sono metricamente identici in latino, se si eccettua la problematica norma di Lange-Strzelecki : vedi quanto ho detto in *Maia* 1968, p. 382 n. 9).

M. Turner : I think Professor T. B. L. Webster has some excellent remarks on the exactness of Menander's language and the generalizing of Terence in *Bull. John Rylands Library* 45 (1962), p. 240. He adduces for instance, Ter. *Andria* 483 *Post deinde quod iussi dari bibere et quantum imperavi, date* spoken by Terence's midwife compared with Menander's (fr. 37 Koe.) καὶ τεττάρων / ὠῶν μετὰ τοῦτο, φιλτάτη, τὸ νεόττιον. Exact observation of detail is the life-blood of the comic style.

M. Handley : Once again, in the controversy over Terence's *tenuis oratio et scriptura leuis*, style and subject appear to be involved together. In the *Phormio* prologue (6 ff.), it is noticeable that he turns his critic's reproach into the form *quia nusquam insanum scripsit adulescentulum / ceruam uidere fugere et sectari canes / et eam plorare, orare ut subveniat sibi.*

IV

FRITZ WEHRLI

Menander und die Philosophie

MENANDER UND DIE PHILOSOPHIE [1]

Da für die folgenden Ausführungen eine knapp bemessene Zeit vereinbart worden ist, möchte ich mich auf einige prinzipielle Überlegungen konzentrieren und eine gegenständliche Stellungsnahme zum Problem nur umreissen. Die Frage nach Menanders Beziehung zur Philosophie ist ohnehin in Gefahr, zerredet zu werden, wenn keine Verständigung über das mit ihr Gemeinte und über die Möglichkeiten, ihr beizukommen, erzielt wird.

Das Problem ist in den letzten Jahren offensichtlich deswegen in den Vordergrund getreten, weil sich die Thematik des neu entdeckten *Dyskolos* mit einer Streitfrage zu berühren scheint, welche in der zeitgenössischen Ethik diskutiert wurde. Dadurch gewann auch die biographische Überlieferung vermehrtes Interesse, nach welcher Menander ein Schüler Theophrasts und Freund des Demetrios von Phaleron gewesen sein soll. Der historische Wert dieser Angaben ist allerdings gering, solange man sie allein nimmt, denn sie könnten auf die Rahmenerzählung eines peripatetischen Dialogs oder eine ähnliche literarische Quelle zurückgehen. Als Bestätigung jedoch würden sie immerhin willkommen sein, falls es gelingen sollte, auf interpretatorischem Wege

[1] *Literatur:*

M. Tierney, *Aristotle and Menander.* (Proc. Royal Irish Acad. 43 (1935/7), 241 ff.)

T. B. L. Webster, *Studies in Menander.* Manchester, 1950, 195 ff.

G. Zuntz, *Interpretation of a Menander Fragment* (Proc. Brit. Acad. 42 (1956), 209 ff.)

P. Steinmetz, *Menander und Theophrast, Folgerungen aus dem Dyskolos.* (Rh. M. 103 (1960), 73 ff.)

A. Barigazzi, *La formazione spirituale di Menandro.* Torino, 1965.

K. Gaiser, *Menander und der Peripatos* (Antike und Abendland, XIII (1967), 8 ff.).

in Menanders Komödien peripatetisches Gedankengut festzustellen.

Unserer Themastellung gemäss haben wir indessen auch nach Beziehungen zu anderen Schulen zu fragen, und an vereinzelten Anspielungen an irgend welche Philosopheme fehlt es durchaus nicht. Da eine gewisse Kenntnis von solchen jedoch in hellenistischer Zeit zur allgemeinen Bildung gehörte, sagen derartige Bezugsnahmen über die Schulzugehörigkeit eines dramatischen Dichters kaum viel aus, besonders wenn sie zur Charakterisierung von Vertretern eines bestimmten Bildungsstandes benützt werden, wie es bei Menander oft geschieht.

Eine sinnvolle Fragestellung kann nach dem Gesagten nur lauten, ob Menanders Kunst als Ganzes einer Gesinnung Ausdruck gebe, zu welcher philosophische Bildung wesentliches beigetragen haben müsse. Bedenkt man dabei jedoch, dass sein Bühnenspiel bei aller Sublimierung alter Komödienderbheit durchaus von der Freude am Menschlich-allzumenschlichen lebt, so scheidet als massgebendes Bildungselement zum Voraus jede triebfeindliche Ethik aus, nächst der platonischen und stoischen sogar die epikureische mit ihrer Forderung einer strengen Kontrolle aller emotionalen Regungen. So bleibt als ernsthafte Möglichkeit eigentlich nur übrig, dass Menander dem Peripatos verpflichtet ist, welcher ohne Verzicht auf sittliche Masstäbe dennoch der ganzen Fülle von Erscheinungen auch des sittlichen Lebens gerecht zu werden versucht hat. Dies verleiht den Berichten über Menanders Beziehungen zu Theophrast und Demetrios von Phaleron eine prinzipielle Glaubwürdigung, und so ist in seinen Menschenschilderungen denn auch eine ganze Anzahl von Zügen namhaft gemacht worden, welche mit solchen bei peripatetischen Autoren übereinstimmen. Da diese jedoch ihrerseits der älteren Komödie Anregungen verdanken, bedürfen solche Gemeinsamkeiten vorsichtiger Deutung, denn sie können auch auf gemeinsame Vorbilder des Dichters und der Philosophen zurückgehen. Mit peripatetischem Einfluss ist also höchstens in solchen Schöpfungen Menanders zu rechnen, die nicht unmittelbar von alter Bühnenüberlieferung bestimmt sind, sondern zur ausschliesslichen Thematik der Neuen Komödie, genauer gesagt unseres Dichters selbst, gehören. Für einen vollen Beweis bedürfte es schliesslich nicht bloss thematischer, sondern auch terminologischer Übereinstimmungen mit der aristotelischen Schule, aber solche sind kaum zu erwarten, da der komische Stil für die Übernahme philosophischen Sprachgutes kaum günstig ist.

Man wird unbedenklich behaupten dürfen, dass Menander wie keiner seiner Zeitgenossen die ethopoetische Kunst beherrschte, den alten Typenschatz der Komödie im Geiste einer neuen Urbanität umzugestalten und entsprechend seiner differenzierten und vertieften Menschendarstellung auch für die Handlung seiner Komödien neue, ernsthaftere Sinngebungen zu finden. Es wird also zu untersuchen sein, ob diese Metamorphose des Bühnenspiels durch Einflüsse der peripatetischen Schule mindestens begünstigt wurde. Wie *Ethik* und *Rhetorik* des Aristoteles sowie die *Charaktere* Theophrasts zeigen, verfügte der Peripatos über eine ebenso reiche Anschauung von den möglichen Ausprägungen der menschlichen Natur wie Menander, und die aristotelische Ethik kam dessen Vorstellungen vom richtigen Verhalten unter Nächsten jedenfalls viel näher als der Individualismus der anderen Schulen. Da den allgemeinen Hintergrund dieser Übereinstimmungen jedoch die gesellschaftliche Kultur des damaligen Athen bildet, muss eine persönliche Lehrbeziehung durch gemeinsames Gedankengut von klarer Umgrenzung erhärtet werden können.

Was Menanders Stellung in der Komödie betrifft, so hat es die antike Kritik unterlassen, seine Kunst von derjenigen seiner Zeitgenossen ausdrücklich abzusetzen. Sie beschränkte sich darauf, die Neue Komödie als Einheit im Gegensatz zur

Archaia zu charakterisieren. Als ihr Hauptmerkmal hob sie dabei zutreffend die Beseitigung alter Derbheiten hervor, und als Mittel dazu scheint sie ebenso richtig den aus der Tragödie übernommenen Anagnorismos beurteilt zu haben. Dieser hat jedenfalls die bei Plutarch (*Quaest. conviv.* VII, 8, 3) gerühmte Lösung des Liebeskonfliktes vorzubereiten, welche darin besteht, das in Armut geratene und von Hetärenschicksal bedrohte Mädchen seinen ehrbaren Eltern zuzuführen und ihm dadurch die Heirat zu ermöglichen. Damit verwandelt sich das alte Streitmotiv mit seinen Erbarmungslosigkeiten in ein Spiel der Irrungen, deren Klärung einen Ausgleich und damit ein für alle befriedigendes Ende der Handlung ermöglicht, wie es der verfeinerte Zeitgeschmack verlangte.

Der antiken Beobachtung bleibt nur das eine beizufügen, dass Menander diese Urbanisierung der Komödie in einem umfassenderen und geistigeren Sinne als die übrigen Dichter verstand, dass sie bei ihm allein oder doch als erstem zu jener neuen Kunst der Ethopoiie und jener Verinnerlichung der Handlung geführt hat, von welcher schon zu sprechen war. Der Theaterzufall des Anagnorismos ist in seinen schönsten Stücken kein bloss äusserlicher Kunstgriff mehr, weil für das umkämpfte Mädchen die Entdeckung seiner bürgerlichen Herkunft mit ihren Folgen dort zur menschlichen Notwendigkeit wird. Nach altem Bühnenherkommen ist dasselbe oft genug blosser Gegenstand des Liebeskonfliktes, und noch in manchen Stücken der Nea tritt es darum nicht einmal selber in Erscheinung. Es bedurfte der Kunst Menanders, um durch die Schilderung seiner Gegenliebe zum Jüngling für sein Schicksal Anteilnahme zu wecken, und diese Humanisierung des Liebesmotivs wirkte sich folgerichtig auf die Zeichnung des jugendlichen Liebhabers aus, was eine Verwandlung der ganzen Komödienthematik nach sich zog. All dies steht mit der urbanen Gesinnung der damaligen Gesellschaft Athens in Einklang, die sich auch in der aristotelischen Ethik spiegelt. Dennoch bleibt die dichterische Leistung Menanders das Geheimnis seines Ingeniums, und in ihrer Allgemeinheit erlauben uns die Übereinstimmungen nicht, mit philosophischer Anregung zu rechnen.

Kaum viel günstiger als mit dem Liebesmotiv verhält es sich mit dem Vater als Widersacher des verliebten Jünglings. Die ältere Komödie pflegte diesem erbarmungslos mitzuspielen, indem sie seine früheren oder gegenwärtigen Sünden ausschlachtete. Dass dies dem empfindlicheren Schicklichkeitsgefühl der Folgezeit anstössig wurde, zeigen verschiedene Umgestaltungen der Thematik in der Neuen Komödie. Menander allein aber gehört jener Vater oder Pflegevater, welcher die Jugend aus reinem Verständnis und ohne für sich selbst etwas erhaschen zu wollen gewähren lässt. Seine Leistung lässt sich der typologischen Entwicklungsreihe vom alten Sünder in der *Asinaria* über den jovialen Junggesellen des *Miles gloriosus* mit seiner etwas verdächtigen Lebensphilosophie bis zum Micio der *Adelphen* ablesen. Nun ist das, was dieser seinem uneinsichtig strengen Bruder Demea über die richtige Erziehung vorträgt, zutreffend mit peripatetischem Gedankengut verglichen worden. Micios Grundsatz, auf Zwang zu verzichten und sich auf freiwilligen Gehorsam zu verlassen, machen das Vater-Sohn Verhältnis zum Modell für jene freiheitliche Staatsordnung, welche Aristoteles als die väterliche der despotischen gegenüberstellt (*NE* 1160 *b* 24 ff. u.a.). Und dass in den *Adelphen* die Pädagogik eines Demea scheitern muss, findet seine Begründung in der ebenfalls von Aristoteles ausgesprochenen Einsicht, dass die Jugend aus irrationalen Impulsen lebt und in besonderem Masse den Trieben unterworfen ist (*NE* 1095 *a* 4; *Rhet.* 1389 *a* 4 ff.), der Erzieher also mit diesen als Naturgegebenheit zu rechnen hat. Auch durch diese Beziehung ist jedoch peripatetischer Einfluss für Menander noch nicht zwingend erwiesen, weil Aristoteles seinerseits auf Anschauungen Bezug nimmt, die zu seiner Zeit Gemeingut gewesen sein müssen. Sein politischer Begriff einer väterlichen Autorität setzt nämlich für den erzieherischen Grundsatz, auf unnachsichtige Härte zu verzichten, eine solche Selbstverständlichkeit voraus, dass er ohne weiteres auf die Staatstheorie übertragen werden konnte.

Mit mehr Zuversicht möchte man peripatetische Interpretation eines allgemeinen Kulturbewusstseins aus dem *Dyskolos* heraushören. Hier wirkt der Zusammenbruch des alten Knemon, welcher geglaubt hat, als zweiter Timon ausserhalb jeder Gemeinschaft leben zu können, wie ein Exempel für jene gegen sophistischen oder philosophischen Autarkiewahn gerichtete Feststellung des Aristoteles, der Mensch sei nicht als Einzelwesen geschaffen, sondern dafür bestimmt, Hilfe von anderen anzunehmen und ihnen zu gewähren.

Man könnte vermuten, es liege an der gelegentlichen Lehrhaftigkeit, welche dem *Dyskolos* anhaftet, dass Menander sich gerade in diesem Jugendstück so unverhohlen zu peripatetischer Lehre zu bekennen scheint. Immerhin darf auch daran erinnert werden, dass in den *Adelphen*, die vermutlich zu seinen reifsten Werken gehörten, aller Wahrscheinlichkeit nach die aristotelische Mesonlehre als Masstab für das Verhalten mindestens des einen unter den beiden gegensätzlichen Erziehern benützt ist.

Damit wären wenigstens zwei Bezugnahmen auf die Ethik des Lykeion gegeben, die sich mit allen gebotenen Vorbehalten als Zeugnis persönlicher Kontakte glaubhaft machen lassen. Und dies erhöht auch die Wahrscheinlichkeit, dass Menander der peripatetischen Charakterologie Anregungen zu verdanken hat. Die Übereinstimmungen in zahlreichen ethopoetischen Einzelzügen, welche zwischen ihm und Theophrast oder Aristoteles geltend gemacht worden sind, bedürfen allerdings erneuter Überprüfung im Lichte der hervorgehobenen Gesichtspunkte.

DISCUSSION

M. Ludwig : In den Komödien Menanders finden sich Begriffe wie ἀτύχημα, προαίρεσις u.ä., die die philosophische Reflexion des 4. Jh. genau definiert hatte. Die Philosophie hatte diese Wörter der Gemeinsprache entnommen. Ich würde gern wissen, ob Sie bei Menander Stellen kennen, wo solche Begriffe nur als philosophische Fachtermini gebraucht werden und ihr Verständnis die Kenntnis ihrer philosophischen Definitionen voraussetzt, oder ob man Ihrer Auffassung nach stets mit dem auskommt, was das allgemeine Sprachverständnis bot.

M. Wehrli : Ich wüsste kein Beispiel zu nennen, welches eine Benützung peripatetischer Begriffe in schulgerechter Terminologie für Menander belegen könnte. Wenn bei ihm überhaupt von philosophischen Anregungen gesprochen werden darf, so beschränken sie sich auf allgemeine Vorstellungen vor allem ethischen Inhalts, welchen er einen der Komödie angemessenen Ausdruck gegeben hat. Mehr ist von ihm als Dichter wohl auch nicht zu erwarten.

M. Turner : Professor Wehrli's caution (the more to be respected since it is the fruit of long reflection by one who is familiar with the philosophical schools of the fourth century as well as with the comic writers) may be illustrated from the idea of ἔλεος. When Getas in *Misoumenos* (316-7) says ; ἀλλ' ἐλεεῖν ὀρθῶς ἔχει τὸν ἀντελεοῦντα, he does not seem remote from the Aristotelian definition, *Rhet.* II, 8, s, 1385 *b* 9 ff. : ἔστω δὴ ἔλεος λύπη τις ἐπὶ φαινομένῳ κακῷ φθαρτικῷ ἢ λυπηρῷ τοῦ ἀναξίου τυγχάνειν, ὃ κἂν αὐτὸς προσδοκήσειεν ἂν παθεῖν ἢ τῶν αὐτοῦ τινα.

Yet the point that Getas is making had been given utterance earlier in the Mytilenean debate as recorded in Thucydides by Cleon, *Thuc.* III, 40, 3.

M. Handley : Following on Professor Turner's point : certainly it is one thing to point to parallels in thought and expression between topics in philosophical writing and topics in Menander, and quite another thing to establish direct derivation or influence. It does however seem worth asking, even when we are dealing with an idea with a long history, how far its appearance in (let us say) Aristotle or Theophrastus can be used to show that it was live and current at the time when Menander grew up and wrote plays. If in fact we are interested in the appeal of Menander to contemporary audiences, can we not use evidence for the currency of particular forms of thought and language without going too far towards presuming their affiliation?

To take another topic: opposition to personal abuse in comedy, and to the freedom of language which went with it, has a very long history by the time we reach the age of Menander, and the reasons why comedy turned away from this side of its tradition are no doubt complex. When he discussed different kinds of joking, Aristotle himself could mark the contrast between ' old ' comedies and those of his own time and could refer to legislation against certain kinds of abuse (*Eth. Nic.* 1128 *a* 16 ff.). When we come to Menander, with his very few references to contemporaries and his very high regard for decency of language, have we room to say that ethical philosophy was one factor which confirmed and strengthened the trend?

M. Wehrli: Die Dezenz der menandrischen Sprache gehört zu den Merkmalen der Neuen Komödie, welche von der allgemeinen Bemühung, volkstümliche Derbheiten abzustossen, bestimmt werden. Eine Verfeinerung der Sitten erklärt diese Erscheinung wohl ungezwungener als philosophischer Einfluss.

Mme Kahil: La volonté de limiter l'indécence, sensible dans la comédie nouvelle, est aussi manifeste dans le costume des acteurs. Par ailleurs le fait que Socrate, Cébès, Simmias apparaissent sur un des panneaux des mosaïques de Mytilène, pourrait témoigner simplement de ce que, dans l'esprit des biographes, Ménandre était associé aux philosophes, notamment à leur maître à tous, Socrate, dont la présence, sur le pavement de Mytilène, viserait à créer une « atmosphère philosophique » autour de Ménandre.

Mlle *Dedoussi :* I should like to ask Professor Wehrli, whether or not he sees the influence of Aristotle's aesthetic theory of drama in Menander's dramatic art and especially in the character drawing.

M. Wehrli : Soweit Beziehungen Menanders zur ästhetischen Theorie des Aristoteles bestehen, brauchen sie nicht unbedingt durch Berücksichtigung derselben erklärt zu werden. Für manches, wie z.B. den Sprechvers, genügt es, darauf hinzuweisen, dass Menander in einer lebendigen Bühnentradition steht, welche nicht lange vor ihm von Aristoteles beschrieben worden ist.

V

CHRISTINA DEDOUSSI

The *Samia*

THE *SAMIA*

I am sorry that the very recent publication of the new text of the *Samia* did not leave me enough time to study it thoroughly. Therefore I am not ready to offer solutions to or suggestions about the various problems, which the new text and the play as a whole present, but I shall rather point out some of the problems, hoping that by discussing them your views and suggestions will throw light on them. These problems concern mainly the plot and the interpretation of the text as well as the analysis of the dramatic motivation of the characters.

There is also a problem which concerns not only the *Samia* but Menander in general. The new texts of Menander have shaken the foundations of the evidence, which was used before for the dating of his comedies. We need to establish a rough history of Menandrean comedy, extended over a period of about thirty years. His dated texts will help in establishing the evolution of Menander's comedy, but this evolution will help in arranging the long fragments in a kind of chronological order. The evidence which has, I think, lost its chronological meaning is the following: 1) The mention of real persons contemporary or older. 2) The use of other metre than the iambic trimeter. 3) The strong comic element (farcical scenes). 4) The traditional material connected with comic types. 5) The presence and the use of monologues. We have now to rely on the internal evidence: the play as a work of art, its plot and its characters express a certain stage in the evolution of their creator.

The only dated play, the *Dyskolos*, is an early play, but all agree that in this comedy the dramatic skill of a genius is already shown, as well as the ability to create individualistic characters. It could not be otherwise, because this is Menander. The prevailing opinion about the date of the

Samia was that it is an early play. In my edition of the play I dated it decisively after the *Dyskolos*, near the year 310 B.C. After reading the new text, not only I am of the same opinion, but I am also inclined to accept an even later date. The mature dramatist reveals himself with the plot and the characters of the play, their behaviors and their thoughts. The criteria of the dating have to be based on the play itself.

I thought it necessary to give these preliminaries in order to be a starting point, in case one wants to turn the discussion on the subject of the dating of the *Samia* and the position of this play in Menander's history as a dramatic poet.

We have a clear idea of the size of the *Samia*. The play appears to be about a hundred lines shorter than the *Dyskolos*, but this difference is reduced by half, considering that about 30% of the lines of the *Samia* are in trochaic tetrameters, while in the *Dyskolos* the proportion is about 16% (trochaic and iambic tetrameters). The trochaic tetrameters take more time in the performance of the play, because not only are they longer verses, but also because they are found in scenes where speech is combined with much actual movement on the stage.

The scene of this comedy is in Athens, there are two houses on the stage, one belongs to the rich Demeas, the other to the poor Nikeratos.

The play begins with a very long prologue spoken by Moschion, one of the characters of the play and not by a divine being or a personified abstraction. The beginning of the prologue is missing and we do not hear the motivation of Moschion's exit. When the text becomes intelligible, we hear that Moschion has committed a sin (ἁμάρτημα) and he is in a difficult situation. His previous life was happy, his father provided him the means to be a distinguished member of society. In return he had always behaved towards his father perfecty well. He was a decent and respectful son. His father fell in love with a Samian ἑταίρα, secretly in the beginning, and he did nothing to take this woman in his possession, because he was ashamed in face of his son. But Moschion found out about it and thought that his father had to take the Samian woman in his possession, otherwise his young rivals could put him in a difficult situation. Here a gap stops the text. We are left with the impression that Moschion helped his father in a way to take this woman in his house as a concubine.

The Samian woman, whose name is Chrysis, was a poor foreigner, a professional ἑταίρα, who decided to live with the rich Demeas as his παλλακή (like Glycera of the *Perikeiromene*). Demeas calls her a free woman (v. 577). Therefore the words τῆς ἑταίρας ἐγκρατής (v. 25) must mean nothing more than ' securing the position of her exclusive lover ' (this in fact he did by taking her into his house and entrusting her with its domestic management). And Nikeratos' words παλλακὴν δ' ἂν αὔριον πρῶτος ἀνθρώπων ἐπώλουν (v. 508 f.) express one of his ' tragic ' exaggerations (see v. 513 and 560 f.). It does not seem to me probable that Demeas bought her from a πορνοβοσκός and that she was his property, or made free afterwards by him, because he would have mentioned it in the scene of her expulsion.

After the gap (v. 35) we hear about the mother of a girl, who was in good relations with his father's concubine (v. 36 ἅβρ]αν?). The women being neighbours and friends used to exchange visits. We understand that Moschion fell in love with the girl (the text here, v. 34, has an obscure expression : συνθλάσας τὸ σημεῖον). One day, almost a year ago, Moschion came back unexpectedly from his father's farm and found a party of women going on. The women were celebrating the Adonia (The word περυσινά, which M. Turner suggests fits well in the beginning of v. 39). Among the guests were, of course, the next door lady and her daughter. It was a merry and noisy party, he could not sleep and took part in it as a spectator. Then—he is ashamed to continue, but what is the use?—the girl became pregnant. He did not deny his responsibilities; he went to her mother and promised her to marry the girl, when his father comes back from his voyage. In the gap after v. 29, he must have mentioned that his father as well as the girl's father were not in Athens and where they had gone. His child was born only a few days ago. He took it and brought it into his house. The text after v. 56 stops at a crucial point. The meaning of v. 55 f. is not clear and the conjecture of a supplement for the beginning of v. 56 is problematic. I do not think that any part of the verb τίκτω suits the context. The good luck for Moschion was the presence of Chrysis in his father's house, because she took up the baby and nobody learned, except the women of the two households, who was the mother of the baby. This arrangement was very convenient, because the real mother could easily visit Chrysis and feed her child. Chrysis offered a great service to Moschion, who must have felt very obliged to her. How did he finish the prologue? And did he leave the stage? We can only make conjectures. Equally unknown is also the beginning of Act I. When Moschion and Parmenon appear on the stage Chrysis is already there. The two are in the middle of an animated conversation. Parmenon announces the arrival of the two fathers (Demeas and Nikeratos) from the Εὔξεινος Πόντος. Now Moschion must speak to his father and ask his consent to marry the poor girl. But Moschion is not only a shy young man, but also a timid one. He simply cannot speak to his father. Parmenon gets angry with him and scolds him. Chrysis joins in the conversation and the three together decide what they are going to do about the baby. Chrysis will go on taking care of it. She will say to Demeas that the baby is his and her child. It was expected that this would make Demeas furious, but they were relying on his love for Chrysis. She is the opposite of Moschion, brave and ready to suffer anything rather than separate the baby from its mother and give it to a poor nurse (v. 84 f.). We do not know how this scene ended. After the gap we find Moschion desperate and terrified. He decides to be alone in an isolated place and prepare a speech. He must find arguments to persuade his father and obtain his consent to marry the poor girl.

Demeas and Nikeratos with slaves carrying their luggage enter. We hear their impressions about the places they came from. This is a place for the dramatist to present Athens with a little traditional encomium (v. 100 f.). Nikeratos' simplicity is made clear with his remark ; the reply he gets from Demeas (v. 106 ff.) shows the humour of the latter. They turn the conversation to a subject they are familiar with : they have decided on a marriage between the son of Demeas and the daughter of Nikeratos, and agree to fix a day for the wedding. But the text stops again. In the gap act I ends and act II begins.

We can guess that act II began with Demeas coming out of his house, having just been told by Chrysis that the baby is his son. After the gap we find Moschion, who came back from the ἐρημία (v. 94). He is so absorbed that he does not notice his father. His rhetorical exercise did not actually take place, because when he was by himself instead of preparing his speech he was dreaming about the day of his wedding—a stupid thing to do at that moment (v. 126). Now he sees Demeas and understands from his appearance that there is something wrong. The ἑταίρα he lives with has born him a child, as if she was married to him. But he is going to send her away from his house (the feminine participle, conjectured to be ἀποφθαρεῖσα must be retained). Moschion is upset and in his embarassment defends the illegitimate child, producing arguments, which are commonplaces (see Soph. fr. 84 and Eurip. fr. 168). The effect is comic, not because of the arguments themselves, but because of the special situation which produces them. The rest of this conversation is unfortunately lost in the gap of the text. After the gap the subject of their conversation is Moschion's marriage. We know from v. 334 f. (τὸν φανέντ' αὐτῷ γάμον ἄσμενος ἀκούσας) that Demeas oppened this conversation by telling Moschion that he had arranged a marriage for him with Nikeratos' daughter. Moschion was unexpectedly relieved, because he gained his cause without any effort. He agrees at once, but he shows an eagerness, which excites his father's curiosity. Moschion now at least must say something, but he simply is unable to do it. In his character we find the theme common to all lovers of comedy, lack of eloquence and persuasiveness, in an elaborate variation combined with timidity. He wishes his father could understand that he is in haste and help him without asking why. His wish is expressed with the optatives of v. 152, which I prefer to be plain optatives (without, of course, a question mark). The effect of Moschion's wish is successful. Demeas ' understands ' (cf. v. 335 f. οὐκ ἐρῶν γάρ, ὡς ἐγὼ τότ' ᾠόμην, ἔσπευδεν) ; he thinks Moschion is very much in love and being himself in the same situation he shows understanding. He decides to run immediately to Nikeratos and arrange the wedding for the same day. Moschion is so glad that he cannot restrain himself. Shall he go and fetch the girl after performing the preliminary rites of the wedding? I think that verses 156-157 suit Moschion better. But Demeas tells him to wait ; They must first see Nikeratos. Moschion feeling guilty and being timid cannot face Nikeratos. He leaves his father alone to take care of the matter and enters the house.

The fragmentary text after the gap is problematic. Who are the speakers here? I agree with Mr. Sandbach that they are Demeas and Nikeratos. Demeas called Nikeratos to come out. It seems to me that Demeas is trying to persuade him that they had already fixed the same day as the day of the wedding, but Nikeratos strongly protests (vv. 170,

173). I cannot see what is the obstacle which makes Nikeratos think that 'it is impossible' (v. 176) to have the wedding on the same day. He says something about his friends (cf. also v. 403). Has he no time to announce the wedding to his friends and invite them? Demeas finally persuades Nikeratos, calls out Parmenon and sends him to the market for the traditional shopping and fetching of a cook. Parmenon cannot understand what has happened so quickly. He says that he is going in to take money. Nikeratos goes in to tell his wife about the wedding before he goes to the market. Demeas comments on Nikeratos, that he is going to have difficulties in persuading his wife to have the wedding on the same day. But I cannot see why. Parmenon shows reluctance to carry out quickly his master's orders. He probably wants first to get some information. The text stops again. Act II ends in a gap with the departure of Parmenon and Nikeratos for the market. Demeas goes in.

The three last acts of the play are almost complete. The old fragments of the Cairo Papyrus and the new ones of the Bodmer Papyrus offer us now a more or less smooth text. In the dramatic structure of the play the third Act contains the development of the action which leads to a failure and disappointment. Demeas opens the act with a long monologue, which is informative as well as dramatic. While he was busy with the preparations of the wedding he overheard that the father of the baby is Moschion. He comes out in a state of alarm. On his way out he sees his concubine suckling the baby. But he cannot even think that Moschion could be able to do such a deed. Parmenon enters with the cook and their traditional comic scene is a small interval. Demeas fails to extract the truth from Parmenon, who has to run away in order to avoid the anger of his infuriated master. Demeas controls himself and tries to face the situation with reasoning. Nevertheless his reasoning leads him to wrong conclusions. Taking into consideration

Moschion's age and former behaviour, he concluded that Moschion is not very guilty; on the contrary Chrysis, the former ἑταίρα and a person of low social level, is alone found responsible and guilty. He decides to throw her out of his house and get rid of her. The execution of his decision follows. It is very important for the dramatic development of the play that Demeas did not tell Chrysis the real reason of his behaviour, but at the same time it is also very well motivated. After this highly emotional scene, to which the presence of the Mageiros adds a comic touch, Nikeratos' appearance and his traditional jokes about the sheep are a change. He consoles Chrysis and takes her in his house.

Act IV, as it is now completed with the new text, is the great surprise in the new *Samia*—and it seems that all new Menandrean texts will contain some surprise. Being the climax of the play, this act has no parallel in Menander's surviving work. The various comic situations succeed each other quickly, 'making the act astonishingly dramatic', and the characters move from one emotional situation to the other, all of them playing equally important parts. The use of the traditional comic and tragic material shows clearly the 'new comedy' style of Menander.

Nikeratos comes out ready to go and speak to his friend. His house is upset, the women are crying. How is it possible now to have the wedding? Moschion comes from the agora. He is impatient and tired of waiting for the time of the wedding. Nikeratos tells him the latest news.

Demeas coming out of his house, where the women are crying, threatens them in order to stop and give a hand to the cook. The wedding must take place. He forces himself to swallow his grief and perform his duties properly. The other two men accost him and Moschion asks him to explain his behaviour to Chrysis. The following scenes spring from the inevitable misunderstanding, because neither Demeas nor Moschion can say openly in front of Nikeratos what each of them implies as the ' truth ' of the story. When at last Demeas full of indignation reveals his secret suspicion, which excites an explosion of Nikeratos' anger, Moschion finds himself in a desperate situation. Now it is impossible to tell the truth in front of the infuriated Nikeratos ; but his silence is taken as a sign of his guilt. This misunderstanding gives Nikeratos time to compare this ' tragic ' situation to the tragic myths of Tereus, Oedipus, Thyestes and to find them now less tragic. He imagines in crescendo a sequence of ' tragic ' events, which he expects to follow Moschion's ' tragic ' deed. He will never give his daughter to such a horrible person—gods forbid ! He would rather accept the failure of having Diomnestos as a son-in-law —an ὁμολογουμένη ἀτυχία—than Moschion. It seems clear to me, although the text here is incomplete (v. 504 f.), that the name Diomnestos has a proverbial meaning (cf. the name Melitides in the *Aspis* 269) ; the difficulty is that Diomnestos appears for the first time in comedy, and his name is not recorded by the collectors of proverbs. Historic persons named Diomnestos, otherwise unimportant, are irrelevant, with one exception, which, I think, can throw some light on this obscure name. A certain Diomnestos is mentioned by Heraclides Ponticus in his work Περὶ ἡδονῆς (fr. 58 Wehrli) quoted by Athenaeus (XII 536 F). The story of Diomnestos, which Heraclides mentions speaking about Kallias, seems to be a popular tradition, fictitious perhaps to a certain degree, with a perpetually exciting subject : the discovery by chance of a buried treasure. We know that Kallias also was connected with the discovery of a buried treasure, hence his adjective λακκόπλουτος (v. *Suda* s.v.).

In Heraclides' story a certain Diomnestos from Eretria found a treasure in a room of his farm house, left there by the Persian general, who had encamped on Diomnestos' field, but was killed with all his army. In the first phase of the story Diomnestos appears as a extremely lucky person. In the second phase the stories of two lucky men (Kallias and Diomnestos) are combined. When the King of Persia sent again an army to destroy Eretria (this is not historically true), the people of Eretria sent away their money. Among them Diomnestos' family sent the treasure to Athens and left it as a deposit to Hipponikos, son of Kallias. But all the inhabitants of Eretria were killed and the treasure of Diomnestos remained in Athens, in the hands of Hipponikos' descendants. Finally then the lucky Diomnestos turned out to be extremely unlucky; he lost not only his treasure but his life also.

The effect of Nikeratos' proverbial use of Diomnestos, as the name meaning great wealth gained and lost by chance, is comic, because it shows his financial concern in front of a 'tragic' situation. The poor Nikeratos realizes only for a moment that he is losing a rich son-in-law. When he goes in to expel Chrysis, Moschion seizes the opportunity to tell his father the truth at last. But now Nikeratos comes out playing a different tragic role; he is the father whose unmarried daughter has a child. Demeas is relieved, but Moschion is dying of fright and runs away, leaving Demeas again to face Nikeratos, who is not easy to handle, because his situation is really serious. He threatens and chases Chrysis, who takes refuge in Demeas' house. Demeas tries various ways: deceit, force, sincerity; till Nikeratos understands that Moschion is the father of his daughter's baby, but he is calmed down by Demeas, because he is assured that the wedding will follow at once. After regaining his humourous disposition Demeas wants to change the mood of the grieved Nikeratos with teasing and jokes. It is his turn to bring similar situations from the tragic myths, and compares Nikeratos to Akrisios, whose unmarried daughter Danae had given birth to a child. Traditional jokes about the parasites are combined.

The wedding, the centre of the action in the *Samia*, has reached the moment of its realization at the end of Act IV, but the end of the play has not come yet, because Moschion has self-respect and cannot bear the thought of his father's suspicions. Therefore he must do something to show the indignation of his wounded self and to punish his father. He would leave the house at once and go to Asia as a mercenary, if he could, but he is in love and his Plangon does not allow him to do any glorious deed. At least he can threaten his father.

Parmenon arrives in the nick of time after his running away. His comic monologue delays a little Moschion's action. Moschion orders him to go in and fetch a cloak and a sword, without giving him any explanation. As happened with Demeas in Act II, Parmenon asks to learn what is the matter and he is reluctant to carry out the order. But he goes in forced by Moschion, who waits imagining the success of his plan, although he admits his inability to persuade. Parmenon comes out without the cloak and the sword. In the house every-thing is ready for the wedding and they are waiting for Moschion. He tells Moschion to go in, because there is nothing to worry about. But Moschion insists and sends him again for the cloak and the sword. Fear and uncertainty about the result of his plan make Moschion irascible and rude and Parmenon gets angry with him. He brings Moschion the things he wanted, but Demeas does not appear yet. Nobody saw Parmenon carrying the sword and the cloak; this seems to ruin Moschion's plan. He is embarrassed till Demeas, after losing his patience, comes out to look for Moschion. Seeing him dressed as a traveller, Demeas understands the situation and with a moving speech begs Moschion to forgive him, forget what has happened that day, and stay. Moschion has succeeded and is completely satisfied, but his success does not last, because Nikeratos comes out. At the sight of Moschion dressed up like a traveller Nikeratos misunderstands him, thinking that his future son-in-law wants to avoid the marriage. He gets angry and threatens to seize and bind him, practicing the rights given to him by the existing law. But Demeas intervenes, begs Moschion to give up the sword and the cloak, and sends Nikeratos to bring out the bride. At once Nikeratos brings the bride followed by her mother, and gives her officially to the bride-groom. From Demeas' house the loutrophoros and the flute player come and join the spectacular nuptial procession.

Demeas, on behalf of the poet, asks the audience to applaud and wishes the goddess Nike to give always her favour to his χοροί, using this word as synonymous to the words ' actors of his plays '. Although the χορός is separated from the drama, it remains an indispensable traditional element of the theatre.

DISCUSSION

M. Turner : Perhaps we may add to the summary of the action a short indication of the artistic methods employed by the dramatist to realize it. The subject of the play is a marriage between the households of two neighbours (a Κηδεία, as the alternative title has it), desired by all the parties to it, and of the obstacles that constantly arise to this marriage. They issue from a series of misunderstandings which are made to arise quite naturally out of each other. In this intricate action, full of ironical situations, surprises and paradoxes, Menander achieves a remarkable degree suspense, and maintains the impetus right to the end of the play. He has also achieved his purpose with economy of characters. Nikeratos' wife and daughter do not appear on the stage till the final tableau.

The action is, in fact, made to grow out of the characters themselves and at the same time reveals them. Demeas misunderstands a situation because he wishes to believe the best of his adoptive son and wants to keep secret his worst suspicions ; Nikeratos because he is slow of comprehension and brusque ; Moschion because he lacks candour (he is a spoiled child) and has a cheerful readiness to hope for the best. There is an irony right from the start that a son should consent to his father taking a mistress and should help him to possess her ; and that in his first interview with his father he should plead the cause, in philosophical terms, of the claim of bastards to human sympathy when the baby in question is his own. Demeas attributes to the urgency of young love his son's instant agreement to the marriage with Plangon, and is therefore ready to fix " today " as the marriage day. When, concealed in the pantry, he has learned that Moschion is father of the child he had been led to believe was his own and also sees Chrysis nursing it, he jumps to the conclusion that Moschion has made love to his own mistress Chrysis. The scene in which the slave Parmenon is questioned but escapes with evasive answers maintains the suspense. Again Demeas draws a wrong conclusion, and rationalizes it : Moschion's conduct he now believes to be due to his desire to escape from a temptress (" my own Helen "). On this is founded his decision to expel her from his household. This decision, as M. F. Wehrli has shown us, tears him in two, for he has a real affection for Chrysis and remembers when she first arrived ἐν σινδονίτῃ λιτῷ. The presence of the cook during this scene, as we have already discussed (pp. 31-33) both prolongs and softens the tension.

At the end of Act III Chrysis with her baby and attendants are shut out by Demeas but given refuge in his house by Nikeratos. The 120 new lines at the beginning of Act IV develop the embroilment, and none of the scholars who have tried to guess at the contents of this lacuna have come anywhere near to the truth, or suggested anything so amusing and imaginative : a scene which (as we can see with hindsight) is a natural enough extension of the earlier misunderstandings. Moschion and Nikeratos join forces ; Demeas is resolved, if he can, to conceal his false suspicions. But Moschion's unexpected request that Chrysis should attend the wedding makes Demeas blurt out that he " knows " the baby to be Moschion's ; and when the latter offers the defense, that his conduct is no worse than that of many others, Demeas bids him tell Nikeratos who is the baby's mother. In this ironical situation Moschion is confused, and it is Nikeratos' turn to jump to the same conclusion as Demeas. He compares Moschion to Phoenix : ' I should have sold any concubine of mine the next day and disowned my son ; and all the barber's shops would have been full of people saying how manfully Nikeratos acted towards " a homicide ".' He then remembers that he has betrothed his own daughter to this " murderer " and leaves the stage outraged. Alone with his father Moschion can confess the truth, and the rest of the act can be allowed full comic (not to say farcical) expression, as Nikeratos, entering and leaving like a top, finds his daughter suckling the baby, and tries to seize it as hostage so as to extract the truth from his wife.

At length Demeas, his urbanity regained, calms Nikeratos down. But the emotional entanglement is not over. Moschion cannot bear to think of the suspicions his father had entertained. It is his turn to be torn in two. Shall he stay, as love for Plangon and oath require? Or go abroad to teach his father a lesson? It is hard to think of the weak-willed Moschion as a successful mercenary soldier. His father's sermon, apologies and entreaties fail to make him change his mind; Nikeratos' brusque orders to lower his sword do succeed. The invocation of the rigour of the law against a seducer of a free citizen woman is dropped, and at last in the final tableau the wedding can go forward.

M. Wehrli: Typologisch nimmt die *Samia* in der Behandlung des Verhältnisses zwischen (Pflege)vater und Jüngling eine so auffällige Sonderstellung ein, dass man chronologische Schlüsse zu ziehen versucht ist. Die auch in anderen Stücken Menanders vorliegende Umwandlung des Konfliktes in ein blosses Missverständnis ist hier mit der umfassendsten Umsicht vollzogen. Ein sachlich begründetes Zerwürfnis wäre durch Demeas Väterlichkeit wie durch Moschions fügsame Art ausgeschlossen; beide stimmen sogar, ohne es zunächst zu ahnen, in den Heiratsplänen für Moschion überein. Ja, der Argwohn des Alten wird gerade durch die reuevolle Verängstigung des Jünglings ausgelöst, der ihm seinen Fehltritt nicht einzugestehen wagt und darum das neugeborene Kind Chrysis unterschieben lässt. Ist diese lückenlose konsequente Motivierung der Handlung ein Beweis für späte Entstehung der *Samia*?

M. Ludwig: Die *Samia* hebt sich als ein einzigartiges Stück aus den übrigen bisher bekannten Komödien der Nea heraus. Ziel der Handlung ist wie sonst auch die Heirat des reichen jungen Mannes mit dem armen Mädchen. Aber weder stellt sich ihr ein Widersacher in Gestalt eines Rivalen oder eines abweisenden Vaters in den Weg, dessen Überwindung oder Ausschaltung das

Problem des Stückes wäre, noch muss eine vermeintliche Hetäre erst durch eine Anagnorisis heiratsfähig werden. Die beiden Haupttypen der Komödie sind damit vermieden. Die Väter haben —das gibt es sonst nirgends—bereits zu Anfang des Stückes (V. 114 ff.) entschieden, dass der junge Mann eben *dieses* Mädchen heiraten soll. Was kann jetzt noch dieser Heirat im Wege stehen? Der Mangel an Vertrauen und Aufrichtigkeit auf Seiten der im übrigen immer gut meinenden Personen verursacht die Verwicklungen der dramatischen Handlung. Die Art, wie hier das Übliche und Herkömmliche bewusst umgangen, ausgespart, ins Gegensätzliche verkehrt wird, scheint mir darauf zu weisen, dass die *Samia* zu den späteren Werken Menanders gehört. Typologisch gehört sie gewiss zu den voraussetzungsreichsten.

U.v. Wilamowitz, *Sitzber. Berlin* 1916, S. 73 : « Die *Samia* war ein Jugenddrama Menanders ». Ein ähnliches Urteil wurde oft vertreten. In ihrem Kommentar sprach sich Mlle Dedoussi bereits für ein nicht allzu frühes Datum aus (*ebda* S. 14, nahe bei 310). Ich begrüsse die zu Beginn ihres Vortrages gegebenen neuen Erwägungen. Die bisher für die Datierung benützten Kriterien scheinen mir in der Tat der Überprüfung bedürftig. Z.B. liegt der Annahme, eine Komödie, die Chairephon nennt, müsse 325-310 entstanden sein, nur eine grobe Schätzung T. B. L. Websters zugrunde (*Cl. Qu.* 1952, S. 22); es ist nicht ausgeschlossen, dass Menander sich auch später noch auf den berühmten Parasiten bezog.

Das Motiv, dass eine Hetäre das Baby eines bürgerlichen Mädchens bzw. einer bürgerlichen Frau für ihr eigenes ausgibt und mit dieser Unterschiebung den Lauf der Handlung entscheidend beeinflusst, hat die *Samia* mit den *Epitrepontes* gemein (etwas anders in *Truc.*). In der *Samia* geschieht sie mit, in den *Epitrepontes* ohne Wissen des Vaters. Bringt sie dort den Anstoss zur Lösung der Verwicklungen, so ist sie hier umgekehrt Anlass für die folgenden Verwirrungen.

M. Sandbach : The obstacles to the marriage that Moschion desires spring from his own actions. The whole of Acts II and

III is initiated by his fathering his own child on his father, not in itself an admirable procedure, although undertaken for a good purpose. He could have intended to reveal the truth when once safely married to Plangon, but there is no hint of this in the play. Then the minor delay of Act V is caused by his desire to punish his father for entertaining false suspicions of him, a project which, as Demeas effectively shows, disregards all the past kindness he had been shown and the attempt, which had gone along with the suspicions, to preserve his reputation.

M. Handley : Is there not this point to the opening situation : that Demeas' involvement with Chrysis and Moschion's involvement with Plangon are accompanied by a certain lack of trust or frankness on *both* sides between father and adopted son ? Demeas fell in love " and understandably, perhaps, he concealed it, he was ashamed " (22 f.) ; Moschion in turn is " ashamed " to confront Demeas with his undertaking to marry the girl (67). The reversal of the expected father/son relationship brought about by Demeas' love affair reminds one of the end of the *Wasps* (where the treatment is much more ostentatiously comic), and of M. Wehrli's discussion of the motif (*Wasps* 1351 ff. ; Wehrli, *Motivstudien* 24). The disappointing result of Demeas' efforts to be a model father recalls a number of points in the fuller study of fathers and sons in the *Second Adelphoi* as adapted by Terence. There, interestingly, the young man's sense of shame before his adoptive father is shown to have its positive as well as its negative side : *erubuit : salua res est* (643 ; cf. 683 f., 690 f. and context).

In looking at the play with the benefit of all the new accessions to its text, one is very much interested to see new points of design emerge. One example : Demeas' extended narrative of the wedding preparations at the beginning of Act III is appreciated in its own right when we come to it, as it has been before. But now that Act IV is present, and we find the same motif taken up at 440 ff., it becomes plain that the detail of the narrative is not simply scene-setting, or description for its own sake, but serves to create a picture in which a significant change can very economically be shown: Demeas now forces the preparations along in spite of himself, and their continuity underlines the revolution in his feelings.

M. Turner: We may similarly note the reference to the use of τρυφή : ἐτρύφησα (v. 7) says Moschion, τρυφᾶν γάρ says Demeas to Chrysis (376). Moschion prides himself on being κόσμιος (v. 18—yet he wasn't!); his father remembers his being κόσμιος (vv. 273, 344).

I should like to ask differents questions. What actually is Moschion doing as he enters to speak the prologue? Does he have some property to occupy his hands? How can he be seen ἄγειν πως σχολήν (20)?

Mlle Dedoussi: The prologue spoken by one of the characters of the play belongs to traditional drama as well as the prologue spoken by a divine being. But while the appearance of a deity has no other motivation than the need of the dramatist to introduce the audience to the plot of the drama, in the case of the appearance of a human being there must be some motivation. In the prologue of the *Mercator* we hear that the usual motivation of the appearance of a young man in a comedy was the need to express his love distress, and problems to the Night, the Gods, etc., in order to relieve his sorrow and ask for pity and help. Since in comedy the characters address the audience, especially in the monologues, it is expected the young man will address the audience, and this is what Moschion does in the *Samia* (v. 5); but he could begin the prologue with an invocation of some divinity. It is understood from v. 61 f. that Moschion left the stage at the end of the prologue, but the motivation of his exit is lost in the gap of the text.

M. Sandbach: A problem that has not been solved by the new text is why Menander made Moschion an *adopted* son. This had given rise to much unbridled speculation, now proved to be false. Have any of those here views on this subject?

Mlle Dedoussi: There was once a theory that Chrysis might have turned out to be Moschion's sister.

M. Sandbach: It is possible that an adopted son would not have the same claim on his father's affections as a son by birth? Demeas' indulgence of Moschion and care for his reputation would then be the more creditable, and he would have the greater reason for reproaching him for ingratitude (vv. 698-710).

Mlle Dedoussi: Why is it necessary to suppose that Chrysis has had a baby? The dramatist wanted to make Demeas certain that Chrysis was the mother of the baby, and the only possible way was to make him see her suckling it (vv. 256 ff.). This does not mean that she was in fact doing so, because Nikeratos also saw his daughter suckling the baby (v. 535 f. and 540 f.) and this shows, I think, clearly that the baby was fed by its real mother. Therefore there was no need for Chrysis to be able to suckle it herself. Demeas implies indirectly that he was mistaken, thinking that Chrysis was in fact suckling the baby, when he tries to persuade Nikeratos that Plangon was playing and not suckling it (v. 542).

Furthermore we can not combine, as a supplement of v. 56, with the adverbial expressions ἀπὸ ταὐτομάτου and καὶ μάλα a verb like ἔτικτεν (Austin tentatively) or τέτοκεν (metrically short). If the birth of a child to Demeas from his ἑταίρα, as a convenient lie, puts him in a most unpleasant situation (the same happens to Charisios of the *Epitrepontes*), why is it necessary to complicate the story, ἔξω τοῦ δράματος, by supposing that Chrysis in fact took the risk and gave birth to a child, who had to die, because there was no place for it in the plot?

M. Sandbach: There may have been some explanation after 118 of why Demeas wished to marry his son to a poor man's daughter. But I think it not out of the question that it was taken for granted that this was in character for him; he was the sort to assist a poor friend in this way. Generosity to poor friends was a custom in Demeas' household, cf. τοῖς φίλοις τοῖς δεομένοις τὰ μέτρια ἐπαρκεῖν ἐδυνάμην (vv. 15-16) a line that may be there partly to prepare the way for this desire to arrange an unprofitable marriage.

Mlle Dedoussi: In vv. 113-115 we hear that the two men, Demeas and Nikeratos, who are friends and neighbours, had decided on a marriage between their children. The decision is ἔξω τοῦ δράματος and there is no need to ask why they so decided. It is clearly stated by the dramatist (vv. 13-16 and 381 f.) that Demeas is a generous rich man. It is unnecessary also to suppose that there must be a benefaction made by Nikeratos to Demeas (the word χάρις—v. 183—does not necessarily support this supposition).

M. Sandbach: Chrysis is a free woman and Demeas treats her as such (vv. 381-382, 577). But a distinction must always be made between the legal position and the practical position of the weaker members of society, among whom foreign women are emphatically to be reckoned. Nikeratos says (508) that he would have sold a *pallake* who had behaved as Chrysis is supposed to have done. There were legal processes for establishing the freedom of a free person who had been *de facto* enslaved (A. R. W. Harrison, *The Law of Athens*, 178-179), but a foreign woman could not benefit by them unless there was some citizen who had enough interest in her to institute them. Thus it is possible that Chrysis, once in Demeas' household, would have been for practical purposes in his power or under his control (25), although not of course his legal property, any more than Dromon and the girl were the legal property of the pirates who were ἐγκρατεῖς of them (*Sikyonios* 3).

M. Handley: Could I return once more to 440 ff. to raise another point of dramatic technique? Demeas' sudden exit from his house interrupts the conversation between Nikeratos and Moschion—at least it does so as far as the audience is concerned. I take it, as I believe M. Sandbach does, that Nikeratos speaks again at 451, when he says σὺ πρότερος, Μοσχίων, πρόσελθέ μου (cf. *BICS* 16, 1969, at p. 105). It may not be determinable whether they are supposed to be talking or whispering to each other while Demeas is speaking, or whether further words were unnecessary; but they have in any case registered Demeas' presence and decided to act. This seems to involve a kind of simultaneous action on the stage. Could I ask whether there is anything comparable in Menander?

M. Sandbach: A passage occurs to me which, although very different from this, has the resemblance that while one character speaks, another conversation must be supposed to go on. At *Misoumenos* 210, Krateia comes out of Thrasonides' house, accompanied by an old woman, in my view her nurse, who is a *muta persona.* Demeas, who is already on stage, cries in surprise ὦ Ζεῦ, τίν' ὄψιν οὐδὲ προσδ[οκωμένην] ὁρῶ; whereupon Krateia says to the old woman τί βούλει, τηθία; τί μοι λαλεῖς; πατὴρ ἐμός; ποῦ;. We must suppose that as Demeas spoke the old woman caught sight of him and broke the girl's train of thought with " look there's your father " or something of the kind.

There seems to be a similar trick at 229, where Getas, who has been speaking to Krateia, continues τί τοῦτο, καὶ σύ, γραιδίον [ ] κ̣α̣λεῖς (λαλεῖς looks much less likely). The old woman must once again be supposed to have said something while Getas was addressing Krateia, and presumably she said it to Demeas. Exempli gratia one might supplement καὶ σύ, γραιδίον, [νῦν δεσπότην] καλεῖς;. By calling Demeas δεσπότης the old woman confirms that he is Krateia's father. That Getas is convinced appears from his politely respectful continuation with the vocative βέλτιστε. In neither place is the old woman allowed to reply to the question addressed to her.

Mme Kahil: a) La description des fêtes d'Adonis, pendant lesquelles a eu lieu le viol, me paraît intéressante. Nous avons sur cette fête, qui comporte ici une *pannychis*, des témoignages archéologiques assez pittoresques (cf. N. Weil, *BCH* 90, 1966, pp. 664-

698 ; D. B. Thompson, *JEA* 50, 1964, pp. 147-163). Contrairement aux Dionysies, Tauropolies, etc., c'est une fête à l'*intérieur* (et non une procession hors de la ville) et cependant la jeune fille y a été mise à mal.

b) Le tableau final de la *Samienne* a pu être fort somptueux : d'après les dernières lignes du texte on peut imaginer l'arrivée de la procession nuptiale avec la joueuse de flûte, la porteuse de loutrophore, les femmes (dont l'épouse de Nicératos). Nous savons que Ménandre aimait ces représentations colorées et pittoresques (cf. le *Dyskolos* et la *Théophorouménè*).

VI

CESARE QUESTA

Alcune strutture sceniche di Plauto e Menandro

ALCUNE STRUTTURE SCENICHE DI PLAUTO E MENANDRO

(con osservazioni su *Bacchides* e Δὶς ἐξαπατῶν)

L'*aetas Menandrea*, inaugurata nel 1958 con la pubblicazione della parte meglio conservata della celebre *papyrus Bodmeriana*, ha prodotto frutti assai ricchi per lo studioso della *palliata*, ed in particolare per lo studioso di Plauto.

La vastità e la difficoltà del tema consigliano di toccare solo alcune questioni, siano esse d'ordine particolare o generale.

Si può riassumere in tre punti, credo, quello che si è appreso grazie alla scoperta del nuovo materiale greco : *(a)* alcuni vecchi problemi o si sono rivelati inesistenti oppure hanno trovato nuove e impreviste vie di soluzione ; *(b)* certe acquisizioni, molto importanti, della critica precedente hanno trovato splendida conferma : per es. i fondamentali postulati del metodo analitico nello studio della *palliata*, anzi, la legittimità stessa di questo metodo non potevano meglio trovare nuovi fondamenti di rigorosa saldezza ; *(c)* infine, il disporre di un materiale di confronto molto più ricco di quello noto sino al 1958 permette alcune considerazioni, almeno in via preliminare e sotto forma di ipotesi di lavoro, circa la struttura rispettiva di νέα e *palliata*, e soprattutto circa i metodi di lavoro di Plauto e degli altri poeti latini.

* * *

Circa il punto (*a*), tutti sappiamo che il finale dello *Stichus* plautino (peraltro già ben analizzato da Webster, *Studies in Menander*, Manchester 1960², pp. 141-142 anche prima delle nuove scoperte) ha svelato buona parte delle sue oscurità di condotta scenica grazie al confronto con *Dysk.* 880 sgg.[1]. La struttura complessiva della commedia plautina dovrà essere esaminata a lungo con attenzione, ma abbiamo almeno la certezza, ora, che gli interventi del flautista sono ricalcati su quelli che dovevano essere nei primi Ἀδελφοί. Al massimo si può pensare che Plauto abbia reso questi interventi più ricchi e articolati di quelli del modello, sebbene proprio il finale del *Dyskolos* manchi di cenni precisi su eventuali interruzioni e riprese dell'accompagnamento auletico.

Circa i rapporti tra commedia plautina e alcuni altri particolari scenici del *Dyskolos* sono state dette cose anche molto inesatte, come vedremo in seguito. Io preferisco far osservare in questa sede come grazie al *Dyskolos* si possa intendere bene anche la scena della *Casina* (IV 3) che prepara il corteo nuziale, e la scena stessa del corteo (IV 4); e la *Casina* risale a Difilo [2]. Ora noi non possiamo dubitare più dell'effettiva

[1] Per un'informazione sulle opinioni della critica prima del 1958, vedi *Menandri quae supersunt* ... II, *ed.* A. Koerte, ... *retractavit* A. Thierfelder, Lipsiae 1959, p. 14 sgg. (Leo aveva pensato a contaminazione), cui si aggiunge l'opportuna messa a punto di Ed. Fraenkel, *Elementi Plautini in Plauto*, Firenze 1960, p. 443; utile il rendiconto di H. J. Mette, *Lustrum* 1965, p. 1 sgg., anche se devono essere respinti i curiosi tentativi di indovinare (alla lettera) il metro di scene menandree perdute, in base a chissà quali criteri (il papiro smentisce tutte le ipotesi circa il Δὶς ἐξαπατῶν) [è strano che in *Lustrum* 1968, p. 553 sg. il Mette non abbia compreso la ragione dei tagli operati da Plauto nel Δὶς ἐξαπατῶν: cfr. invece oltre, p. 206 sgg.]). È innegabile che le coincidenze tra *Stichus* e *Dyskolos* indeboliscono l'ipotesi della contaminazione, senza escluderla. (Per il *Dyskolos* ho tenuto presenti in modo particolare le edizioni commentate di E. W. Handley, London 1965; J. Martin, Paris 1961; M. Treu, München s.d. [1960]; e il comm., senza testo, di F. Stoessl, Paderborn 1965; per le questioni sceniche e metriche del finale è assai utile la diligente trattazione di F. Perusino, *Il tetrametro giambico catalettico nella commedia greca*, Roma 1968, pp. 131 sgg. e soprattutto 138 sgg.).

[2] Su Difilo, oltre alle classiche trattazioni di G. Jachmann, *Plautinisches und Attisches*, Berlin 1931, p. 105 sgg. e Ed. Fraenkel, *Elementi*..., p. 281 sgg. vedi T. B. L. Webster, *Studies in Later Greek Comedy*, Manchester 1953, p. 152 sgg.; F. Della Corte, *Da Sarsina a Roma*, Firenze 1967², p. 119 sgg. (con riferimenti bibliografici); sulla ψυχρότης, forse inesistente, fa ora acute considerazioni il Barigazzi, Macone e i prologhi di Difilo, *RFIC* 1968, p. 390 sgg.; problemi particolari tocca E. Fantham, Terence, Diphilos and

presenza in scena del *tibicen*, al quale, anzi, va attribuito, con la tradizione manoscritta (cfr. gli apparati di Leo e Lindsay), il primo ritornello nuziale (v. 800) : *hymen hymenaee o hymen*. Come il flautista del *Dyskolos* non fa parte dell'azione, nel senso che entra ‘ dalla comune ’ — come diremmo noi — anche se Geta gli si rivolge come a un personaggio (cfr. le note *ad l.* di Handley e Stoessl), così il flautista della *Casina* è presupposto già in scena, senza speciali accorgimenti tecnici, nel momento in cui Lisidamo ed Olimpione si rivolgono a lui mentre attendono il corteo. Ma Plauto (o già Difilo ?) rompe l'illusione scenica più di Menandro, perchè il flautista intona egli stesso il ritornello che invece poco dopo è affidato ai soli Lisidamo ed Olimpione (v. 808 ; oppure è cantato, il ritornello, a n c h e dai due personaggi, o l t r e che dal *tibicen* ?). Ad ogni modo sembra sicuro che anche qui Plauto ha ripreso un particolare tecnico del modello. E' infatti più che probabile che Difilo non lasciasse priva di un adeguato accompagnamento musicale la scena del corteo nuziale, sebbene l'uso di veri metri lirici nella scena difilea corrispondente a *Casina* IV 4 sia ipotesi difficilissima, se non impossibile (certo i vv. 815-846 sono, metricamente, quanto di più plautino si possa immaginare).

Nella *Casina* il momento d'inizio del suono del *tibicen* è chiarissimo. Nello *Stichus*, invece, il *tibicen*, che è in scena almeno dal v. 715, ha di certo iniziato a suonare da prima. L'invito a bere si giustifica scenicamente solo pensando che il *tibicen* mostri in qualche modo, con una mimica appro-

Menander, *Philologus* 1968, p. 196. Non mi soffermo su *Dysk.* 432 sgg. perchè è sicuro che qui la flautista non suona o, se inizia, smette subito : il testo è sempre in trimetri giambici. Un noto passo della *Theophoroumene* (v. 28) è troppo incerto perchè possa essere discusso qui (αὔλει od αὔλει ?) : vedi *Menandri Comoediae quae exstant, recognovit*... D. Del Corno, I, Milano s.d (1965), pp. 432-433 ; è difficile che il PSI che apparirà definitivamente nel vol. XV sia un frammento della monodia attestata da *Schol. ad Eur. Andr.* 103 : cfr. Pavese, Un frammento di mimo in un nuovo papiro fiorentino, *SIFC* 1966, pp. 63-69 (ma vedi Handley, *BICS* 16 (1969), 95 sgg.).

priata, di non voler esercitare l'arte sua ... a bocca asciutta (anche se poi sembra schermirsi): Sagarino e Stico, che trincano gagliardamente, lo invitano allora ad unirsi alla festa. Il flautista potrebbe essere entrato in scena al v. 683, uscendo con Sagarino e Stico dalla casa di Epignomo, e sarebbe, in questo caso, tra i figuranti che preparano il festino degli schiavi (almeno in un primo momento). Però, considerando *Dyskolos* e *Casina* ~ Κληρούμενοι, questa mi pare ipotesi debole, e preferisco pensare che il flautista fosse già vicino alla scena, pronto per intervenire, se caso, nell'azione : un passo dello *Pseudolus*, che vedremo, ci testimonia la possibilità di interventi auletici anche fuori dell'azione.

Dobbiamo, ad ogni modo, tener presenti due fatti :

(a) non si riesce a precisare quando, nello *Stichus*, il flautista inizi a suonare: forse al v. 702, in cui il metro passa da tr^7 a ia^8? Oppure al v. 707, in coincidenza con l'emistichio greco?

(b) a differenza di quanto sappiamo sino ad ora per Menandro, il flauto accompagna, in Plauto, anche, se non principalmente, parti in tr^7 : prescindendo dal ritornello nuziale (probabilmente esclamazione *extra metrum*), in tr^7 è la scena IV 3 della *Casina*, in tr^7 (fatta eccezione per i vv. 702-705) è la scena V 5 dello *Stichus*. In particolare non sono concepibili senza musica, in questa commedia, i deliziosi versi 729-730, vera e propria canzoncina popolare da osteria :

haec facetiast, amare inter se riualis duos,
uno cantharo potare, unum scortum ducere.

Inoltre le singolarità metrico-prosodiche di tutta la scena (cito un po' a caso: il proceleusmatico *ăgĕ sĭquĭd* nel v. 715 ; la ' correptio ' *éripe ĕx óre* del v. 718 ; il problematicissimo v. 736, in cui paiono violate a bella posta le più severe norme del verso plautino ; una certa abbondanza di longa bisillabici ' strappati ' fuori delle abituali preferenze dell'autore) sembrano anch'esse suggerire la presenza c o n t i n u a di un accompagnamento musicale che le giustifichi. Del resto Plauto, se fa precedere la brevissima scena conclusiva da un preludietto musicale, al ritmo del quale gli schiavi danzano (il flauto ha cessato di suonare almeno con il v. 761 e ripiglia dopo il v. 768), e scrive questa scena in giambi ' lunghi ', riprendendo cioè il metro del finale del *Dyskolos* e verosimilmente presente anche nel finale dei primi 'Αδελφοί, Plauto, dico, inserisce tra due coppie di ia^7 (770-771, 774-775) due *versus Reiziani* (772-773), ritmicamente omogenei al contesto, ma ignoti ai Greci. Plauto di Sarsina ribadisce la sua sovranità sui *numeri innumeri*. Sia chiaro infatti, per quanto detto qui e altrove, che supporre un'influenza vera delle usanze metriche di Menandro su Plauto è cosa addirittura risibile. Tra l'altro, le commedie in cui appaiono tetrametri giambici catalettici (il solo *Dyskolos*) e tetrametri trocaici catalettici (abbondanti parti, ora, nella *Samia*) accanto ai trimetri giambici sembrano appartenere solo ad un momento giovanile dell'arte del poeta (ma resta da stabilire bene la cronologia della *Samia*, in cui, se non ci sono tetrametri giambici, larghe sono le parti in tetrametri trocaici). Di *Ps.* 573-573a parleremo in altro contesto.

Sempre rimanendo nel settore dei problemi o risolti o avviati a soluzione, direi che luce importante è venuta sulle questioni relative al *Poenulus* dal *POxy* 2654.

La struttura generale del *Poenulus* è ancora molto problematica, anzi questa commedia è, a mio parere, la più complessa tra quelle di Plauto che ci siano giunte, anche per questioni di tradizione manoscritta [1]. Sappiamo tutti che la

[1] Ancora una volta la problematica oggi dibattuta risale a G. JACHMANN, *Plautinisches*..., p. 195 sgg. e Ed. FRAENKEL, *Elementi*..., p. 253 sgg., accanto ai quali va messo W. H. FRIEDRICH, *Euripides und Diphilos*, München 1953, p. 233 sgg. ; per la bibliografia più recente vedi H. J. METTE, *art. cit.*, pp. 143-144 (a pp. 95-98 un tentativo di ricostruzione dell'originale, supposto, con Arnott [vedi p. 189, n. 1], di Alessi).

possibilità di una derivazione da Menandro si fondava — oltre che su di una identità di titolo (pur non completa) e trascurando le conclusioni che si potrebbero ricavare da un passo oscuro del prologo (vv. 53-55) — sulla forte analogia di situazione scenica fra i vv. 210 sgg. Turner del *Misoumenos* (già v. 12 sgg. Koe.) e i vv. 1292 sgg. della commedia plautina (e di questa si vedano anche i vv. 1253 sgg.). L'analogia di situazione sussiste anche se nella seconda parte del v. 216 Turner (v. 18 Koe.) si continua il discorso di Geta escludendo la presenza di Trasonide, come già aveva fatto Webster (*Studies in Menander*, cit., p. 19 n. 3) e fanno ora Mette (*art. cit.* pp. 156 e 158) e lo stesso Turner, meglio interpretando la tradizione manoscritta (in sostanza rappresentata dal *PBerol* 13281, perché il *POxy* 2656 è, al v. 216, proprio lacunoso dopo le parole ἐξῆλθεν ἔξω, dopo le quali Wilamowitz e Koerte ponevano l'intervento di Trasonide) [1]. La scoperta del *Sikyonios* sembrò recare una nuova conferma di paternità menandrea per il *Poenulus*. Il *Sikyonios*, come tutti sappiamo, mostra nei vv. 342 sgg. una situazione che è molto affine a quella di *Poe.* 1096 sgg., anzi i vv. 359-360 del *Sikyonios* sono quasi identici a *Poe.* 1107 sgg. (sfrutto qui e altrove il materiale raccolto da Kassel nella sua ammirevole edizione), mentre non mancano le possibilità di altri confronti (*Poe.* 372 ~ *Sik.* 197 ; *Poe.* 86 ~ *Sik.* 355), seppure molto meno indicativi. Forti di ciò, potevamo anche trascurare il fatto che nessuno dei frr. del Καρχηδόνιος di tradizione indiretta (frr. 226-233 Koe.) trova riscontro nella pur lunghissima commedia plautina (così, assai bene, Mette, *art. cit.*, p. 143).

[1] Accettando la presenza del soldato c'è il rischio di creare un dialogo ' a quattro ' che parrebbe estraneo a Menandro (ma il finale delle *Bacchides* = Δὶς ἐξαπατῶν? Non è chiaro Mette, *art. cit.*, p. 54). Si noti che l'Antamenide plautino, pur concedendo che il Sarsinate l'abbia vivacemente colorito in modo tutto suo, non ha niente a che fare con Trasonide, Polemone o Stratofane.

D'altra parte l'amico e collega W. G. Arnott, in un articolo molto acuto [1], ha riproposto la derivazione del *Poenulus* dal Καρχηδόνιος di Alessi. In modo particolare (ha fatto osservare Arnott) il fr. 263 Kock di Alessi trova rispondenza nei vv. 522-525 del *Poenulus*, i quali dal canto loro appartengono a quella ' azione di Collibisco ' che io non ritengo ancora del tutto illegittimo distinguere dall' ' azione di Annone ' nella struttura della commedia. Ma ognuno vede, a questo punto, che tenendo fermo da un lato ai raffronti menandrei (piuttosto connessi con l' ' azione di Annone '), dall'altro a quelli con Alessi (legati con l' ' azione di Collibisco ') si poteva proporre un'ipotesi piuttosto audace : non solo una sicura *contaminatio*, ma addirittura una *contaminatio* tra i due Καρχηδόνιος, l'uno di Alessi, l'altro di Menandro!

Il *POxy* 2654 semplifica, ora, di molto i termini della questione. Se i vv. 4-10 (in cui i vv. 7-8 coincidono con i due vv. sentenziosi che formano il fr. 228 Koe.) non ci illuminano troppo, i vv. 31-39 (comunque si legga il v. 39), unitamente alla parola σκάφη che si legge nel v. 25, ci permettono di indovinare un'azione ove né il luogo in cui questa si svolge, né i nomi dei personaggi, né (come fa osservare Turner) la situazione, soprattutto, in cui questi si trovano hanno niente in comune con il *Poenulus* (vedi *POxy*, vol. XXXIII, London 1968, p. 3). Menandro è adesso da escludere come fonte, o una delle fonti, del *Poenulus* (il problema dell'eventuale *contaminatio*, anche della sola scena I 2, non è interessato, di per sé, da quanto ricavabile dal nuovo papiro). Ma che peso dare, a questo punto, ai già visti riscontri, non certo impugnabili, con situazioni sceniche chiaramente ritornanti nei menandrei *Sikyonios* e *Misoumenos*? Evidentemente lo stesso che diamo, *mutatis mutandis*, a quelli

[1] The author of the Greek original of the ' Poenulus ', *RhM* 1959, p. 252 sgg. ; Alessi come modello dello *Pseudolus* è ora proposto, in un dotto articolo, da T. Mantero, Lo *Pseudolus* plautino e i frammenti dello Ψευδόμενος di Alessi, *Maia* 1966, p. 392 sgg.

che, per es., ci sono tra *Dyskolos* ed *Aulularia* [1], *Dyskolos* e *Adelphoe* od *Eunuchus* di Terenzio (nelle parti sicuramente menandree), con in più l'avvertenza che in questi casi ci si muove nell'ambito della tecnica teatrale menandrea, mentre nel caso del *Poenulus*, che al Καρχηδόνιος di Menandro non risale, dobbiamo considerare, più ampiamente, tutta la νέα.

La νέα è, infatti, un repertorio, forse il più vasto e ricco esistente nelle letterature occidentali, di situazioni sceniche fisse, variamente combinate secondo norme strutturali che non sarà difficile formulare mano a mano che cresce il materiale di studio. Per es. nel *Sikyonios* abbiamo la scena dello svenimento di Cichesia, per la quale si sono potuti confrontare *Tri.* 1091 sgg. (meno calzanti i riscontri con *Mil.* 1332 e *Tru.* 366, che tuttavia sono variazioni del medesimo τόπος); il v. 374 del *Sikyonios* è direttamente confrontabile con *Curc.* 235, ma nessuno pretenderebbe di cogliere derivazioni plautine dal *Sikyonios*. E c'è di più. I rapporti tra Difilo e Menandro non sono chiarissimi (cfr. Webster, *Studies in Later Greek Comedy*, cit., p. 160 sgg.), ma si può credere, con buona verosimiglianza, che il modello della *Rudens* sia posteriore agli 'Επιτρέποντες. Se non sapessimo che la *Rudens* risale a Difilo, avremmo anche potuto pensare, fondandoci sulla scena dell'arbitrato, che anch'essa risalisse a Menandro, e precisamente ad una commedia in cui questo poeta riprendesse, con le debite variazioni, il τόπος dell'arbitrato e del successivo ἀναγνωρισμός con questo legato [2]. Si noti, per l'appunto, che *Misoumenos* e *Sikyonios* hanno riscontro con il

[1] La derivazione di questa commedia da modello menandreo è giusta *communis opinio* : cfr. H. J. METTE, *art. cit.*, pp. 195-196, ma cfr. l'opinione di F. H. SANDBACH, *supra*, pp. 97-98.

[2] Vedi su questo problema anche le osservazioni di G. MONACO, La scena dell'arbitrato e del riconoscimento nel *Rudens* plautino, *PP* 1947, p. 319 sgg. Partendo dalla considerazione tipologica della νέα e della palliata, da tempo consueta agli studiosi (esemplari in tal senso sono le *Motivstudien zur griechischen Komödie* di F. WEHRLI, Zürich 1936 ; vedi anche il materiale presentato dal METTE, *art. cit.*, pp. 100-105), occorre giungere allo studio delle funzioni dei personaggi nella morfologia della commedia (*supra*, pp. 30-31).

Poenulus nelle scene più stereotipe tra quelle che la νέα offre, quelle, cioè, di riconoscimento. Esse erano così scontate, ormai, che Menandro, poeta raffinato come pochi, non trova di meglio che stilizzarle in un linguaggio in cui, con funzione chiaramente ironica, abbondano gli echi di parlar tragico : penso a *Sik.* 369 sgg., a *Perik.* 349 sgg. (in cui il fenomeno è vistoso, considerando la struttura del dialogo e le particolarità metriche), e, nella sua funzione di preparazione dell' ἀναγνωρισμός, al discorso del carbonaio Sirisco, un vero capolavoro di etopea e ironia umanissima del poeta. Salvo, dunque, il caso di riscontri particolarmente significativi o di larga estensione, resta sempre come poziore, almeno in via di cautela metodica, l'ipotesi della presenza di *loci communes*, variamente adoperati prima dai poeti della νέα e poi da quelli della *palliata*.

* * *

Ho già detto prima, anticipando il secondo punto della mia esposizione, che il più recente materiale menandreo ha confermato importanti postulati della critica analitica o comparativa che dir si voglia. D'altra parte questa critica, occorre dirlo, soffriva della mancanza di un ampio confronto diretto tra un testo comico greco e la sua ' versione ' latina o, meglio, ' barbara '. I frammenti del Δὶς ἐξαπατῶν, di cui Handley ci ha generosamente messo a parte, giungono quindi a noi come un tesoro da molto tempo invano cercato.

Il *vortere* latino dei testi letterari greci è uno dei poli d'interesse della filologia classica da Leo in poi. Com'è evidente, il concetto di *vortere* è amplissimo : può essere visto sotto l'angolatura del codice linguistico, vale a dire delle possibilità espressive del latino nei secc. III e II a. C ; (vedi per es. Traina, Terenzio ' traduttore ', *Belfagor* 1968, p. 341 sgg., che riconsidera i pochi riscontri diretti fra Menandro e Terenzio ch'è possibile istituire), oppure sotto quella, più vasta, della struttura compositiva, di cui l'elemento linguistico è solo uno dei fattori [1].

Il collega Handley, nella προέκδοσις preziosa dei più estesi frammenti del Δὶς ἐξαπατῶν, ha già fatto da par suo molte osservazioni confrontandoli con le *Bacchides* che ne derivano [2]. Io cercherò di esaminare i frammenti menandrei, per quello che di essi è noto, sotto qualche altro punto di vista, solo in parte riprendendo quanto già trattato da Handley.

E' noto (vedi n. 1) che le versioni poetiche latine di testi greci tendono fortemente al patetico, in modo particolare quelle del teatro arcaico. In esse il πάθος soverchia e non di rado sacrifica l'ἦθος. Questa caratteristica appare anche nella ' versione ' plautina del Δὶς ἐξαπατῶν. Vediamone qualche esempio.

[1] La filologia classica italiana ha studiato il problema con ricchezza di idee, producendo contributi importanti : sono classici i lavori di S. Mariotti (*Livio Andronico e la traduzione artistica*, Milano 1952 ; *Lezioni su Ennio*, Pesaro 1951 = Torino 1963[2] ; *Il Bellum Poenicum e l'arte di Nevio*, Roma 1955 ; Letteratura latina arcaica e alessandrinismo, *Belfagor* 1965, p. 35 sgg.), cui si aggiungono le ricerche di A. Traina (Pathos ed ethos nelle traduzioni tragiche di Ennio, *Maia* 1964, p. 659 sgg. ; Ramenta philologa de uertendi ratione poetarum Latinorum, *Mem. Acc. Patavina*, 74 (1961/62) p. 116 sgg.) ; le finissime osservazioni sparse qua e là, con mano doviziosa, dal Barchiesi, *Nevio epico*, Padova 1962 ; lo stimolante contributo di I. Mariotti, Tragédie romaine et tragédie grecque : Accius et Euripide, *MH* 1965, p. 206 sgg. ; sempre di A. Traina si vedano le importanti note a *Comoedia, antologia della Palliata*, Padova 1966[2] (particolarmente interessante quanto osservato circa Menandro fr. 333 e Cecilio Stazio v. 143 sgg. R[3]). Per questioni generali si tenga presente il saggio premesso di A. Ronconi alla versione italiana di Terenzio (Firenze 1960). Sullo stile di Menandro mi sembra ora esemplare quanto ha detto F. H. Sandbach, *Menander's Manipulation of language for dramatic Purposes* (qui come terzo ' exposé ', pp. 111-143).

[2] *Plautus and Menander : a Study in Comparison...*, ecc., London 1968 ; poco frutto si ricava da J.-M. Jacques, Ménandre inédit : la ' Double fourberie ' et la ' Samienne ', *Bull. Ass. G. Budé* 1968, p. 213 sgg., ov' è indebitamente pubblicata (in versione francese approssimativa) anche parte del materiale del Δὶς ἐξαπατῶν ancora inedito ; per lo *status quaestionum* sino al 1964 vedi la mia edizioncina delle *Bacchides*, Firenze 1965 (Nota introduttiva, *passim*) ; E. Salvadori, Nuovi frammenti del Dìs Exapatôn, *Maia* 1969, pp. 86-92 riprende l'opuscolo di Handley, cit., riassumendolo, come ho fatto io in *RFIC* 1968, p. 502 sg.

I vv. 11-13 di Menandro sono indubbiamente molto vivaci. In essi abbiamo tre frasi tutte con verbo all'imperativo, rivolte da Padre-Filosseno[1] a Sostrato-Mnesiloco: ἐκκάλει ... νουθέτει ... σῶσον. Anche la clausola del v. 13 (οἰκίαν φίλην φιλῶν), con figura etimologica ed allitterazione, contribuisce alla tensione stilistica che adeguatamente esprime l'indignazione del vecchio. Ma Plauto (v. 494) è più colorito ancora: *regere animum atque ingenium* è frase solenne, che non corrisponde alla fondamentale *mediocritas* del λεκτικόν menandreo. Al congiuntivo esortativo *regas* segue nel v. 495 un imperativo (*serua*), il quale traduce direttamente σῶσον, ma αὐτόν non è reso con *illum* od *eum*. Plauto è stato più patetico e ... più pedante: αὐτόν si è geminato in una coppia di sostantivi (*sodalem* e *filium*), ciascono dei quali rappresenta ... una parte di Mosco-Pistoclero: questi, infatti, è *sodalis* di Sostrato-Mnesiloco e *filius* di Padre-Filosseno. In Menandro non c'è υἱός, a meno che di un accusativo υἱόν non sia traccia il ν che si legge subito dopo la lacuna nel v. 12 (col. I v. 51). Il v. 499 di Plauto va letto dopo il 495, secondo l'ordine conservato da P ed ora confermato dal papiro. Ma se Λυδέ, προάγωμεν è reso con *Lyde, sequere me*, cui s'aggiunge (forse per completare il verso) la replica *sequor* del pedagogo, niente c'è nel testo greco dell'enfatico *in te ego hoc onus omne impono* con cui Padre-Filosseno conclude la sua tirata prima di chiamar via il pedagogo (l'ordine del discorso è lo stesso in greco ed in latino).

Anche la prima replica di Lido mostra una certa sovrabbondanza (all'emistichio εἰ δὲ κἀμὲ καταλίποις; corrisponde l'intero v. 496), ma è soprattutto nei vv. 497-498 che Plauto, di nuovo, ha reso più marcati, più grassi direi, i contorni dell'elocuzione greca. Nei vv. 15-16 di Menandro ci sono due soli imperativi rispetto ai tre del testo latino (nel quale

[1] Il papiro non ci dice che nome avesse in Menandro il padre di Mosco-Pistoclero: cfr. E. W. Handley, *op. cit.*, pp. 8-9 e p. 21 n. 15 (per Criside-Bacchide); C. Questa, *ed. cit.*, p. 4 e n. 5; K. Gaiser, *WS* 1966, p. 194.

preferirei la successione *i cura concastiga*, in modo da avere un tricolon ascendente con alliterazione tra secondo e terzo membro), sebbene il livello stilistico del Δὶς ἐξαπατῶν sia qui un tantino più risentito che non in precedenza (penso all'uso di ἐλαύνω); non a caso chi parla è il pedagogo, le cui parole Menandro soffonde di benevola ironia con il farle solennemente ammonitrici.

Il v. 17 ci mostra un altro caso del procedimento stilistico plautino visto più sopra. Se αἰσχύνει è reso con *dedecorat* (ma precisato anche con *flagitiis suis*; il verbo *dedecorare* torna in Plauto solo in *Tri.* 298), ἅπαντας ἡμᾶς τοὺς φίλους si trasforma in Plauto in un tricolon quanto mai enfatico: *tu me amicosque alios* (l'emendamento di Camerario si impone). La semplicità di fondo dello stile menandreo non è gustata da Plauto, il quale, pur conservando i gangli essenziali del testo greco (si noti la precisione con cui sono tradotti i verbi σῶσον, καταλίποις, αἰσχύνει), ne ha sviluppato le suggestioni foniche in un discorso dove predomina l'ornato. Non voglio neppure pensare che quest' αὔξησις complessiva sia dovuta a banali motivi metrici, cioè all'uso di un verso ' più lungo ' qual'è il tr⁷ rispetto al trimetro giambico. Il processo semmai, è l'inverso: anche l'uso di un metro più sonoro e — forse — anche ad orecchio latino meno dialogico e più orchestico dei giambi si iscrive nella ricerca della fastosità lessicale e metrica.

Sappiamo che i vv. 31-90 di Menandro contenevano due dialoghi, separati da fine d'atto, tra Sostrato-Mnesiloco e Demea-Nicobulo; e sappiamo che Plauto ha tagliato le due scene menandree riassumendone alla meglio il contenuto nei vv. 520-525 e 530-533 (Handley, *op. cit.*, p. 13 sg.). Sui modi di questo riassunto e sulle importanti conseguenze che il taglio plautino ha avuto circa la struttura della commedia ci soffermeremo poi (oltre a tutto Handley ha soltanto accennato al contenuto di questo brano, ancora inedito, né mi è possibile far serio ricorso ad indebite indiscrezioni di altri).

Per ora è importante ai nostri fini l'esame dei vv. 18-30 e 91-102 comparati ai vv. 500 sgg. di Plauto. Si tratta di due monologhi, il primo dei quali è completo (il v. 30 è infatti ' didascalico ' nel suo secondo emistichio, che annuncia l'entrata di un personaggio da identificare in Demea-Nicobulo), non meno del secondo, se ricordiamo con Handley (*op. cit.* p. 14) che l'ancor inedito v. 90 annuncia la partenza per l'agorà-foro di Demea-Nicobulo. Completezza dei monologhi significa però, nel nostro caso, che di essi noi constatiamo con chiarezza inizio e fine : il loro testo, quello del primo in particolare, è purtroppo in condizioni non buone.

Per quello che si riesce a vedere, Menandro esprime con vivacità, duttilità di stile e abilità scenica l'incoerenza dei pensieri dell'innamorato deluso, che oscilla, prima e dopo d'aver restituito il denaro al padre, tra la stizza nei suoi propri confronti, l'ira per la creduta fedifraga, la delusione nei confronti di Mosco-Pistoclero, anch'esso creduto traditore. Dal secondo emistichio del v. 18 in poi la figura della cortigiana domina il discorso di Sostrato-Mnesiloco : essa è ' sfacciata ' (ἰταμή), è pronta a giurare e spergiurare, come Menandro adombra elegantemente nella frase εἰς μέσον τε πάντες οἱ θεοὶ ἥξουσι. Con il secondo emistichio del v. 23 Sostrato-Mnesiloco riconsidera il suo stato, riprendendo il monologo con un'esortazione a se stesso (ἐπάναγε, Σώστρατε) certo un po' solenne ; in seguito, dopo un accenno per noi oscuro ad una ' servitù ' (d'amore?), il giovane esprime la decisione di rendere il denaro al padre. Altrettanto fine è il secondo monologo, successivo ai due dialoghi tra padre e figlio. Menandro ci mostra un Sostrato-Mnesiloco sempre pieno di rancore nei riguardi di Criside-Bacchide, di cui, con tormentoso piacere, il giovane immagina l'avidità delusa. Un accenno a Mosco-Pistoclero prepara opportunamente l'apparizione di questo personaggio, ed il successivo dialogo che chiarirà l'equivoco.

Ai due monologhi di Menandro Plauto risponde — prima novità — con uno solo (dei vv. 530-533 parleremo dopo), e questo inizia subito con una differenza : il poeta latino ha soppresso la formula ' didascalica ' d'avvio (ἤδη 'στιν οὗτος φροῦδος ;) che pure egli, quando vuole, sa riprendere dai modelli o comunque usare (vedi per es. *Ps.* 397 *illic hinc abiit, tu adstas solus Pseudole*, ecc.). E le differenze tra Menandro e Plauto si fanno poi sempre più marcate. Il monologo plautino ha solo due veri punti di contatto con il Δὶς ἐξαπατῶν : il primo, più generico, è tra i vv. 500-501 e 99-102 ; il secondo, molto stretto, è tra i vv. 515-519 e 25-29, i quali si ricostruiscono proprio grazie al confronto col testo latino (oltre che dall'essere ripresi nei vv. 91 sgg., giusta una tecnica menandrea illustrata da Handley, *op. cit.*, p. 20 n. 8).

Al monologo plautino presiedono criteri ben diversi da quelli che sottostanno al monologo menandreo. La prima coincidenza, abbiamo detto, è generica :

καὶ τὰ μὲν ἔγωγ' ὀργίζομαι
τὰ δ' οὐκ ἐκεῖνον τοῦ γεγονότος αἴτιον
ἀδικήματος νενόμικα, τὴν δ' ἰταμωτάτην
πασῶν ἐκείνην

inimiciorem nunc utrum credam magis
sodalemne esse an Bacchidem incertum admodumst.

I versi di Menandro, come dicemmo, preparano il rientro di Mosco-Pistoclero, che al v. 103 appare sulla soglia della casa delle etère, e concludono il secondo monologo di Sostrato-Mnesiloco. In Plauto, invece, il concetto ch'essi esprimono è stilizzato in una *sententia* di valore e forma più generale, che apre l'unico monologo, ricollegandosi psicologicamente a quello che Sostrato-Mnesiloco ha saputo nella scena precedente. I vv. 500-501 di Plauto mostrano bene la loro funzione di riassunto e spiegazione. Nel monologo Plauto non fa mai menzione, come Menandro del resto, di Mosco-Pistoclero (a parte l'*illum* del v. 502), ma il poeta latino ha creduto opportuno chiarire bene al suo pubblico la situazione psicologica che s'è creata tra i due giovani dopo le false informazioni che Sostrato-Mnesiloco ha ricevuto da Lido e Padre-Filosseno [1].

Successivamente Plauto di Sarsina ha proceduto in modo diverso (come, lo vedremo subito) ed è ritornato a Menandro, quasi traducendolo alla lettera [2], solo alla fine del monologo (i vv. 519 a-c sono doppia redazione dei vv. 512-514; i vv. 520-525 non sono più vero e proprio monologo), là dove nel testo del Δὶς ἐξαπατῶν è esposto un fatto di importanza essenziale allo svolgimento della vicenda : la decisione di Sostrato-Mnesiloco di restituire il denaro al padre. Qui, certo, agisce la suggestione della scena menandrea, tagliata dal poeta latino e ridotta a riassunto, in cui, subito dopo la fine del primo monologo, Sostrato-Mnesiloco portava ad effetto il suo proposito incontrando il padre, ma ciò non toglie valore al fatto che, ristrutturando in uno i due monologhi greci, Plauto abbia preso da Menandro due sole ' pietre da costruzione ', proprio quelle essenziali al processo dell'azione : una, meno importante, è quella dei vv. 99-102, resa generica e posta a capo dell'unico monologo ; l'altra, molto più importante, è il brano in cui Sostrato-Mnesiloco decide di restituire il denaro. Apparentemente questa seconda ' pietra ' conserva il posto originario, ma è illusione ottica, perchè l'altro monologo menandreo illumina molto bene sul rovello che, secondo il poeta greco, continua a divorare Sostrato-Mnesiloco pur dopo la spiegazione col padre. Le

[1] Si tengano presenti le pagine di J. BLÄNSDORF, *Archaische Gedankengänge in den Komödien des Plautus*, Wiesbaden 1967.

[2] Circa πιθανευομένη al v. 27 (cfr. v. 93) ed il *subblandibitur* di Plauto cfr. E. W. HANDLEY, *op. cit.*, p. 12 ; come ha visto anche Handley, il v. 519 va letto con Camerario : *tum cum mihi ‹illud› [blandiri] nihilo pluris referet* ; *blandiri* è glossa in textu di *illud*, ricavata dal *subblandibitur* precedente.

dimensioni psicologiche del personaggio sono molto diverse, e diversa è, infatti, in Menandro la funzione dei vv. 25-29: nel Δὶς ἐξαπατῶν Sostrato-Mnesiloco trova un momento di fermezza nel va e vieni di sentimenti che lo agitano e continuano ad agitarlo; nelle *Bacchides* i versi esprimono il superamento definitivo dell'incertezza ed un fermo proposito subito realizzato. Tanto alla fine che al principio del suo unico monologo Plauto pare chiaramente dominato da esigenze di precisione espositiva e psicologica, vuole che al suo pubblico siano ben evidenti le cause delle azioni di Sostrato-Mnesiloco.

Resta da esaminare, a questo punto, quella parte del monologo delle *Bacchides* che non ha riscontro preciso nella parte conservata di Menandro. In essa possiamo distinguere tre sezioni: vv. 502-508, 509-511, 512-515.

Menandro ci ha dato nei vv. 91-103 un altro degno esempio della sua peculiare tecnica del monologo [1]. Plauto, come abbiam detto, non lo ha seguito, ed ha costruito i suoi versi secondo una struttura differente, ma non meno raffinata, che si fonda sui *lapsus linguae* del parlante. Per quattro volte Sostrato-Mnesiloco inizia un discorso contro Criside-Bacchide, e per quattro volte, con comico ἀπροσδόκητον, il discorso si trasforma in dichiarazione d'amore per l'infida cortigiana (leggo *meo* nel v. 503). Il gioco dei *lapsus* è particolarmente elegante nel v. 508, dove *mendicet* sembrerebbe aver per soggetto Criside-Bacchide, e invece vien seguito dal vero soggetto, l'inopinato *meus pater*. In questa sezione del monologo la lingua di Plauto è semplice e piana, in modo che l'attenzione degli spettatori si concentri tutta sulla sorpresa che riserva loro la sintassi.

[1] Menandro fa monologare il suo personaggio, mettendogli in bocca citazioni, dirette, del discorso (qui immaginario) di un' altra persona (lo stesso procedimento in *Sik.* 175 sgg., *Mis.* 302 sgg.). Terenzio si terrà fedele anche in questo al suo modello (cfr. *And.* 215 sgg.; *Hec.* 816 sgg.; *Heaut.* 223 sgg.), ma su differenze e somiglianze rispetto a Menandro vedi ora, molto fine, il saggio di B. DENZLER, *Der Monolog bei Terenz*, Diss., Zürich 1968.

Un monologo di questo genere è un *unicum* in Plauto. D'altro canto la lunga e bella scena tra Lisidamo e Pardalisca nella *Casina* (III 5) è tramata anch'essa dai comici *lapsus linguae* del vecchio, cui più d'una volta l'ossessione erotica fa sostituire se stesso ad Olimpione nel dialogo con la schiava. Ciò fa pensare, com'è del resto logico supporre, che i poeti della νέα usassero con una certa ampiezza di un artificio dialogico capace di effetti comici notevoli [1].

Ad ogni modo resta il fatto che Plauto nella parte più significativa del monologo del suo personaggio ha messo da parte Menandro e procede da solo. Proprio da solo? Questa conclusione parrebbe del tutto legittima sapendo che appunto nei monologhi il poeta latino si è prese le più ampie libertà rispetto ai modelli greci (è inutile citare ancora le classiche pagine di Fraenkel). Si considerino, inoltre, i vv. 509-511 (seconda sezione di questa parte del monologo), i quali, se hanno un'indubbia funzione di raccordo rispetto alla terza sezione, non sono per questo meno tipicamente plautini nella rottura dell'illusione scenica e dello stato psicologico del personaggio. Essi anticipano, con chiara allusione, lo sviluppo futuro della vicenda (molto bene in questo senso Handley, *op. cit.*, pp. 14-15). I vv. 512-515, dal canto loro, preparano in forma immaginosa la decisione di Sostrato-Mnesiloco, che i vv. 515-519 esprimono con perfetta evidenza traducendo Menandro alla lettera o quasi, come vedemmo. Il v. 514 è molto plautino e patetico nella sua forte sequenza di allitterazioni (*m*endicum *m*alim *m*endicando uincere). Allora, altra prova che abbiamo versi, sicuramente, di Plauto di Sarsina? Sarà bene non abbandonare una certa cautela metodica. Non solo il confronto tra Δὶς ἐξαπατῶν e *Bacchides*

[1] Diverso è il caso, naturalmente, di un personaggio che corregge se stesso dopo un *lapsus* che suscita il riso: per es. *Ps.* 841 sgg. Al nostro passo si possono accostare *Bacch.* 193, *Cis.* 67, dove però il procedimento stilistico appare una volta sola: cfr. quanto osserva P. FLURY, *Liebe und Liebessprache bei Menander, Plautus und Terenz*, Heidelberg 1968, p. 72, che, pur senza esaminare *Bacch.* 503 sgg., nota come Menandro ignori lo stilema plautino.

è possibile soltanto per l'estensione di poco più di cento versi, ma da quanto fatto sapere da Handley circa la parte ancora inedita del papiro e da quanto diremo appresso sembra che Plauto abbia usato a distanza brani o, piuttosto, spunti e immagini del testo greco (il termine ' contaminazione a distanza ' è di Mariotti e Ronconi) [1] : se Plauto avesse preso qui a modello, anche solo come falsariga strutturale, un monologo di altra parte, a noi ancora ignota, del Δὶς ἐξαπατῶν? Forse quest'ipotesi potrà venire in seguito allontanata o esclusa grazie al confronto tra i vv. 104-112 di Menandro e i vv. 534-562 di Plauto, ma è bene tenerla almeno presente.

Osserviamo ora alcune conseguenze sceniche derivanti dall'ampio taglio plautino. Il poeta romano ha riassunto due scene del modello in otto versi e mezzo : vv. 520-525, il primo emistichio del v. 530 ed i vv. 532-533. La funzione meramente connettiva dei vv. 520-525 si sorprende nell'andamento un po' trascurato dello stile (vedi le fastidiose ripetizioni *causa mea* v. 521, *mea causa* v. 523, *causa mea* v. 524). Lasciando per ora da canto la questione di Demea-Nicobulo, che Plauto ha fatto letteralmente sparire come personaggio recitante in questa parte della commedia, diremo che il taglio ha prodotto un'altra diversità di situazione. In Menandro Sostrato-Mnesiloco è già in scena quando Mosco-Pistoclero esce dalla casa di Criside-Bacchide, in Plauto accade il contrario : appena Sostrato-Mnesiloco è entrato dal padre, Mosco-Pistoclero esce dalla casa delle etère. I vv. 526-529 delle *Bacchides* riprendono sì i vv. 102-103 di Menandro, ma nel Δὶς ἐξαπατῶν Mosco-Pistoclero dice fra sé una frase brevissima e subito dopo scorge l'amico, mentre in Plauto lo stesso personaggio si rivolge prima a Criside-Bacchide, che si deve immaginare in casa dietro la porta.

[1] Cfr. S. Mariotti, *Livio Andronico* ... cit., p. 47 n. 1 e poi A. Ronconi, Antiche traduzioni latine da Omero, *SIFC* 1962 (ora nel volume *Filologia e linguistica*, Roma 1968, p. 109 sgg. : vedi p. 124).

Plauto è stato più menandreo di Menandro in questo particolare scenico, che egli ha certo imparato dal frequente riapparire nelle commedie dell'Ateniese (ma non solo in queste, c'è da credere: vedi Handley *ad Dysk.* 206-211, 427-429, 541-546 ecc.; per Plauto cfr. Fraenkel, *op. cit.*, p. 155 n. 1). Il ricorso a quest'espediente è un ripiego quasi disperato. Con solo quattro versi, infatti, Plauto deve 'riassorbire' gran parte del tempo che si presuppone necessario a Sostrato-Mnesiloco per rendere il denaro al padre Demea-Nicobulo, e spiegare in più a questo la faccenda di Efeso. Abbiamo questa volta la prova più sicura, io credo, della rinuncia plautina a dividere in atti le commedie e dell'assenza di intervalli, in esse, che, appunto, consentissero 'riassorbimento di tempo'. Se Plauto avesse conosciuto intervalli di tal genere [1], nessun momento delle *Bacchides* sarebbe stato più adatto di questo ad ospitarne uno: Sostrato-Mnesiloco entra dal padre e l'intervallo avrebbe supplito al taglio delle scene operato da Plauto 'riassorbendo' il tempo. Poichè il poeta latino non conosce intervalli del genere, è costretto a far uscire subito Pistoclero dalla casa di Criside-Bacchide, prestandogli qualche parola di circostanza per allungare il discorso, in modo che Sostrato-Mnesiloco possa uscire lui, nel frattempo, dalla casa del padre. E sempre per rendere meno brusca la saldatura tra i due tronconi menandrei è necessario che Sostrato-Mnesiloco, uscito dalla casa del padre, riprenda nei vv. 530-533 un concetto dei precedenti vv. 520-525 (il perdono per Crisalo), facendolo precedere da un solenne quanto lapalissiano *reddidi patri omne aurum* e da una striminzita considerazione su Criside-Bacchide, ch'è quanto resta dell'agile, vario, movimentato secondo monologo di Menandro. A questa inver-

[1] Su questo problema sono fondamentali le pagine di J. Andrieu, *Le dialogue antique*, Paris 1954, pp. 39-44, 55-56, 69 sgg. (con ricca bibliografia), che ora trovano luminosa conferma da quanto si ricava dal Δὶς ἐξαπατῶν; vedi inoltre W. Beare, *The Roman Stage*, London 1955², p. 188 sgg.

sione delle entrate di Mosco-Pistoclero e Sostrato-Mnesiloco Plauto è stato costretto proprio dall'inesistenza nel suo teatro — come istituzione — di lunghe scene vuote con valore di intervallo tra ' atto ' ed ' atto '. E ancora : i vv. 530-533 di Sostrato-Mnesiloco sono detti mentre Mosco-Pistoclero muove già verso la casa dell'amico per cercarlo (v. 529 *ibo ut uisam huc ad eum si forte est domi*), ma, sempre per lasciare un po' di tempo ancora a Sostrato-Mnesiloco ed ' illudere ' lo spettatore con la rapidità convenzionale del tempo scenico, Plauto non ha potuto consentire a Mosco-Pistoclero di vedere subito il *sodalis*.

Infine il dialogo si avvia, ed ecco un caso in cui si può supporre (cfr. anche Jacques, *art. cit.*, pp. 221-222) una piccola ' contaminazione a distanza '. I vv. 104-105 (τί κατηφὴς καὶ σκυθρωπός, εἰπέ μοι / καὶ βλέμμα τοῦθ' ὑπόδακρυ;), qui senza riscontro, sembrano riapparire in bocca a Siro-Crisalo in *Bacch.* 668 668a 669 (*numqui nummi exciderunt, ere, tibi/quod sic terram optuere?/quid uos maestos tam tristisque esse conspicor?*) : era Menandro a ripetersi, in qualche modo, oppure Plauto ha tralasciato prima il testo greco per ricordarsene poi?

Altre vistose differenze ci attendono, mentre per ora prescindiamo dai vv. 540-551, circa i quali è lecito avanzare varie soluzioni, tutte metodicamente corrette (vedi Handley, *op. cit.*, p. 18 e p. 21 n. 18 e quanto aggiungerò dopo).

Osserveremo in via preliminare che nei vv. 534-535 appare una metafora militare (*hostis ... contollam gradum*) ignota a Menandro, la quale, nel suo colorito paratragico, dà un avvio al dialogo più ridanciano, in fondo, di quello menandreo. Par quasi che Plauto voglia far intendere che il malumore di Sostrato-Mnesiloco è violento sì, ma destinato a durare ben poco. Ma c'è poi un fatto molto più importante. Per quanto riusciamo a vedere, non senza difficoltà, dai vv. 108 e 110, Sostrato-Mnesiloco non perde tempo, in Menandro, a dire a Mosco-Pistoclero di aver ricevuto da lui un grave torto. Il v. 112, anzi, lascia supporre, con la replica di Mosco-Pistoclero (λέγεις δὲ τί;), che venisse subito dopo una rapida esposizione dei fatti da parte di Sostrato-Mnesiloco, vale a dire che il dialogo si avviasse secondo lo schema di quello plautino dei vv. 560 sgg. Se le cose stanno così, è allora evidente che in Menandro non c'era — o non c'era in questo punto, per la solita riserva metodica — niente che potesse essere avvicinato ai vv. plautini 536-539 e 552-559. In questi versi c'è un vero e proprio γρῖφος, condotto con abile κλῖμαξ ascendente, che culmina nel ' rivelatore ' v. 560 : " Pistoclero, il falso amico sei tu, tu mi hai distrutto ".

Sino ad ora le amplificazioni plautine del dialogo erano discernibili grazie a indizi piuttosto costanti, che è stato merito di Fraenkel riconoscere, ed era quasi dogma rifiutare a Plauto la capacità di scrivere un dialogo capace di far veramente progredire l'azione. Ora, non è che nei versi delle *Bacchides* senza riscontro nel Δὶς ἐξαπατῶν l'azione progredisca veramente, ma almeno essa giunge — seppure in un ambito molto ristretto — ad un punto nodale : Sostrato-Mnesiloco dice a Mosco-Pistoclero di credersi da lui tradito, e questo particolare è essenziale al progresso della scena (in cui, ad un certo punto, Plauto riprende finalmente Menandro). Più interessante è che il dialogo non mostra i soliti ' agganci ' plautini (per es. ripetizione a distanza di un verso quasi identico), né i riempitivi buffoneschi indubbiamente peculiari del poeta latino.

In questa situazione di marcata indipendenza dal modello greco (che sussiste anche se ci trovassimo di fronte ad una ' contaminazione a distanza ', ma è ipotesi, questa, molto faticosa), non solo i vv. 502-515 paiono di Plauto soltanto, ma il problema dei vv. 540-551 può essere risolto nel senso ad Handley apparso poziore : questi versi sono anch'essi plautini. Invece l'ipotesi che un grammatico antico li avesse espunti perché non avevano corrispondente nel Δὶς ἐξαπατῶν mi par da escludere : troppe cose, allora, avrebbero dovute essere espunte dalle *Bacchides* ! Forse i versi saranno stati tagliati in qualche replica, e questo *textus breuior*, chissà come testimoniato, può aver suscitato i dubbi dell'antico filologo [1].

In siffatto intrico, abbastanza curioso, di somiglianze e differenze, che valore ha l'omissione plautina delle scene tra padre e figlio, parzialmente ancora conservate nel papiro ? Del taglio abbiamo visto alcune conseguenze, ma, in fin dei conti, perché Plauto ha soppresso i due dialoghi ?

Si può suggerire qualche risposta.

Il Δὶς ἐξαπατῶν difficilmente avrà superato il migliaio di versi, mentre le *Bacchides* arrivano a 1211, cui occorre aggiungere una prima scena e un prologo (a quanto pare), di cui, nel complesso, abbiamo poco più di trenta versi. Non sbaglieremo di molto attribuendo alla commedia latina, in origine, circa 1350 versi o poco più. Se per le *Bacchides* ogni serio sospetto di *contaminatio* è caduto, resta la sicurezza di altri interventi plautini. Essi non sono soltanto documentati adesso grazie al nuovo papiro, ma già acquisiti dalle sapienti ricerche della critica. Gli interventi plautini non appaiono soltanto nella veste metrica (frammenti, vv. 612-669, ultimo ' atto ' e così via), ma in aggiunte al testo (a volte le due cose coincidono). Faccio un esempio perspicuo a tutti : nei vv. 925 sgg. abbiamo una smisurata ' gonfiatura ' dei pochi versi che nel testo greco Siro-Crisalo poteva dire, anzi certo diceva, all'uscita dalla casa delle cortigiane. Ma una commedia di Plauto è scritta per un pubblico che vuole divertirsi, al quale non si può imporre una sosta nel teatro più lunga di un certo limite, e d'altra parte Plauto ha una concezione ' per scene ' del suo teatro, nel senso che la sua fantasia è

[1] J. M. Jacques, *art. cit.*, p. 221 n. 1 nota una certa somiglianza di contenuto di questi versi con il pap. 65 *GLP* di Page [in realtà per i vv. 540-551 non mi sento di escludere una ' contaminazione a distanza ' : vedi la discussione tra il collega Del Corno e me in *Maia* 1970 anche circa questioni toccate qui a p. 190 sgg. ed il fr. 65 *GLP*].

stimolata dalle singole situazioni ben più che dall'organico complesso della trama. In questo caso (ne abbiamo ampie prove), le ἀπάται di Siro-Crisalo a Demea-Nicobulo, l'arrivo dell'ἀλαζών Cleomaco, le grida di vittoria di Siro-Crisalo e quelle di furore del beffato Demea-Nicobulo lo stuzzicano molto di più (suscitandone la fantasia verbale, metrica e insomma di uomo di teatro fra i più scaltri) delle complicate spiegazioni tra padre e figlio, certo interessanti per un poeta introspettivo e psicologico come Menandro, ma insipide nel contesto di un'altra civiltà teatrale. Oltre al fatto che le due scene dovevano essere un po' troppo simili tra loro, perché soffermarsi su di un fatto ormai drammaticamente poco significante quando urgeva la divertente vicenda dell'ἀπάτη di Siro-Crisalo? Plauto ha lasciato trapelare i suoi veri interessi quando ha fatto preannunciare, rapidamente, a Sostrato-Mnesiloco il seguito della *fabula* : ricordate i vv. 509-511 ? Questa maniera di lavorare, del resto, è proprio quella che per Plauto ci è testimoniata dal prologo della *Casina* in versi (64-66) che io credo senz'altro plautini, ma ai quali la questione della paternità nulla toglie quanto al valore documentario ; e da un passo terenziano che ci si conferma di ammirevole precisione (*Ad.* 9-11). Procedimenti non diversi ha usato il Sarsinate nel fare latine *(Cistellaria)* le menandree Συναριστῶσαι, come ha mostrato il collega Ludwig (sopra, pp. 43 sgg.).

Dal punto di vista della condotta scenica il taglio dei dialoghi tra padre e figlio ha prodotto, oltre all'abolizione della fine d'atto menandrea senza che questa venisse supplita da altra pausa, una notevole imprecisione nei movimenti di Demea-Nicobulo (per quanto è lecito sospettare). Era già stato osservato che Demea-Nicobulo, uscito di scena per andare al foro al v. 348 delle *Bacchides* (secondo indicazioni risalenti di certo al testo menandreo [cfr. Handley, *op. cit.*, p. 20 n. 11 ; il papiro smentisce quanto supposto dal Webster, *Studies in Menander*, cit., p. 129]), è presupposto rientrato in casa già ai vv. 520 sgg., per non dire al v. 761. Ora constatiamo che in Menandro le cose si svolgono in modo non diverso, ma più complesso. Nel Δὶς ἐξαπατῶν, infatti, Demea-Nicobulo, uscito di scena per cercare nell'agorà-foro Sostrato-Mnesiloco dopo il colloquio con Siro-Crisalo (= *Bacch.* 348), vi torna (Δὶς ἐξαπατῶν v. 30) e incontra finalmente il figlio, che gli restituisce il denaro (io suppongo quindi un'uscita ed un rientro di Demea-Nicobulo n e l c o r s o d e l m e d e s i m o a t t o: vedi più oltre la discussione seguita alla mia comunicazione : p. 226 sgg.). Entrato in casa con il figlio, il vecchio ne esce — dopo la fine dell'atto II — ancora con il figlio, che poi lascia per andare un'altra volta nell'agorà-foro (v. 90). D'altra parte è vero che nel prosieguo dell'azione (*Bacchides* ormai, perché il papiro si interrompe) Demea-Nicobulo è ritornato a casa (*Bacch.* v. 761 sgg.), uscendo dalla quale egli vede Siro-Crisalo, che egli non ha più incontrato da quando il figlio gli ha raccontato la faccenda dell'oro di Efeso (v. 770 sgg.). Il problema si sposta, ma resta in sostanza quello già segnalato dalla critica : come rientra Demea-Nicobulo dalla s e c o n d a andata al foro, in modo da incontrarsi con Siro-Crisalo, nella cui ἀπάτη deve ingenuamente cadere ? Qui occorre distinguere, almeno per un poco, tra Δὶς ἐξαπατῶν e *Bacchides*. Per Menandro io credo possibile, almeno in teoria, un rientro ' tacito ' di Demea-Nicobulo, purché tra il rientro (che non viene presentato agli spettatori, ma dev' essere da questi supposto) ed il successivo incontro del vecchio con lo schiavo si collochi una fine d'atto (in questo caso, il terzo) che permetta la verosimiglianza dell'evento. Occorre però dire che, sino ad ora, ci manca in questo senso qualunque termine di paragone nelle commedie di Menandro che possiamo leggere. Piuttosto, dove porre, in Menandro, la fine del terzo atto ? Dopo la scena tra i due giovani, quindi dopo il v. 572 di Plauto, è impossibile : l'ipotesi del Mette (*art. cit.*, p. 52) è smentita dal papiro perché il terzo atto sarebbe troppo corto. Si potrebbe allora accettare l'ipotesi di Webster (*Studies in Menander*, cit., p. 130) e, giudicando i vv. 610-611 ' cemento plautino ', credere che Menandro ponesse fine d'atto dopo il brevissimo monologo che chiude la scena di Mosco-Pistoclero con il Parassita (su cui vedi ancora Webster, *Studies* ..., cit., pp. 129-130). Ma anche quest'ipotesi offre difficoltà. Al terzo atto del Δὶς ἐξαπατῶν possiamo infatti attribuire circa duecento versi, almeno come ipotesi di lavoro [1]. Poiché il secondo atto del Δὶς ἐξαπατῶν finisce con la seconda colonna di papiro, il terzo inizia con la terza colonna e potremmo ricostruirlo così: nei primi ventotto versi di questa colonna (cioè vv. 63-90 di tutto il papiro) è, od era, il secondo dialogo tra padre e figlio, omesso da Plauto ; nei vv. 29-40 (=91-102 di tutto il papiro) è il secondo monologo di Sostrato-Mnesiloco : siamo già a quaranta versi complessivi. Al dialogo di spiegazione tra i due giovani io attribuirei circa trenta versi, di cui dodici sono più o meno bene ancora conservati dal papiro stesso, mentre gli altri possono essere immaginati leggendo i vv. 560-572 di Plauto, dove, anche per necessità di tener ben chiaro l'intrigo, il poeta latino non pare essersi concesso molte libertà (si noti che l'accordo con Menandro riprende proprio al v. 560). Ricostruito così il contenuto dei primi settanta versi di Menandro, cosa attribuire ai restanti centotrenta circa ? L'entrata del Parassita e il dialogo di questo personaggio con Mosco-Pistoclero occupano, in Plauto, ventotto versi e, se i vv. 573-588, a quanto pare, ' traducono ' Menandro [2], i rimanenti 589-605 ospitano ' scurrili ' allargamenti plautini. Le successive scene plautine (3 e 4 del quarto ' atto ') formano

[1] Il terzo atto del *Dyskolos* ha 192 vv. ; circa 180 quello degli *Epitrepontes* ; più di 200 quello della *Samia* ; già 178 quello dell'*Aspis*, mutilo nella conclusione. Resta aperta, e *uideant doctiores*, la questione della cifra ΤΞΔ = 364 scritta in fondo alla seconda colonna del papiro del Δὶς ἐξαπατῶν : cfr. E. W. Handley, *op. cit.*, p. 16 (vedi ora la discussione qui alle pp. 223 sgg. e quanto preciso in *Maia* 1970).

[2] Confronta i vv. 581-583 con *Epitr.* 717-719.

centocinquanta versi circa. Se, nell'insieme, togliamo alle prime quattro scene del quarto 'atto' delle *Bacchides*, e specialmente al monologo-*canticum* di Siro-Crisalo, le sicure aggiunte plautine, possiamo facilmente ridurre i circa centottanta versi di Plauto a quei centotrenta versi, più o meno, che sono necessari per completare l'estensione del terzo atto di Menandro. Nel Δὶς ἐξαπατῶν, dunque, la fine del terzo atto era o dopo la conclusione del ' terzetto dell'inganno ' (v. 760 di Plauto), o subito dopo il breve monologo di Siro-Crisalo (vv. 761-769 di Plauto, da intendersi però senza i vv. 768-769, perché la scena deve rimanere vuota). Ma a questo punto è veramente necessario supporre un rientro ' tacito ' di Demea-Nicobulo, in Menandro, consentito dalla fine del III atto? L'ipotesi può essere del tutto superflua, poiché il quarto atto di Menandro poteva avere — all'immediato inizio, o dopo i versi corrispondenti a *Bacch.* 761 sgg., sempre senza i versi corrispondenti a 768-769 — il rientro di Demea-Nicobulo dal foro. Se leggiamo i vv. 761 sgg. di Plauto (allontanando idealmente i vv. 768-769) ci accorgiamo che niente in essi, come nei successivi vv. 770 sgg., ci costringe per forza a supporre Demea-Nicobulo che esce di casa (non è certo tale il v. 794). Le parole che il vecchio dice (vv. 770-771) non potrebbero essere quelle di un personaggio che ritorna dal mercato ancora pieno di stizza? Niente vieta, mi pare, di credere per l'appunto Siro-Crisalo in attesa non già di un padrone che esca di casa, ma di un padrone che torni dal mercato. In questo caso la variazione apportata alle mosse di Demea-Nicobulo è opera di Plauto (vv. 768-769) e si spiega benissimo. Tagliate le due scene con il figlio e ridottele ad un misero riassunto che necessariamente presuppone Demea-Nicobulo in casa a ricevere l'oro maltolto dalle mani del figlio pentito, a Plauto non è più lecito far ritornare il vecchio dall'agorà-foro, fosse quest'evento, nel testo greco, rappresentato direttamente o presupposto per convenzione teatrale. La restituzione dell'oro al padre — in casa — è un fatto essenziale, che condiziona tutto il successivo svolgersi degli inganni, ed era ricordato troppo bene, per questo, dal pubblico, e fosse pure il pubblico di Plauto e non di Menandro. Inoltre Sostrato-Mnesiloco, restituendo l'oro, si preoccupa anche della sorte di Crisalo : ecco un altro particolare, legato all'incontro in casa tra padre e figlio, che Plauto ha messo in evidenza, forse aggiunto di suo, e che il suo pubblico ricordava non meno bene! Il pubblico di Plauto, insomma, sebbene poco sensibile ad esigenze di coerenza strutturale e d'intreccio, difficilmente avrebbe tollerato di veder riapparire dal foro quel vecchio che un momento importantissimo della commedia presuppone, poco prima, in casa a parlare col figlio. Con ciò abbiamo ottenuto un altro risultato. Quale che fosse il modo in cui, presso Menandro, Demea-Nicobulo tornava dalla sua seconda andata all'agorà-foro, i vv. 768-769 sono ' cemento plautino ', per dirla con Webster : essi sono il modo con cui Plauto ha abolito la fine d'atto che nel Δὶς ἐξαπατῶν doveva essere o subito prima o subito dopo il brevissimo monologo di Siro-Crisalo. Resta in piedi, quindi, la vecchia difficoltà, già segnalata dal Baar (cfr. la mia edizione, p. 15 n. 16) : Nicobulo, uscito di scena al v. 348, è supposto in casa al v. 520. Quest' incongruenza è effetto del taglio della prima scena col figlio, quella che precede la fine del II atto (in Menandro). Plauto ha supposto Demea-Nicobulo tornato ' tacitamente ' a casa (seppure egli ha badato al particolare) non perché a lui una fine d'atto lo consentisse, ma perché la prima uscita del vecchio è drammaticamente priva di rilievo, tale da non disturbare la ' coscienza teatrale ' dello spettatore latino che, non meno del suo autore preferito, gusta lo spettacolo soprattutto per scene, curandosi soltanto dei punti salienti dell'intreccio. L'incongruenza, nel complesso, è meno stridente, in questo caso, di quella famosa che si crea ai vv. 925 sgg., quando i movimenti di Nicobulo sono, come consta da un pezzo, del tutto imprecisati e quasi assurdi proprio a causa dell'intervento di Plauto nel modello greco [1]. Ci sarebbe forse, per spiegare la diversità di situazione tra il v. 348 e i vv. 520 sgg., la possibilità di ricorrere all'ipotesi di un rientro di Demea-Nicobulo attraverso l'*angiportum*, in modo che il pubblico in qualche modo vedesse il vecchio, ma, a parte le difficoltà intrinseche dell'ipotesi, non vedo quando quest'azione muta poteva avvenire, così da essere seguita dagli occhi degli spettatori [2].

Plauto, dunque, s'interessa alle singole scene, non al complesso organico della commedia. In questa sua concezione del teatro va inquadrata anche la rinuncia agli atti delle commedie menandree (e della νέα in genere), già ragionevolmente affermata da studiosi come Andrieu e Beare (cfr. p. 201, n. 1) ed ora documentata come meglio non si potrebbe.

Tuttavia proprio nella commedia tratta dal Δὶς ἐξαπατῶν, le *Bacchides*, s'è voluta vedere, ai vv. 107 sgg., traccia più o meno esatta e diretta della presenza di un coro di tipo menandreo e della conseguente divisione in atti ; e circa l'intermezzo auletico dello *Pseudolus* (vv. 573-573a) s'è pensato sia un sostitutivo del coro greco, implicante una vera pausa, istituzionale, nell'azione della commedia, tale che essa si ripeteva, qui e altrove (anche se non menzionata dal poeta) a regolari intervalli, così da produrre una divisione in atti comparabile a quella dei testi greci.

Il passo dello *Pseudolus* non è paragonabile direttamente a *Dyskolos*, *Casina* e *Stichus*, com'è stato fatto troppo sommaria-

[1] Da quanto ho detto è chiaro che io non posso seguire H. J. Mette, *art. cit.*, pp. 52-53 nel porre la fine dell'atto menandreo dopo i vv. corrispondenti a *Bacch.* 913-924 ; io credo (con T. B. L. Webster, *Studies in Menander*, cit., p. 131) che la fine dell'atto menandrea fosse dopo l'inganno di Siro-Crisalo (v. 1075 di Plauto), in modo che il quinto atto si aprisse con il monologo di Padre-Filosseno, seguito dal monologo ' apparente ' di Demea-Nicobulo, rientrato fuor di sé dall'agorà. Si tratta, in Plauto, di 314 versi, che si riducono di molto eliminando le fiorettature del poeta latino nei dialoghi ed il grande monologo mitologico (riserve metodiche suscita in me l'art. di H. D. Jocelyn, Chrysalus and the Fall of Troy, *HSPh* 1968, p. 135 sgg.).

[2] Per la questione vedi W. Beare, *op. cit.*, p. 252 sgg. ; G. E. Duckworth, *The Nature of Roman Comedy*, Princeton 1952, pp. 87-88.

mente, perché ostano alcune differenze di fondo. L'intermezzo dello *Pseudolus* viene preannunciato agli spettatori, come il coro menandreo ; esso viene eseguito, in quanto intermezzo, a scena vuota, come il χοροῦ μέλος menandreo, ben diversamente dalla funzione, integrata alla vicenda che si svolge, che il suono del *tibicen* ha in *Dyskolos*, *Casina* e *Stichus*. Non riesco quindi a capire come si sia potuto pensare che Plauto per l'intermezzo dello *Pseudolus* avesse in qualche modo in mente il *Dyskolos* [1]. Quanto a *Poenulus* (*aduocati* dei vv. 504-816) e *Rudens* (i pescatori dei vv. 290 sgg.), queste commedie sono casi ben diversi, come tutti sappiamo. Nel teatro latino le scene in questione potevano essere realizzate con una sorta di corifeo che parlasse e alcuni figuranti che mimassero ; poi, e questo vale per la *Rudens*, i pescatori non vengono preannunciati quale coro con quei versi ' didascalici ' caratteristici per noi di Menandro, ma non di lui solo (cfr. Handley *ad Dysk.* 230-232) ; inoltre nella *Rudens* c'è omogeneità metrica fra il piccolo coro e la scena successiva, in cui Tracalione dialoga con esso : non c'è, insomma, cesura nell'azione e tanto i pescatori quanto gli *aduocati* si comportano come un singolo interlocutore [2].

[1] A torto accettai (ma non senza qualche riserva) un sostanziale avvicinamento di *Ps.* e *Dysk.* nella mia edizione, cit., p. 12 e n. 12 : ora me ne pento. Sagge ed equilibrate le posizioni del Beare, *op. cit.*, pp. 202-203 (la parte di Pseudolo, incredibilmente lunga, deve essere interrotta per ragioni teatrali) e dello Swoboda, De numero histrionum partiumque in comoediis Plautinis quaestiones, *Eos* 1957/58, pp. 83-85.

[2] Nei vv. 504 sgg. il cosiddetto coro degli *aduocati* entra annunciato sì da Agorastocle con versi ' didascalici ' (molto plautini nello stile), ma è Agorastocle stesso a condurlo in scena, mentre in Menandro il coro, se è annunciato, entra però a scena vuota ; poi, nei vv. 814-816 il cosiddetto coro annunzia la propria uscita, anche qui contro ogni consuetudine menandrea. Pur concedendo ad Alessi una tecnica diversa e la possibilità di una partecipazione all'azione del coro da lui impiegato (cfr. fr. 48 *GLP* Page ?), una così prematura uscita di scena di un vero coro sembra impossibile (la presenza degli *aduocati* non comporta, comunque, cesure nell'azione) ; il Mette, *art. cit.*, p. 96 attribuisce anche al Καρχηδόνιος di Alessi un coro di νεανίσκοι ὑποβεβρεγμένοι : in base a quali indizi ?

Nell'insieme noi dobbiamo tener fede alla testimonianza di Diomede (*GLK* I p. 491), contro cui nulla possono le oscure notizie del *Liber Glossarum* (presso Kaibel, *CGF* p. 72, 19-20) né i dubbi di Andrieu (*op. cit.*, p. 43) circa Evanzio III 1 (p. 18, 15-17 W.): il coro era assente dalla commedia latina nella funzione di intermezzo fisso e organico. Nell'ipotesi contraria le testimonianze latine sulla difficoltà di *dirimere actus quinquepartitos* (nel senso che i tardi grammatici latini e Donato in particolare dànno al termine *actus*: cfr. Andrieu, *op. cit.*, p. 38-44) non avrebbero senso (vedi, tra le altre, le testimonianze di Varrone fr. 307 Fun., Evanzio III 1 p. 18 W.). Vanno però visti da vicino due passi di Donato. Il primo dice (*Praef. Andr.* II 3, pp. 38-39 W.) che in certi punti dell'azione la scena è vuota *ab omnibus personis, ita ut in ea chorus uel tibicen obaudiri possint. quod cum uiderimus, ibi actum esse finitum debemus agnoscere.* Il secondo è interessante, direi, per la sua puerilità (*Praef. Andr.* III 6 p. 40 W.): *illud nos commouere non debet, quod in horum actuum distinctione uidentur de proscaenio non discessisse personae quaedam, sed tenere debemus ideo Terentium uicinitatis mentionem fecisse in principio, ut modico receptu et adesse et abesse personam intellegamus. nihil ergo secus factum est ab antiquis, qui ad hunc modum Terentianas fabulas diuiserunt.* Il primo passo ha trovato, per quanto riguarda il coro, un esegeta perfetto in Leo (Der Monolog in Drama, *Abhandl. der k. Ges. der Wiss. zu Göttingen*, 1908, H. 5, p. 55), il quale ha chiarito che Donato menziona il coro solo perché lo conosce usato da Menandro e lo trova attestato nell'edizione menandrea da lui posseduta. Ma il suono del *tibicen*? Il passo di Donato ed i vv. 573-573a dello *Pseudolus* parrebero sorreggersi a vicenda: se non c'era il coro, si dirà, c'erano a sostituirlo regolari intermezzi auletici. Ma questo ragionamento è sbagliato. Se il coro greco fosse stato normalmente, istituzionalmente sostituito, nella *palliata*, da un intermezzo auletico con la medesima funzione, i grammatici latini avrebbero avuto in questo un facile mezzo per *dirimere actus quinquepartitos*. Ma ciò non avveniva. Lo dimostra il silenzio di tutte le altre commedie a noi conservate su eventuali intermezzi del genere, silenzio che si contrappone (ora lo vediamo bene) alla regolarità con cui il coro è annunciato in Menandro ; lo dimostra la tradizione grammaticale latina, che abbiamo scrutato ; lo dimostra la ricerca dei moderni (per es. la dissertazione di Georgine Burckhardt) [1] ; lo dimostra, ora, la maniera in cui Plauto si è comportato nell' adattare il Δὶς ἐξαπατῶν alle esigenze della sua scena : dove meglio si sarebbe introdotto un intermezzo auletico se non là dove era necessario 'riassorbire' un bel po' di tempo scenico ? Io ammetto però che i versi dello *Pseudolus* siano esemplati su modello greco, genericamente, o addirittura che, in questo caso, ricalchino e sostituiscano un corrispondente intermezzo corale greco, ma anche così l'intermezzo auletico dello *Pseudolus* ha un valore del tutto diverso, ed è motivato da più d'una ragione eccezionale, che vari studiosi, da Jachmann ad Andrieu e Beare, hanno saputo ben cogliere [2]. Si noti, poi, un fatto che ai miei occhi ha peso decisivo : nello *Pseudolus* l'intervallo non presuppone riassorbimento di tempo.

Veniamo ora alle *Bacchides*. La presenza eccezionale del coro in questa commedia è stata supposta da Leo confrontando il v. 107 con i vv. 33-35 degli Ἐπιτρέποντες [3]. Lindsay, successivamente (bibliografia in appar. *ad l.* della mia edi-

[1] *Die Akteinteilung in der neueren griech. und in der röm. Komödie*, diss., Basel 1927 (tutta l'abbondante bibliografia in J. ANDRIEU, *cit.* a p. 201, n. 1).

[2] Per un'informazione e una discussione della abbondante bibliografia vedi, meglio di ogni altro, l'art. di T. MANTERO citato p. 189, n. 1 ; se *Ps.* 573 sgg. ricalcano una fine d'atto greca nello stesso punto, certo questa non era la prima : Plauto ha quindi applicato al *tibicen* versi ' didascalici ' caratteristici, a quanto sappiamo, solo del primo intermezzo corale.

[3] Cfr. F. LEO, Χοροῦ, *Hermes* 1908, p. 308 sgg.; *id.*, Χοροῦ bei Plautus, *Hermes* 1911, p. 292-294 ; la ricca bibliografia successiva è discussa in G. E. DUCKWORTH, *op. cit.*, p. 100 n. 69 ; vedi anche J. ANDRIEU, *op. cit.*, pp. 77-78 sgg. e, sopra, p. 211, n. 1.

zione), emendò il verso in modo che l'annuncio del coro risultasse tanto perspicuo quanto lo è in Menandro, per cui invece della vulgata (cui mi sono attenuto ancora io, meritando le obiezioni di Arnott, *Gnomon* 1967, p. 137 e O. Skutsch, *CR* 1967, p. 40)

simul huic nesciocui, turbare qui huc it, decedamus <*hinc*>

si dovrebbe leggere

simul huic <*nos*> *nesciocui turbae, quae huc it, decedamus* <*hinc*>.

Alla luce dei frammenti del Δὶς ἐξαπατῶν mi pare che tanto l'ipotesi leonina della presenza eccezionale di un coro, quanto l'ipotesi della Burckhardt circa una pausa qualsiasi dell'azione da paragonarsi a *Ps.* 573-573a (*diss. cit.*, p. 14) siano entrambe da respingere. Una rarità tecnica di questo genere avrebbe costretto Plauto a seguire fedelmente la struttura del modello, di cui gli atti divisi dai χοροῦ μέλη erano elemento essenziale. Ciò non è avvenuto. D'altra parte un Plauto che, come abbiamo visto, si comporta con tanta disinvoltura di fronte al testo di Menandro, per quale ragione in questo singolo passo si sarebbe dovuto sentire le mani così legate da conservare meccanicamente un verso del testo originale? Più di uno studioso ha visto nel v. 107, infatti, 'a piece of over-litteral translation of the Greek model' (Arnott, *rec. cit.*, p. 137). Ora è un fatto che Menandro non solo annuncia l'entrata del coro, ma specifica con chiarezza la qualità delle persone che il coro compongono (in *Epitr.* 33 sgg. abbiamo l'ὄχλος ὑποβεβρεγμένων, in *Perik.* 71 sgg. i μεθύοντα μειράκια, in *Dysk.* 230 sgg. i problematici παιανισταί, in *Asp.* 247 ancora un ὄχλος ἀνθρώπων μεθυόντων). In Plauto, invece, il v. 107, comunque lo si legga, è generico : o annuncia un *hic nescioquis* che le ragazze non vogliono o non possono incontrare per convenzioni sceniche, oppure una *nescioqua turba*, non meglio precisata, contro quello ch'è l'uso menandreo. Ma in tale genericità si deve vedere il segno della trasformazione plautina della fine d'atto menandrea, di cui, fuor di dubbio, il v. 107 è una traccia. Preannunci il verso una singola persona (testo vulgato) o una *turba* (così con Lindsay, ma Plauto non dice altrove *turba turbat* [cfr. Lodge s.v.] : *Bacch.* 1076 è ovviamente altra cosa), è chiaro che si tratta — non può trattarsi d'altro — di Pistoclero che ritorna (o di Pistoclero con la sua *pompa* : cfr. v. 114). Il verso di Menandro (in cui può benissimo aver figurato la parola ὄχλος, sì che Lindsay non avrebbe, allora, tutti i torti) è stato conservato, ma solo parzialmente conservato, ed adattato ad altra funzione dopo essere stato reso generico nel suo contenuto. Questa maniera di arrangiare l'azione (già intuita da Andrieu, *op. cit.*, pp. 64 e 72) è tipicamente plautina e non è diversa da quella che abbiamo potuto toccar con mano nei vv. 520 e 530-533. Anche questa volta — si noti — è l'assenza di intermezzi corali e di regolari, istituzionali sue forme sostitutive (come un'aulodia) a costringere Plauto di Sarsina ad un' ' accelerazione ' molto sensibile del tempo degli eventi fuor di scena [1]. Casi simili non sono rari, del resto, sulla scena latina : basti pensare a quel ch'è accaduto, secondo l'ipotesi ormai tradizionale di F. Skutsch e G. Jachmann, quando Terenzio ha soppresso l'intermezzo corale del menandreo *Heautontimoroumenos* [2].

[1] Esempi in J. Andrieu, *op. cit.*, p. 69 sgg.

[2] F. Skutsch, Χοροῦ bei Terenz, *Hermes* 1912, p. 141 sgg. = *Kleine Schriften*, Berlin 1914, p. 480 sgg. ; G. Jachmann, *Plautinisches...*, cit., p. 245 sgg. e art. *P. Terentius Afer*, *RE* VA, 9 (1934), c. 634 (per altri contributi e la diversa opinione di H. Drexler, vedi la discussione di H. J. Mette, *art. cit.*, pp. 136-137). Si può condividere l'opinione di F. Leo, *Hermes* 1908, pp. 310-311 secondo cui Plauto ha anche scritto brevi scene per supplire gli aboliti intermezzi corali, ma questo conferma, appunto, una preferenza di Plauto per il δρᾶμα *continuum* (secondo Leo tale funzione avrebbe anche la scena del *choragus* nel *Curculio*, su cui vedi ora, come su altri problemi della commedia, la discussione, con bibliografia, di E. Fantham, The *Curculio* of Plautus : An Illustration of Plautine Methods in Adaptation, *CQ* 1965, p. 84 sgg.); sui rapporti tra la divisione in atti di Menandro e Terenzio negli *Adelphoe* vedi

DISCUSSION

M. Handley : Could I raise a first question about the *tibicen*? There seem to be several different ways in which pipers are connected with plays. First, the piper may be simply an accompanist, ready to pipe when needed, but quite uninvolved in the play. In Menander's time, he may still have worn a special traditional costume (I have mentioned some examples in a note on *Dysk.* 880). Secondly, from references in our texts, as well as from monuments, we have examples of pipers in dramatic scenes (for example, Parthenis at *Dysk.* 432 f. and another girl-piper, as I should suppose, in *Theophoroumene* : *BICS* 16 (1969) 88 ff.). Where these pipers were actually called on to play, I imagine there was more than one possibility of providing the music. It could be that the stage-piper merely mimed, while the tune came from the accompanist ; that the stage-piper actually played ; or even—all this is theoretical—that the accompanist was able to leave his post and change into dramatic costume to take the part. But there is still another class of cases, in which the accompanist is actually brought into the play, against the dramatic illusion : he is addressed by Getas at *Dysk.* 880, one remembers. Could we ask how the Plautine instances which Professor Questa has discussed respond to this sort of classification ?

(Suite de la dernière Note de l'entretien Questa.)

le buone osservazioni di K. Gaiser in appendice (pp. 141-144) a O. Rieth, *Die Kunst Menanders in den 'Adelphen' des Terenz*, Hildesheim 1964. In linea generale, la divisione in atti attestata nei mosaici di Mitilene (su cui vedi le pregevoli osservazioni, qui appresso, di Mme Kahil) dimostra che la struttura in μέρη sopravviveva in ambiente greco, ciò che non stupisce. Ma riflette essa una pratica teatrale ancora effettiva (i mosaici sono del III sec. d.C. e rappresentazioni della *Theophoroumene* sono attestate in Atene per il medesimo periodo), oppure è l'eco di testi scritti, nei quali i μέρη erano indicati dalla indicazione riccorrente χοροῦ? Questa è attestata dal papiro del *Sikyonios* (III sec. a.C.) al Cairense degli *Epitrepontes* ecc. (V sec. d.C.). Il problema, comunque, non riguarda la *palliata*.

M. Questa: Il collega Handley ha toccato un punto molto difficile. Innanzi tutto dobbiamo chiederci se la scena romana fosse organizzata come la scena greca, così che in essa fossero conservate le varie consuetudini di questa circa il flautista. Per lo *Pseudolus* siamo sicuri che il *tibicen* non interveniva nell'azione scenica *(tibicen uos interea delectaverit)*. Per lo *Stichus*, ho ammesso la possibilità che il flautista entrasse con i figuranti o comparse che preparano il banchetto (vedi sopra p. 185), sebbene potesse anche essere invitato solo in seguito a prendere parte ai veri e propri avvenimenti della scena (v. 715, ecc.). Per *Casina*-Κληρούμενοι, io potrei credere che all'aprirsi della casa di Lisidamo (vv. 796-797) si vedesse già pronta almeno una parte del corteo nuziale, tra i componenti del quale poteva benissimo essere il *tibicen* (questo poteva accadere già in Difilo, in cui la scena del corteo doveva avere elementi musicali anche se non veri versi lirici). Ma ai miei occhi il problema del *tibicen* nel teatro latino si complica con quello dei cantica (assenti come norma nella νέα: le pochissime eccezioni testimoniate non contano). Il *tibicen* doveva avere una funzione importante, non paragonabile di sicuro, questa volta, a quella che aveva nella νέα. Nello *Pseudolus*, per es., il flautista poteva benissimo preparare musicalmente l' 'aria di bravura ' che Pseudolo attacca appena tornato in scena (v. 574 sgg.). Certo il *tibicen* era importante, se ce ne serbano il nome didascalie plautine e terenziane (con buona pace di Mattingly, i cui dubbi circa le didascalie tutti conosciamo).

M. Wehrli: Herr Questa ist durch seine Interpretation plautinischer Szenen zur Feststellung von Freiheiten gegenüber dem griechischen Original gelangt, welche nach Zweck und Umfang mit der von Ed. Fraenkel gekennzeichneten Arbeitsweise der Römer durchaus übereinstimmen. Anderseits hat Herr Questa auch auf lateinische Dialogpartien hingewiesen, in welchen die Vorlage getreu widergegeben wird, und sogar von vereinzelten Anregungen gesprochen, die Plautus für seine *cantica* in griechischen Komödien finden konnte. Nötigen solche Annäherungen nach Herrn Questas Meinung dazu, die Gesamtvorstellung von Plautus' Eigenständigkeit zu korrigieren, welche Ed. Fraenkel durch sein Buch *Plautinisches in Plautus* begründet hat?

M. Questa : Sì, io ritengo che il libro di Fraenkel (ed, insieme, quello di G. Jachmann, che vorrei vedere presto tradotto in italiano) sia sempre fondamentale. Fraenkel ha indicato la *via regia* per un giusto *accessus ad Plautum* e le recenti scoperte menandree gli dànno, fondamentalmente, piena ragione. Non è necessario che ripeta i particolari, ma vorrei far osservare che proprio confrontando *Bacchides* e Δὶς ἐξαπατῶν abbiamo la prova che Plauto, da solo, *non* fa procedere l'azione. Per far questo, ha bisogno del modello greco. Plauto ha tradotto alla lettera quelle parti di Menandro che fanno procedere la vicenda (restituzione dell'oro al padre ; dialogo di spiegazione tra Sostrato-Mnesiloco e Mosco-Pistoclero). In questa commedia, però, c'è anche qualcosa di inaspettato rispetto ai criteri di Fraenkel (vv. 502-514 ; vv. 535-559), ma si tratta, da quel che riusciamo a vedere, di questioni limitate assai. C'è infine da ricordare che le *Bacchides* sono una commedia della vecchiaia di Plauto (vedi la mia edizione, pp. 1-6), scritta quando il poeta è completo padrone del mestiere *anche* per quanto concerne le strutture drammatiche (ma sempre in ciò che lo interessa più da vicino, e con le disinvolte trascuranze circa Menandro che, come vedemmo, si è concesso).

Circa la questione dei *cantica* è evidente che Menandro o Difilo possono soltanto aver suggerito qualche spunto. Nella stessa scena finale dello *Stichus* i particolari tecnici desunti presumibilmente dal modello (gli 'Αδελφοὶ α') sono immersi in un'atmosfera molto plautina, come ho detto. Si tenga anche conto del virtuosismo metrico che Plauto mostra all'inizio della commedia. Purtroppo il finale del *Dyskolos* è stato paragonato all'ultimo ' atto ' del *Persa* e persino dello *Pseudolus* : chi lo ha fatto non conosce né Menandro né Plauto.

M. Handley : I should like to ask whether, in the course of his studies of Plautine manuscripts, Professor Questa has found any more evidence for the distinction of scenes according to the manner of their performance, as by the letters C and DV.

M. Questa: No, una revisione dei mss. plautini non mi ha condotto a particolari scoperte. A parte la maggiore o minore antichità, per es., dell'annotazione EBRIUS posta accanto al titolo di scena che precede *Ps.* 1246, le uniche indicazioni sceniche a noi note sono medievali. Per es. il revisore del cod. D (*Vat. Lat.* 3870), che io indico con la sigla D^3, il quale dev'essere stato anche il ' direttore ' dello *scriptorium* dove è stato approntato il codice, non solo fa congetture al testo (a volte così giuste, benchè facili, da concordare con A : esempi per lo *Pseudolus* darò in *SIFC* tra non molto), non solo aggiunge sigle di personaggi, dove omesse dall'antigrafo, basandosi direttamente sul dialogo, ma dove ha identificato (o crede) un monologo aggiunge a margine *secum* (vedi il mio apparato a *Bacch.* 349, 606, 1053). Il fatto era già noto (cfr. Andrieu, *op. cit.* pp. 148 e 149 n. 1), ma il controllo dei manoscritti ha permesso di mostrarne più esempi e chiarirne la paternità (Andrieu parla a torto di D).

M. Ludwig: Bei Menander gab es zwischen Szenen leere Bühne mit und ohne Chorauftritt (sog. Aktschluss bzw. Szenenschluss). Da bei Plautus der Chorauftritt ersatzlos wegfiel, gab es keine motivierte Hervorhebung bestimmter Szenenschlüsse mehr, sondern eine kontinuierliche Bühnenhandlung, innerhalb deren die Bühne natürlich von Fall leer wurde. Im allgemeinen wird Plautus die « leeren Szenen » seiner Originale beibehalten haben. Der Δὶς ἐξαπατῶν-Papyrus zeigt, dass er solche « leere Szenen » auch beseitigen konnte, indem er zwei in eine zusammenzog. Der Fall der *Bacchides* war wahrscheinlicherweise nicht singulär. Aber es blieb doch sicher immer eine Ausnahme. Es mussten besondere Gründe im Einzelfall vorliegen. Was sind die speziellen Ursachen für die Beseitigung des Szeneneinschnitts an unserer Stelle? Wurde er primär erstrebt oder war er die Konsequenz einer andere Ziele verfolgenden Änderung des Plautus?

M. Questa : Io credo che si debba rispondere a due quesiti. In generale io tengo per fermo che Plauto *non* conosce divisione in atti come istituzione, come qualcosa, cioè, di paragonabile ai μέρη di Menandro. Soprattutto egli non conosce ‘ entr’actes ’ con significato ai fini dello svolgimento della vicenda, ad es. per ottenere ‘ résorption de temps ’ (il termine è di Andrieu e altri, tra cui la Frété). Per quanto concerne i rapporti con i modelli greci noi dobbiamo ammettere che a ‘ scena vuota ’ greca potesse corrispondere ‘ scena vuota ’ latina ; a ‘ scena vuota ’ con χοροῦ μέλος, e quindi fine del μέρος del testo greco, ‘ scena vuota ’ latina (di regola, non solo senza coro, ma senza monodia del *tibicen*) ; e che anche tagli e aggiunte plautine creassero, eventualmente, nuove situazioni sceniche (il Δὶς ἐξαπατῶν è una prova). Per quanto concerne il singolo caso Δὶς ἐξαπατῶν-*Bacchides* si può ben pensare che Plauto abbia soprattutto eliminato scene vuote e intervalli per accelerare la vicenda e giungere ai punti di questa che più stuzzicarano la sua fantasia (come ho detto : vedi p. 204 sgg.). Io non credo che Plauto tendesse ad eliminare con particolare attenzione scene vuote ed ‘ entr’actes ’ greci (ma teniamo anche presente Leo, *Hermes* 1908 p. 311 circa *Cap.* 461-497 : vedi sopra p. 215, n.2). Attendiamo, ad ogni modo, di vedere cosa ci diranno nuove scoperte di papiri. Io ho constatato un fatto, in questa commedia, che ho cercato di spiegare riferendomi agli usi della scena romana dei tempi di Plauto.

Mme Kahil : Le public de Plaute ne s’attendait pas à des « actes », mais il ne semble pas impossible qu’un certain public soit allé voir « du Ménandre », sinon à Rome, du moins en Italie grecque. Au cours du dernier siècle de la République, alors qu’on connaissait encore Plaute, certains Romains se rendaient probablement à Athènes, où Ménandre était joué !

M. Questa : Nel III e II sec. a. C. non credo che il pubblico della città di Roma — per cui Plauto scrive — andasse ad ascoltare Menandro. Certo a Roma non lo ascoltava, anche se qualche spettatore poteva aver assistito in città greche dell'Italia meridionale o della Grecia stessa, a rappresentazioni comiche di testi della νέα ad opera dei τεχνῖται. Queste, anzi, Plauto le ha viste egli stesso di sicuro, ma un conto è quello che facevano i Greci, un conto è quanto fa egli stesso. E poi : sappiamo noi forse *come* fossero rappresentati Menandro e gli altri dai τεχνῖται greci? Oggi molti testi classici del teatro europeo, divisi nei cinque atti creduti veramente ' classici ' ed obbligatori dai loro autori (Molière o Goldoni, Racine o Alfieri), vengono rappresentati in ' due tempi '. Ricordo cosi uno splendido *Don Juan* di Jean Vilar, un *Avare* ancora di Vilar o l'*Oreste* di Alfieri quale lo presentò molti anni fa il Visconti. Menandro, dunque, sarà sempre stato rappresentato diviso nei cinque μέρη con intermezzi corali? Per i testi da leggersi il caso è diverso : il papiro del *Sikyonios* (III sec. a. C.) mostra che Plauto poteva aver innanzi a sé copie di Menandro in cui già figurava l'annotazione ΧΟΡΟΥ. Il problema, se vogliamo, si complica con la questione della rappresentazione dei testi plautini, da supporsi avvenuta sino alla fine della repubblica, se Cicerone spesso allude a testi comici nelle sue orazioni ; se Roscio era famoso come attore nella parte di Ballione, se a Ballione è paragonato Antonio da Cicerone nella *II Filippica* (6, 15). Considerando anche i mutamenti prosodici del latino, *come* avranno recitato Plauto?

M. Handley : I do think that Madame Kahil's question is an interesting one, especially if we think of it in terms of poets and theatrical tradition as well as in terms of audiences. After all, if we believe our traditional account, Livius Andronicus came from Tarentum, where he would have been well placed to know Greek theatrical practice ; Naevius, with his epitaph *plenum superbiae Campanae*, is also someone who is likely to have known Greek plays in production as well as from copies—and both wrote tragedies as well as comedies. Moreover, might not guilds of actors, as at Tarentum, be expected to preserve theatrical tradition and possibly to pass it on to their Latin-speaking colleagues and successors? But in general, on the elimination of act-breaks by Plautus and Terence, I find Professor Questa's discussion very satisfying, as I do on many other points.

M. Questa: Lei fa una domanda molta acuta. Certo, Livio Andronico e Nevio vengono da un ambiente o greco o vicinissimo ai Greci e quindi possono essere stati molto più sensibili alle abitudini della commedia greca, ivi compresa quella del coro. Non è chiaro per quale motivo il coro sia scomparso dalla *palliata*, ma non è meno sicuro che è scomparso. Potrebbero, forse, esserci state ragioni speciali: c'era, prima di Livio, Nevio e Plauto, una tradizione, non letteraria ma efficace, di teatro comico senza coro; in più, il χοροῦ μέλος non era connesso con l'azione, nella quasi totalità dei casi (Alessi è altra cosa), sì che si può concepire benissimo (l'ho detto prima) una rappresentazione di Menandro senza intervalli lasciati al coro. Invece i testi tragici avevano un coro che partecipava all'azione molto più direttamente, almeno fino a quell'Euripide tanto amato dalla scena romana arcaica; di contro, non esisteva una tradizione tragica nazionale (il cosiddetto teatro etrusco ha l'aria d'essere una favola, e comunque sarà stato anch'esso di origine sicuramente greca). Inoltre il coro sembra essere stato d'impaccio anche a un poeta come Ennio, se è credibile che questo poeta riservasse al coro il solo settenario trocaico (vedi però Skutsch, *Studia Enniana*, London 1968, p. 161). Del resto, abbiamo prove sicure di tragedie dei grandi Ateniesi rappresentate con coro più o meno ridotto: vedi quanto dice Jocelyn, *The Tragedies of Ennius*, ecc., Cambridge 1967, p. 19 n. 5. Il *PSorb* 2252 è istruttivo: è del III sec. a. C. (quasi contemporaneo di Plauto e contemporaneo di Livio Andronico e Nevio) e contiene l'*Ippolito* di Euripide senza parti corali.

M. Sandbach: I should very much like to hear Professor Questa's views on the passage in *Curculio* which is ascribed to *choragus*. Does this replace a χοροῦ μέλος in the Greek? If so, why did Plautus abandon his usual practice of writing an undivided play?

M. Questa: La scena del *choragus* è qualcosa di eccezionale. Essa può aver benissimo sostituito un intermezzo corale (l'idea è di Leo, già ricordato rispondendo prima al collega Ludwig), ma certo non dimostra che Plauto dividesse in atti le sue commedie. La scena può trovare una sua ragione considerando che il *Curculio* è una della commedie più ... noiose di Plauto, nel senso che essa presenta, senza rilievo particolare, i personaggi più risaputi nell'intreccio più risaputo. Plauto può aver sentito il desiderio di variare un po' il solito intreccio. In ogni caso, come nello *Pseudolus* l'intermezzo auletico, così qui la parte del *choragus* non corrisponde certo al *primo* intervento del coro. La scena ha un sapore aristofanesco, di παράβασις, e probabilmente dovrebbe essere studiata in rapporto all'influenza che Aristofane ha qua e là su Plauto. Del resto niente vieta di credere che Plauto abbia adattato alle esigenze del suo teatro scene in cui il coro agiva veramente (questo però non avviene nel *Poenulus*: cfr. p. 211, n. 2) pur eliminandolo come intermezzo: sui problemi del *Curculio*, oltre a quanto detto a p. 215, n. 2 del mio 'exposé', si vedrà molto profitto la recentissima edizione di G. Monaco (Palermo 1969), per più ragioni ammirevole (utile anche il comm. di F. Bertini, Bologna 1969).

M. Handley: Among the problems in the Δὶς ἐξαπατῶν fragments which one would like to see cleared up, there is the number ΤΞΔ (364) found at the foot of column II. My own inclination was to think of it as a total for verses in the act, but on any view there seem to be problems, and I wonder if anyone has arrived at an answer.

M. Questa: Nel mio exposé (p. 207, n. 1), esprimo chiaramente il mio imbarazzo di fronte alla nota sticometrica : esso non è inferiore a quello che ha provato Lei. Il problema non è molto diverso da quello del *Sikyonios* (cfr. Kassel, Menanders Sikyonier, *Eranos* 1965, pp. 12-13), ma, direi, è più complicato, in quanto la cifra è, o vorrebbe essere, precisa. Si possono dare due interpretazioni: *(a)* la cifra rappresenta la somma dei versi dei primi *due* atti di Menandro, ma in questo caso dobbiamo supporre che Plauto abbia aggiunto molto, moltissimo al testo greco. Teniamo fermo che i versi greci corrispondenti a *Bacch.* 107 sgg. segnavano indubbiamente, in Menandro, fine del primo atto. Se diamo allora al II atto di Menandro la lunghezza media di 180 versi circa e sottraiamo da questo totale i 53 versi che in qualche modo si leggono nelle prime due colonne, restano per Menandro 130 versi circa, ai quali dovrebbero corrispondere i vv. 109-493 di Plauto, cioè 384 versi: il rapporto è del tutto insolito e poco credibile. Si può allora pensare: *(b)* che 364 sia la somma dei versi del *solo secondo atto* menandreo. In questo caso, sottratti i 53 vv. superstiti, restano 311 versi, ai quali corrispondono i 384 di Plauto già calcolati. Questo mi sembra più facile e nel complesso preferibile come ipotesi, visto che non le si oppongono vere difficoltà, se non la inusitata lunghezza del secondo atto del modello greco.

M. Turner: The common view about stichometric letters or numbers (Kurt Ohly, *Ztschr. f. Bibliothekswesen* Beiheft 61, 1928) is that they represent the scribe's figuring of the number of lines/verses or στίχοι that he has copied so that he may be paid in full. It must be said that this view is a hypothesis only. Such numbers commonly appear in two forms: 1) as totals, whether of lines written on a single page (e.g. the Pierpont Morgan *Iliad*) or at the end of a book (e.g. of Homer, of Sappho, of Menander's *Sikyonios*, even a speech of Demosthenes); 2) as a running number, usually in the left margin. In the latter case, the numbers are normally rounded off to every hundred verses. There seems to be no parallel example as yet in an ancient manuscript, whether on papyrus or parchment, of a total of the number of verses in a particular section of a work. It would not, however, be repugnant to common sense or what is known of other stichometric notation to suppose that ΤΞΔ here meant "I have written 364 verses so far, and shall require to be paid for that number".

M. Ludwig: 364 Zeilen als Umfang der ersten beiden Akte bei Menander wäre an sich durchaus möglich. In der *Samia* hatten sie zusammen ungefähr diese Grösse. Beim Δὶς ἐξαπατῶν ständen dem aber ca. 650 Verse in den *Bacchides* gegenüber. Es ist nicht zu sehen, wo und wie Plautus insgesamt 300 Verse hinzugefügt haben sollte. Vielleicht ist deshalb eher ein überlanger zweiter Akt des Δὶς ἐξαπατῶν vorzuziehen. Auch der zweite Akt der Συναριστῶσαι, dem bei Plautus ca. 540 Verse entsprechen, war wohl schon bei Menander länger als gewöhnlich (dann aber von Plautus noch zusätzlich erweitert, s. oben).

M. Questa: Sono contento di vedere il collega Ludwig condividere la mia idea. Le sue cifre coincidono con le mie. Il 364 è il numero dei versi di due atti di Menandro; Plauto risponde, come Ludwig ha mostrato, con circa 650, cioè con i versi 35-525 (= 490), cui si aggiungono i 34 frammenti delle prime due (?) scene e poco più di un centinaio di versi del tutto perduti : come Ludwig dice, circa 650. Ripeto invece che credo il rapporto 364: 650 (circa) del tutto ... allarmante e tale da costringerci a pericolosi voli di fantasia circa il modo di lavorare di Plauto, almeno in questa commedia. Sono grato a Ludwig per il suo prezioso riscontro con *Synaristosai - Cistellaria.*

M. Handley: I wonder if we are to make anything of the fact that our 364 stands at the same point as the critical signs *diple* and *coronis* to the left of the column? The question arises because one context in which we do meet exact totals for sections of a play is in metrical scholia, where the description does include references to critical signs and other " landmarks " of the text.

An example could be Schol. on Ar. *Clouds* 814: Κορωνὶς ἑτέρα ὁμοία, οἱ δὲ στίχοι ἰαμβικοὶ τρίμετροι ἀκατάληκτοι οε', ὧν τελευταῖοι

πρὸς πάντα τὰ δίκαι' ἀντιλέγειν δυνήσεται

ἐπὶ τῷ τέλει κορωνὶς καὶ ἑξῆς τὸ χοροῦ.

At *Clouds* 889 (the point in question) we have : διπλῆ καὶ κορωνὶς ἀποχωρησάντων τῶν ὑποκριτῶν· μέλος δὲ τοῦ χοροῦ οὐ κεῖται, ἀλλὰ γέγραπται μὲν ἐν μέσῳ χοροῦ, καὶ ἕπεται, κτλ.

Such a systematic description of Menander, if ever compiled, could hardly, one feels, have been of great *metrical* interest. But there may be room to keep our minds open to the possibility of a scholarly tradition of reckoning verses as well as a scribal one. The problem, however, if we try to think of a second act (or two acts) of 364 lines based on Plautus, will partly be one of entrances and exits, will it not?

M. Questa : Io preferisco lasciare alla Sua competenza la questione delle note sticometriche, per la quale occorre, mi pare, quella specifica esperienza di papirologo che a me manca. Posso soltanto farle notare che — forse per caso — la tradizione manoscritta di Plauto conosce in un caso una nota colometrica (numero dei versi di un *canticum*) : veda quanto, dopo Ritschl, osserva Leo in apparato a *Tri.* 275a circa il codice B. Si tratta forse di caso, come ho detto, ma l'annotazione sembra antica, perché A coincide con B nel dividere, in pratica, il *canticum* nello stesso numero di στίχοι, (nessuna nota colometrica è però in A). Ciò conferma tuttavia quello che Lei dice, perché per Menandro non si poneva il problema di scrivere e computare gli στίχοι di parti liriche dalla complessa disposizione ἐν εἰσθέσει ed ἐν ἐκθέσει. Per quanto concerne le entrate e le uscite dei personaggi, io penserei che un numero lungo di versi come 364 potrebbe facilitare le cose. Sembra essere legge che un personaggio, uscito ad un certo punto, non possa ritornare che nell'atto seguente (di Menandro o altro testo greco ; per i Latini il problema non esiste poiché non conoscono atti). Ma il papiro ci mostra (v. 30) Demea-Nicobulo già di ritorno dal foro-agorà nel corso del secondo atto. D'altro canto io credo con Lei (l'ho detto nel mio exposé) che l'uscita di scena per il foro-agorà di Demea-Nicobulo in *Bacch.* 348 sia di Menandro e non di Plauto. *Bacch.* 107-109 riproducono, con i debiti adattamenti, la fine del primo atto di Menandro, nel quale non si vede assolutamente come potesse comparire Demea-Nicobulo. Questi, infatti, esce di casa, comparendo in scena per la *prima* volta in *Bacch.* 235 (le sue sono, chiaramente, tipiche parole di autopresentazione di un personaggio), dunque già nel corso del secondo atto del modello greco. Stando così le cose, noi dobbiamo ammettere, almeno per il momento, che uno stesso personaggio potesse uscire di scena (annunciando l'uscita : *Bacch.* 348) e ritornarvi (Δὶς ἐξαπατῶν v. 30) nel corso dello stesso atto. La legge è dunque infranta? Parrebbe di sì, ma l'infrazione può essere giudicata tanto più tollerabile se l'atto è lungo, come è almeno lecito supporre fosse il secondo del Δὶς ἐξαπατῶν.

M. Handley : It is true that from the present state of the text one cannot be certain where the old man is coming from at Δὶς ἐξαπατῶν 30. At 89 f. in the new Act, it does seem that we have him going to the market with the words ταῦ[τ'] ἄπειμι πρὸς ἀγορὰν / [πρ]άττ[ων· ὅ]τι πράττῃς (-εις P) ἄ[λ]λο δέδοται τοῦτό σοι, and hence it is very likely that he is returning from there at the point represented by 768 ff. of *Bacchides.* Professor Questa must, I think, be right to recognize Plautine alteration at 768-769 ; and the following encounter with Syros-Chrysalus is interestingly parallel with the encounter with Sostratos-Mnesilochus (so far as one can follow it) at Δὶς ἐξαπατῶν 30-63—both, as it seems, on return from the market. It may then be that comic capital was made of the old man's repeated excursions, and that he is allowed —perhaps exceptionally in this play—the licence of going and coming back within the Act. The idea of an Act-break after the point represented by 384 has been supported on the ground that Lydus needs to fetch Philoxenus from off-stage between there and 405 ; but however little we trust the detail of the intervening monologue by Mnesilochus as a guide to the original, it is possible to imagine something like it which would resolve any apparent improbability in Lydus' movements.

M. Questa : Sono felice di vedere che Lei approva la mia ipotesi circa i vv. 768-769. Possiamo allora credere che Demea-

Nicobulo, in Menandro, tornasse dall' ἀγορά al principio del quarto atto e che incontrasse Siro-Crisalo davanti a casa propria. Il mutamento di situazione, quindi, è opera di Plauto, a ciò costretto dal contenuto dei suoi vv. 520 sgg.

M. Handley : Plautus' *uos me sequimini, Ba*, 525, suggests that in adding a retinue of slaves, he imagined the scene differently from Menander. I wonder if Professor Questa has a view of this? If he is right that at *Bacchides* 107 ff. Plautus followed Menander's words, but used them in a different function, we might think that he was doing the same with the repeated ἀκολούθει of the Greek here.

M. Questa : La *pompa* che accompagna Sostrato-Mnesiloco può non essere un problema : o le comparse attendevano un po' appartate che il dialogo e poi il monologo finissero (il pubblico, in sostanza, li dimenticava nel frattempo), oppure Plauto si è ricordato solo alla fine della scena di un particolare del Δὶς ἐξαπατῶν e l'ha riprodotto più o meno alla lettera con la solita disinvoltura. Con Demea-Nicobulo ha fatto di peggio : talvolta si potrebbe concordare con Orazio !

VII

LILLY KAHIL

Remarques sur l'iconographie des pièces de Ménandre

REMARQUES SUR L'ICONOGRAPHIE DES PIÈCES DE MÉNANDRE

Au terme de ces Entretiens, il n'est pas inutile de faire appel à l'archéologie et de considérer les enrichissements qu'elle est susceptible d'apporter à la connaissance de Ménandre. Un auteur antique, en effet (ou un auteur moderne) n'est pas simplement le créateur d'une littérature en quelque sorte abstraite : il dépend profondément de la réalité qui l'entoure, réalité humaine et réalité matérielle, et cela est particulièrement vrai pour un auteur dramatique qui s'adresse à un public donné, qui est obligé de se plier aux exigences d'un genre donné, et aussi au cadre dans lequel ses œuvres seront exécutées. C'est le cas pour Ménandre, d'autant plus que la Comédie nouvelle a multiplié les possibilités de l'action théâtrale. D'où l'intérêt spécial que présente ici une enquête sur la documentation iconographique, enquête qui s'attache en premier lieu aux représentations dans l'art figuré de scènes tirées de l'œuvre de Ménandre.

Or si, depuis bien longtemps, on avait formulé maintes hypothèses à propos d'un certain nombre de documents, qu'il s'agisse de reliefs ou surtout de mosaïques et de peintures, qu'on attribuait à des pièces de la Comédie nouvelle [1] et parfois à Ménandre, les découvertes de ces dernières années, et surtout celles de Mytilène, permettent d'envisager ce problème d'une manière nouvelle. C'est pourquoi il convient d'aborder cette enquête non point selon l'ordre chronologique des images, mais en présentant d'abord un ensemble tardif, celui justement de Mytilène, qui a l'avantage considérable de regrouper un grand nombre de documents

[1] L'excellent ouvrage de A. Simon, *Comicae Tabellae*, 1938, avait déjà formulé un certain nombre de ces attributions. Mais l'étude capitale est celle de T.B.L. Webster, *Monuments illustrating New Comedy*, 1re éd. 1961, 2e édition 1969, qui rassemble, classe et attribue un matériel considérable.

et de désigner par des inscriptions les pièces, les actes et souvent les acteurs. Ainsi, partant du connu, nous pourrons remonter vers l'inconnu et formuler, sur la base de certitudes acquises, un certain nombre d'hypothèses concernant des documents plus anciens.

L'ensemble le plus complet, le plus intéressant, dont nous disposions à l'heure actuelle, concernant l'iconographie des pièces de Ménandre, est constitué par la série des mosaïques découvertes par Sérafim Charitonidis, Ephore des Antiquités, à Mytilène, dans une maison dont ont été fouillées, en 1961 et en 1962, deux pièces principales et, partiellement, un portique [1]. La grande pièce du nord-ouest, une sorte de salon muni d'un trône bâti, était ornée d'une mosaïque figurant Orphée charmant les animaux ; la grande pièce du nord-est, de dimensions analogues (6,50 m × 5,50 m), présentait une mosaïque dont la disposition indique qu'il s'agissait d'un triclinium : la partie laissée libre par les lits comportait dix panneaux, avec, en particulier, le portrait de Ménandre, Thalie, et sept scènes de comédie. Ces deux salles donnaient au sud sur ce qu'on doit considérer comme l'aile d'un portique : cette dernière a été dégagée seulement sur une longueur de 8,50 m et une largeur de 2,50 m ; son pavement de mosaïque comporte, dans l'axe, une bande décorée de panneaux carrés. Il paraît vraisemblable, encore que la fouille ait été arrêtée à cet endroit par la présence de maisons modernes, que ce couloir-portique faisait, à son extrémité ouest, retour vers le sud : en effet le dernier panneau à l'ouest diffère des autres par ses dimensions (plus faibles), par son

[1] Cf. S. Charitonidis, *Praktika* 1961, p. 212-214 ; *Praktika* 1962, p. 134-141 ; *Praktika* 1963, p. 158-159. La mort accidentelle de S. Charitonidis en 1965 n'a pas permis l'achèvement de la fouille ; l'ensemble déjà fouillé vient de paraître dans *Les Mosaïques de la Maison du Ménandre à Mytilène* (S. Charitonidis, L. Kahil, R. Ginouvès), *Antike Kunst*, Beiheft VI, Berne 1970, auquel on doit se reporter pour les illustrations en couleur et en noir et pour les descriptions détaillées. S. Charitonidis avait bien voulu associer R. Ginouvès et moi-même à la publication de cet ouvrage que nous dédions à sa mémoire.

sujet (il s'agit d'un masque isolé, et non d'une scène de comédie) et par son orientation (il est destiné à être vu de l'est, comme probablement toute la série de panneaux de ce côté) [1].

En abordant les panneaux de la salle à manger, il faut s'attarder un instant sur le portrait du poète, qui en ouvre la série, non point pour en esquisser une étude iconographique indépendante, mais parce que ce premier panneau est, en fait, intimement lié aux autres, et se rattache aux mêmes problèmes généraux. Ménandre est ici figuré en buste, le visage presque de face, mais pourtant légèrement tourné vers la droite ; il est désigné par l'inscription Μένα/ν-δρος. Une particularité physique frappe immédiatement : tandis que l'œil droit est dessiné de face, la pupille gauche est ramenée dans l'angle interne, indication qui n'est pas due à quelque maladresse du mosaïste, mais à la volonté de figurer nettement un strabisme qui correspond à ce que nous savons par la tradition littéraire : Ménandre était, comme le dit la *Souda*, στραβὸς τὰς ὄψεις. Dans l'iconographie du poète, encore si discutée, ce panneau de Mytilène, qui porte le nom de Ménandre, occupe désormais une place de choix. Certes, la mosaïque de Princeton, 40.435 [2], comporte elle aussi une inscription donnant le nom du poète, qu'elle présente en compagnie de Glykèra et de la Comédie (ces deux noms aussi sont inscrits) ; mais elle nous apprend peu de choses sur son apparence physique. A la même inspiration que cette mosaïque se rattachent un certain nombre de reliefs, dont le plus remarquable est celui du Latran-Vatican, inv.9985, datant du Ier siècle de notre ère [3] : le poète comique, torse nu, est assis vers la droite, tenant dans la main gauche un masque de jeune homme, et on voit sur la table les masques d'une jeune femme et d'un vieillard, tandis qu'à droite une jeune femme debout a été interprétée

[1] Pour le plan de la portion déjà fouillée de la maison cf. *Praktika* 1962, p. 135, fig. 1.

[2] Cf. Webster, *Monuments illustrating New Comedy*², p. 171, ZM 4.

[3] Cf. Webster, *ibid.* p. 212, IS 10.

soit comme Glykèra, soit comme une personnification de Skènè, soit comme une Muse ; le poète est très évidemment Ménandre, la mosaïque de Princeton le montre bien, mais nous n'avons pas davantage ici un portrait à proprement parler. Cependant le visage mobile, fin, les joues creusées, la pomme d'Adam saillante, conviennent à l'apparence générale du personnage telle que les textes nous invitent à l'imaginer, et concordent aussi dans l'ensemble infiniment mieux avec le portrait de Mytilène que, par exemple, une mosaïque de Thuburbo Majus, au Musée du Bardo, n° 1396 [1], pièce encore peu connue qui figure certainement le poète : un jeune homme assis vers la gauche tient un rouleau, et deux masques comiques sont posés sur un meuble devant lui. Il est remarquable que le type de représentation des documents de Princeton et du Latran ait survécu fort longtemps, puisqu'on le retrouve sur un lagynos du Musée du Caire, datant d'environ 300 après J.-C., provenant de Moyenne-Egypte [2], et dont le prototype est connu par un plâtre alexandrin conservé au Musée de Kaboul [3] : sous un arbre, un poète est assis devant une Muse tenant les masques d'un jeune homme, d'un esclave et d'une jeune fille. Pourtant, si on veut trouver des documents iconographiques directement comparables avec la mosaïque de Mytilène, plutôt que vers les mosaïques ou les fresques comme celle de la Casa del Menandro [4], c'est vers les portraits en ronde-bosse qu'il faut se tourner, par exemple ceux de Boston, de Dumbarton Oaks, de Philadelphie et de Venise [5]. Il est aisé de comparer les particularités de ces visages avec celles du Ménandre de Mytilène ; d'autre

[1] *La mosaïque gréco-romaine*, 1965, p. 129, fig. 8 et *Les Mosaïques de la Maison du Ménandre*, pl. 16, 1.

[2] Cf. L. Ghali-Kahil, *Monuments Piot*, 51, 1960, p. 81, fig. 8 ; Webster, *ibid.*, p. 178, EV 17.

[3] Webster, *ibid.*, p. 178, ET 65.

[4] Fresque figurant le jeune poète assis : cf. G. Richter, *Portraits of the Greeks*, II, 1965, p. 228, n° 7, fig. 1515.

[5] Richter, *ibid.*, p. 233.

part, si on regarde par exemple le buste de Venise, qu'on a parfois considéré à tort comme un portrait de Virgile, on peut y retrouver une manière identique de présenter le vêtement. C'est là une confirmation éclatante de l'attribution à Ménandre de toute la série établie autour de ce buste. Mais la mosaïque de Mytilène, qui semble constituer un reflet fidèle de ces sculptures, doit se rattacher à un prototype dont les autres panneaux permettent de mieux comprendre la nature.

En effet, après ce portrait, commence la série des pièces figurées, avec le *Plokion*, acte II (Πλοκίου μ/έ(ρος) β'). Trois acteurs sont en présence, identifiés par des inscriptions. Le premier à gauche est Μοσ/σχί/ων, (Moschion), la main gauche cachée dans le manteau, comme pour la plupart de ces personnages, la main droite levée à hauteur de la poitrine ; sa chevelure pourpre et chamois comporte, derrière la *speira*, une masse de laquelle tombent sur les épaules des mèches jaunes et beiges ; le masque lui-même est de tonalité rose ; l'acteur porte deux tuniques superposées, avec une ceinture, un manteau et des chaussures noires. Au centre, Λά-χης (Lachès), vieillard à chevelure blanche, fait un grand geste vers la droite, en direction de Κρω/βύ/λ/η (Krobylè), dont le visage est de tonalité claire, et qui porte une tunique inférieure blanche, une tunique supérieure bleue, et un petit manteau verdâtre. L'inscription indique qu'il s'agit d'un épisode de l'acte II du *Collier*. Le fr. 333 Koe. nous apprend que Krobylè est une femme mariée, riche et dominatrice, qui essaie de contraindre son époux à accepter, pour son fils, un mariage auquel le jeune homme répugne car il a violé une jeune fille pauvre ; à cette intrigue se mêle une seconde, concernant le père et une esclave qu'il a dû renvoyer. Le panneau de Mytilène montre ou bien Lachès reprochant à Krobylè, en présence de Moschion son fils, de l'avoir obligé à se séparer de son esclave, ou bien — et c'est l'hypothèse la plus vraisemblable — Krobylè qui vient de dévoiler les projets matrimoniaux qu'elle forme pour Moschion et le père qui prend la défense du jeune homme réticent. Comme nous sommes seulement à l'acte II, il semble improbable que les parents connaissent déjà l'affaire de l'enfant attendu par la jeune fille violée. Ce panneau, en tout cas, confirme le nom de Krobylè, et même, d'une certaine manière, son apparence physique, avec le long nez dont parle le fragment ; et il nous apporte deux nouveaux noms, ceux de Lachès, mari de Krobylè, et de Moschion, son fils.

Le troisième panneau soulève un problème très difficile. Trois personnages se tiennent debout, sans masques : Σωκράτ/ης (Socrate) au centre, entre Σιμμί-/ας (Simmias) et Κέβη/ς (Cébès), tous désignés par des inscriptions ; mais aucune inscription ne désigne la pièce, ni un acte éventuel. Socrate et ses interlocuteurs dans le *Phédon*, vêtus de la tunique et du manteau, se présentent à nous, dans l'attitude typique de philosophes enseignant : avant-bras droit levé, index et majeur pointés, la main gauche serrant un rouleau, attitude dans laquelle l'art paléochrétien figurera les disciples du Christ, par exemple sur une mosaïque de l'église Sant' Andrea in Catabarbara [1]. Comment expliquer cette évocation socratique dans une série de panneaux destinés à glorifier Ménandre et ses comédies ? On remarquera que si les personnages ne sont pas masqués, il y a cependant une volonté certaine, de la part du mosaïste, de montrer Socrate sous un aspect typique, comparable par exemple à l'hermès de Naples [2], avec le front dégarni, le nez épaté ; pourtant, en général, les mosaïques ne sont guère précises (Cologne et Apamée) [3], celle de Baalbeck faisant exception [4]. L'hypothèse la plus simple est d'imaginer que le panneau ne figurerait pas une récitation

[1] Cf. W. Oakeshott, *The Mosaics of Rome*, 1967, p. 254, fig. 8.

[2] Pour la question de l'iconographie de Socrate, cf. Richter, *Portraits of the Greeks*, I, p. 109, 111.

[3] Cf. Richter, *ibid.* fig. 572, et fig. 569.

[4] Richter, *ibid.*, fig. 571.

du dialogue socratique, pratique pourtant attestée [1] (car cela impliquerait que l'artiste, qui n'a pas voulu montrer ses personnages masqués, a cependant donné à celui qui jouait le rôle de Socrate un aspect physique « socratique »), mais il évoquerait le véritable dialogue entre Socrate et ses disciples. Le *Phédon* est en effet un des dialogues socratiques les plus célèbres, celui qui traite de l'immortalité. Cette image, dans un ensemble glorifiant la comédie de Ménandre, mettrait donc en valeur d'une part le caractère dramatique du dialogue socratique, que les Anciens soulignaient déjà, tout comme les aspects poétiques du dialogue platonicien [2] ; d'autre part le rapport entre la comédie ménandréenne et l'esprit socratique. Et l'on peut supposer que, placé à un endroit privilégié, entre le portrait de Ménandre et la tête de Thalie, ce panneau pouvait faire partie de l'illustration du *Bios* du poète, précédant l'illustration de ses pièces. La présence du *Plokion*, immédiatement auparavant, s'expliquerait dans ce cas par la nécessité d'installer quatre panneaux dans la première série, tout en réservant le premier et le dernier (les plus en vue) à Ménandre et à Thalie.

Pour cette Thalie précisément, désignée par l'inscription Θά-λεια, il suffit d'indiquer ici qu'elle porte un masque, très probablement un masque de vieillard à en juger par la couleur [3], ainsi que la baguette avec laquelle on la représente si souvent. De nombreuses comparaisons seraient possibles car, tandis que les Muses en pied sont rares, leurs bustes sont fort répandus [4].

Le panneau suivant (Pl. I A) montre une scène de la *Samienne*, tirée de l'acte III : Σαμίας. μ/έ(ρος) γ'. Trois personnages sont figurés, au centre Δη/μέ/ας (Déméas), le vieillard, de

[1] Plut. *Quaest. conv.* : VII, 8, 2.

[2] Arstt. *Poet.*, 1447*b* 10.

[3] Le masque est de tonalité jaune avec des cheveux blancs.

[4] Cf. K. Parlasca, *Die römischen Mosaiken in der Schweiz*, 1959, pp. 141-144, qui a rassemblé une documentation très riche à ce sujet.

trois quarts vers la droite, fait un geste de reproche violent en direction d'une jeune femme, Χρυσίς (Chrysis), qui tient dans ses bras un enfant emmailloté. A gauche, un cuisinier (Μά-γ/ειρ/ος) assiste à la scène. L'image figure le moment capital de l'acte III : Dèméas chassant Chrysis et l'enfant (vv. 157-158 Koe. = *P. Bodmer XXV*, vv. 372-373) ; seule manque la vieille nourrice, personnage muet. Le panneau, dès avant la publication du *Papyrus Bodmer*, nous apprenait que le *mageiros* assistait effectivement à la scène, contrairement à certaines interprétations, et c'était là un apport majeur de la mosaïque ; mais seul le nouveau papyrus pouvait attester les interventions de ce personnage. Enfin, l'inscription du panneau montre que, pour le titre de la pièce, le premier éditeur avait bien raison : la *Samienne* est une comédie à double titre, le second étant, comme on l'a démontré récemment, *Kèdeia* [1].

Le panneau suivant (Pl. II) représente les *Synaristosai*, acte I : Συναριστωσῶν / μ/έ(ρος) α'. Quatre personnages sont en scène, trois femmes assises autour d'une table, et, à l'extrémité gauche, un enfant debout dont on ne voit que la tête. La femme de gauche est désignée par l'inscription Φιλαι/νίς (Philainis) ; elle lève dans la main droite une coupe, et son visage grimaçant, jaune vif, est celui d'une vieille femme, d'une proxénète, que nous connaissons par d'autres masques encore. Derrière le dossier de son siège, un enfant rejette la tête en arrière, comme pour mieux apercevoir la scène. Le personnage central est désigné par l'inscription Πλαγ/γών (Plangon) : c'est la pseudo-korè ; à droite, Πυθ/ιάς, (Pythias), est caractérisée comme une hétaïre, en particulier par l'ornement de sa chevelure. C'est grâce à la *Cistellaria* de Plaute, qui adapte les *Synaristosai*, que nous pouvons comprendre l'intrigue, encore que les noms aient été modifiés dans la pièce latine : Philainis est la *lena* ; Pythias, sa fille, y est appelée Gymnasium ; Plangon est devenue Selenium. L'acte s'ouvrait,

[1] R. KASSER et C. AUSTIN, *Papyrus Bodmer XXV*, *Ménandre*, *La Samienne*, p. 25, n. 2.

vraisemblablement, chez Ménandre déjà, par le spectacle de ces trois femmes attablées. Mais d'un autre côté, ce panneau de Mytilène apparaît particulièrement intéressant dans la mesure où il remonte avec certitude à un prototype ancien : dès le premier coup d'œil, il évoque une autre mosaïque fort célèbre, un des panneaux de Dioscouridès conservés au Musée National de Naples (Pl. III) [1]. Cette œuvre, qui date de la fin du second siècle avant J.-C., dérive elle-même d'un original de la première moitié du IIIe. Marx, puis Webster [2], avaient déjà suggéré que cette mosaïque devait illustrer le début des *Synaristosai* ; mais le panneau de Mytilène donne à cette interprétation, qui n'avait pas toujours été acceptée, une confirmation définitive : c'est bien la même scène qu'il représente, simplement inversée, la vieille femme étant, sur le panneau de Naples, à droite, et sa fille à gauche ; le petit personnage qui apparaît, dans les deux cas, derrière l'entremetteuse, est une petite esclave, comme l'indique le fragment 385 Koe. L'apport du panneau de Mytilène est donc considérable : il nous donne, dans leur version originale, les noms des protagonistes de la pièce de Ménandre, dont nous n'avions que la transcription latine (pour deux d'entre eux seulement) ; il nous permet aussi de reconnaître avec certitude l'inspiration d'une des plus belles œuvres de la mosaïque hellénistique. Enfin il pose, comme cette dernière, un problème important pour l'histoire de la mise en scène : ces deux images suggèrent en effet, sans cependant que l'on puisse l'affirmer avec certitude, que ce repas se passait sur scène, soit sur l'estrade en avant du décor, soit à l'intérieur de l'une des maisons, visible à travers l'entrée [3].

Le septième panneau illustre l'acte II des *Epitrépontes* : 'Επιτρεπόντων μ/έ(ρος) β' (Pl. I B). Cinq personnages sont figurés :

[1] Naples, n° 9987, cf. WEBSTER, *l.l.*, p. 183, NM 1.

[2] Cf. WEBSTER, *Greek Theater Production*, p. 23.

[3] Cf. WEBSTER, *ibid.*, p. 25-26, qui reprend toute la discussion. Cf. aussi *supra*, pp. 36-39.

trois acteurs masqués et deux personnages secondaires. Au centre, le vieillard Σμει/κρίν/ης (Smikrinès) apparaît entre un esclave, le berger Σύρος (Syros), avec son bâton recourbé, à gauche, et, à droite, 'Αν/θρα/κεύ/ς (Anthrakeus), le charbonnier, qui porte un masque d'esclave, alors que son vêtement pourrait désigner un affranchi. A l'extrême droite une femme, personnage muet, est figurée plus petite ; elle serre dans ses bras un enfant. Il est évident qu'il s'agit de la grande scène de l'acte II, la scène même de l'arbitrage, qui a donné son nom à la pièce. Le charbonnier, désigné dans ce panneau sous le nom d'Anthrakeus (et non sous celui de Syriskos, transmis par le texte), s'est rendu en ville pour payer ses redevances à Chairestratos. Il rencontre Daos (ici Syros), qui lui a confié un petit enfant, mais non les signes de reconnaissance, et il les lui réclame : tous deux décident de demander au premier venu d'arbitrer le conflit ; c'est précisément Smikrinès, le propre grand-père de l'enfant, né de sa fille Pamphylè (vv. 125-127 Koe.). Le panneau montre donc ici aussi le passage essentiel qu'il fallait choisir pour illustrer la pièce. On notera l'emploi du nom générique Syros pour Daos, nom pourtant habituel pour les esclaves, et d'un nom de métier, Anthrakeus, pour désigner celui que les manuscrits appellent, très probablement, Syriskos.

Le huitième panneau du triclinium montre une scène de l'acte II de la *Théophoroumènè* : Θεοφορουμένης μ(έρος) β' (Pl. IV). Il figure trois hommes et un enfant : à gauche, Λυσί/ας (Lysias), dans un vêtement qu'on pourrait au premier abord interpréter comme celui d'un esclave, danse allègrement, une cymbale dans chaque main ; au centre, l'esclave Παρμ-ένω/ν (Parménon) fait de la main droite un geste de surprise ; à droite, un autre jeune homme, Κλει-νί/ας (Kleinias), tient dans la main droite un objet arrondi, jaune vif, qui pourrait être un instrument de musique, peut-être un tambourin. A l'extrême droite, le petit personnage porte un objet très difficile à distinguer, un bâtonnet recourbé, peut-être quelque instrument de musique. Pour cette pièce encore mal connue, le panneau de Mytilène est extrêmement important. D'après le papyrus fragmentaire, Lysias propose à Kleinias, qui est probablement amoureux de la jeune fille « possédée », une épreuve destinée à vérifier si elle l'est réellement, ou s'il s'agit d'une simulatrice ; il semblerait qu'ils miment un chœur de Corybantes [1] : ils ordonnent à la flûtiste de jouer, si l'on admet que αὔλει (v. 26) est bien un impératif, et non un indicatif comme le voudraient certains éditeurs (Körte). C'est ici que devrait se situer le panneau de Mytilène : la Théophorouménè elle-même n'y apparaît pas encore, ce qui à première vue pourrait surprendre ; il figure l'invitation à la danse, scène dont le pittoresque et le comique ont dû frapper les Anciens. Récemment, E. W. Handley a attribué à la pièce un autre fragment de papyrus avec l'entrée de la jeune femme, chantant un hymne à la Mère des Dieux [2]. Par ailleurs, le panneau de Mytilène évoque le second panneau de Dioscouridès au Musée de Naples [3], où l'on reconnaît habituellement soit des musiciens ambulants, soit une danse en l'honneur de Cybèle ; or, bien qu'ici la distance entre les deux versions soit plus grande que pour les *Synaristosai*, c'est bien d'une scène toute proche de la même pièce qu'il doit s'agir : le personnage qui heurte les cymbales pourrait être Lysias ; un autre joue du tympanon ; le petit personnage est présent, mais Parménon manque à Naples, tandis que la joueuse de flûte est absente à Mytilène, à ce qu'il semble. Le moment n'est donc pas exactement le même, mais l'atmosphère en est très proche. Parmi les apports du panneau de Mytilène, on soulignera qu'il permet d'écarter définitivement l'hypothèse d'un Lysias *senex* ; il confirme la présence

[1] Cf. l'étude si pénétrante de E. W. Handley, Notes on the Theophoroumene of Menander, *BICS*, 16, 1969, p. 92-93.

[2] V. Bartoletti, *Dai Papiri della Società Italiana*, 1965 n° 1 ; Pavese, *SIFC*, n.s., 34 (1962), p. 21 ss. ; Handley, *ibid.*, p. 96 et n° 22.

[3] Naples 9985 ; Webster, *Monuments illustrating New Comedy*², p. 183, NM 2.

d'un Kleinias ; il nomme Parménon l'esclave, qui assistait à cette scène majeure du second acte ; et surtout il nous introduit dans l'atmosphère de cette pièce, au genre mêlé. Son succès semble avoir été durable : des jetons de plomb d'Athènes, datant du IIIe siècle, ne portent-ils pas l'inscription Θεοφορου/μένη, ce qui atteste que la comédie était encore jouée en public à cette époque ? [1]

Le neuvième panneau figure une scène du 4e acte de l'*Encheiridion* : 'Ενχειριδίου. μέρος. δ'. Deux vieillards, Στ/ράτω/ν (Straton) et Δέρ-σιπ/πο/ς (Dersippos), brandissent chacun de la main droite un poignard, tandis qu'au centre l'esclave Κέρ/δω/ν (Kerdon) tient un objet difficile à reconnaître, une bourse peut-être (ou une clef ?). Il s'agit très probablement de la scène qui a donné son nom à la pièce, puisque chacun des vieillards tient un poignard, qui pourrait constituer un signe de reconnaissance : les acteurs, en effet, ne semblent pas se menacer. L'objet que porte Kerdon est mystérieux : le nom du personnage évoque le lucre, et ce qu'il tient pourrait constituer la récompense pour les signes de reconnaissance ; mais il ne s'agit là que d'une hypothèse. Le *PSI* 99 donne les noms de Straton, Kerdon et Doris : le panneau de Mytilène rend très vraisemblable l'attribution de ce fragment à l'*Encheiridion*. Enfin, le nom Dersippos pourrait être une graphie de Derkippos, qu'on trouve dans un autre fragment de Ménandre (fr. 639 Koe.).

Le dixième panneau illustre une scène de l'acte V de la *Messénienne* : Μεσσηνίας μ/έ(ρος) ε'. Un jeune homme, Χαρ/εῖ/νο/ς (Charinos), semble écarter violemment deux esclaves, Σύρος (Syros) et Τίβι/ος (Tibios), à moins qu'il ne cherche à les entraîner avec lui. L'image se rapporte certainement à une scène capitale, mais on ne sait comment l'interpréter. E. W. Handley a attiré mon attention sur l'épisode qui termine le *Dyskolos*, et qui pourrait fournir une situa-

[1] Cf. M. Crosby, *Agora* X, 1964, p. 122.

tion analogue : Sicon et Gétas cherchent à entraîner Cnémon dans la danse ; mais ici la main droite de Charinos, qui a saisi le poignet de l'esclave, semble indiquer que c'est plutôt lui qui a l'initiative de l'action.

Le portique sud montre, après un masque posé sur une étagère dans le premier panneau (un masque d'esclave très probablement, d'après sa coloration rougeâtre), une nouvelle série de pièces, mais cette fois le nom des personnages n'est pas inscrit. C'est d'abord l'acte III des *Kybernètai* : Κυβερνη-τῶν / μ/έ(ρος) γ'. La représentation est d'autant plus difficile à interpréter que les fragments conservés ne nous donnent, sur l'intrigue, que fort peu de renseignements. Le personnage de gauche, qui semble agenouillé, pourrait à la rigueur être un jeune homme, mais plutôt une jeune femme, à en juger par sa chevelure partagée ; la ligne ondulée qui apparaît à la base de la représentation, dans une surface bleutée, semblerait évoquer la mer, à laquelle le titre de la pièce fait évidemment penser. Les deux autres figures, un jeune homme au centre et un vieillard à droite, tendent le bras vers celle de gauche, mais leur geste ne peut être exactement interprété : menace, exhortation, ou secours ? Pour le moment, il ne paraît pas utile de multiplier les hypothèses à ce sujet : on peut au moins rappeler la possibilité d'une scène de naufrage, tel que celui que présuppose le début du *Rudens*.

Le troisième panneau représente la *Leukadia* : Λευκαδίας. L'acte n'est pas indiqué. Trois acteurs sont en présence : celui de gauche, que son masque semble désigner comme un vieillard, fait un geste d'étonnement, d'admiration ou de ferveur religieuse. Le personnage du centre, qui porte sur la tête une couronne de feuillages, tend une palme : son costume, avec la tunique supérieure très longue, paraît indiquer qu'il s'agit d'une femme, peut-être la prêtresse dont il est question au fr. 257 Koe. Le personnage de droite, plus petit parce qu'un peu en retrait, semble être un esclave, d'après la couleur de son masque, mais il porte sur la tête un voile qui se justifierait dans la perspective d'une scène religieuse. Une petite figure, à droite, comme juchée sur une base, pourrait éventuellement être interprétée comme une statue de culte, si nous sommes bien au sanctuaire d'Apollon à Leucade, mais l'objet qu'elle tient est d'une interprétation extrêmement difficile : s'agit-il d'un temple en miniature, évoquant les bâtiments que, dans l'iconographie byzantine, certains dédicants portent dans leurs mains ? L'hypothèse pourrait paraître trop audacieuse : elle ne saurait en effet s'appuyer sur aucun parallèle contemporain. Le fait que l'acte n'est pas indiqué pourrait n'être pas imputable à une négligence du mosaïste, mais au fait que le panneau évoquerait le prologue de la pièce, dont il nous permet au moins d'imaginer l'ambiance religieuse, ambiance dont on a vu qu'elle caractérise souvent les comédies de Ménandre [1].

Le panneau suivant illustre une scène du dernier acte du *Misouménos* : Μεισουμένου μέ(ρος) ε'. Ici encore, les noms des personnages manquent, ce qui ne contribue point à faciliter l'interprétation ; en outre, certains masques et certains costumes sont plus difficiles à reconnaître que partout ailleurs. Le costume de l'homme de gauche est semblable à celui des esclaves, et son visage est aussi de tonalité rouge : il serre une écharpe autour de son cou ; le personnage du centre tente de l'en empêcher ; à droite se tient une femme, dont l'apparence rappelle celle d'une concubine, en particulier à cause de la coiffure avec un diadème multicolore. Grâce aux travaux de E. G. Turner [2], l'intrigue de la pièce est mieux connue : nous sommes ici à la fin, et le geste du personnage qui essaie de s'étrangler inviterait à penser aux vers qui pré-

[1] Il suffit de songer au *Dyskolos*, à la *Théophoroumènè*, etc. ... Si les cultes officiels ne jouent pas un grand rôle dans les pièces de Ménandre, les cultes plus populaires et même les superstitions religieuses y sont maintes fois mentionnés.

[2] E. G. Turner, New fragments of the Misoumenos of Menander, *BICS*, suppl. 17, 1965, et *POxy*, XXXIII, 1968, nº 2656-2657.

cèdent le dénouement : Thrasonidès songe à se suicider et Dèméas l'en empêche en lui accordant la main de sa fille (vv. 443-445). Mais il faudrait que le personnage de gauche soit un soldat, ce qui n'est pas certain ; et les vers 443-445, d'ailleurs *restitués*, pourraient simplement signifier « je m'étrangle de rage », le mot étant pris au figuré. Plusieurs autres hypothèses semblent plausibles : si le personnage de gauche est l'esclave Gétas, comme le suggère K. Schefold, on pourrait admettre qu'il mime la tristesse de son maître, en présence de Dèméas, au centre ; si on admet en revanche, avec Webster, que le personnage du centre est Thrasonidès (le costume et le masque présentent, en effet, par rapport à la série des vieillards, des différences difficilement explicables), le geste de l'esclave devient très difficile à comprendre, et la présence de la jeune fille ne s'explique plus, à moins qu'on admette que l'esclave Gétas raconte à Thrasonidès l'acceptation de Krateia et de son père, et que celle-ci apparaît en même temps à droite pour matérialiser en quelque sorte l'histoire, la rendre plus sensible (elle est d'ailleurs nettement à l'arrière-plan). C'est un problème à certains égards semblable que pose un moule à gâteaux d'Ostie, daté du IIIe s. de notre ère, où il n'est pas impossible de reconnaître les mêmes personnages [1].

Enfin, le dernier panneau du portique figure une scène du *Phasma*, acte II, Φάσματος / μέ(ρος / β' : une jeune fille apparaît dans l'embrasure d'une porte aux deux battants écartés, devant un personnage âgé, au centre, qu'accompagne un jeune homme à droite. Il s'agit très probablement de la seconde apparition de la jeune fille devant le jeune homme, dont les textes nous indiquent qu'il s'appelait Phidias, en présence de son père qui la voit, lui, pour la première fois. L'image pose d'ailleurs une difficile question d'optique théâtrale : il semble que la porte représente le « passage », aménagé

[1] WEBSTER, *Monuments*..., p. 222, II, 80.

en chapelle, dont il est question dans le texte (il est décrit dans le prologue) ; il paraît bien en effet qu'une telle apparition, d'une importance dramatique capitale, devait être figurée sur la scène ; mais, on le voit, la porte ne signifie pas, comme dans les conventions théâtrales habituelles de l'Antiquité, la séparation entre l'extérieur et l'intérieur d'une maison : elle se trouve ici à l'intérieur de la maison, ou, plus précisément, elle fait communiquer deux maisons voisines ; et force est bien de convenir que la réalisation pratique de cet arrangement soulève quelques problèmes sur la scène.

Cet extraordinaire ensemble de Mytilène, qu'on peut dater de la seconde moitié du IIIe siècle de notre ère, méritait d'être étudié en premier lieu, à cause de sa richesse et de sa cohérence : ne donne-t-il pas onze images de comédies de Ménandre, avec dix fois le numéro de l'acte [1] dont une scène est figurée (l'indication manque seulement pour la *Leukadia*), et, dans le triclinium, sept fois le nom des personnages ? De plus, la fouille n'est pas achevée ; de nouveaux panneaux peuvent donc encore venir allonger la liste des pièces figurées. Pourtant, d'autres documents montrent que ces mosaïques de Mytilène ne constituent pas une exception. On connaît depuis plusieurs années une mosaïque d'Ulpia Oescus, en Bulgarie, qui représente une scène des *Achaioi* de Ménandre : l'acte n'est pas indiqué, et les quatre personnages (dont l'un n'est pas masqué) ne sont pas désignés par des inscriptions, aussi ont-ils été diversement interprétés. On voit au centre un vieillard assis, à gauche et à droite un jeune homme debout, et au second plan un quatrième personnage, celui qui précisément ne porte pas de masque. L'interprétation

[1] Le problème est évidemment de savoir si cette division en actes à Mytilène est tardive (comme cela est le cas pour Térence) ou non, mais en fait, pour Ménandre, il semble permis de supposer que cette division date déjà de l'époque hellénistique ; parmi les arguments à l'appui de cette thèse, on doit mentionner qu'un papyrus du *Sikyonios*, de l'époque hellénistique, connaît déjà une division en actes.

A. Samia, Acte III (Mosaïque de Mytilène)

B. Epitrepontes, Acte II (Mosaïque de Mytilène)

Synaristosai, Acte I (Mosaïque de Mytilène)

Synaristosai, Acte I (Mosaïque de Dioscouridès, Musée national, Naples)

Theophoroumene, Acte II (Mosaïque de Mytilène)

« légendaire », qui reconnaissait dans cette mosaïque une scène homérique, est maintenant condamnée par la découverte du *POxy* XXVII, 2462, qui donne, parmi d'autres titres de Ménandre, Ἀχαιοὶ ἢ Πελοπο[ννήσιοι. Il s'agit donc bien d'une comédie mettant en scène des contemporains du poète, et on pourrait imaginer que le héros de ces *Achaioi* était un soldat, comme dans le *Misouménos* ou dans la *Périkeiroménè*, soldat qu'on reconnaîtrait dans le personnage de gauche de la mosaïque.

A une date toute récente, la mission autrichienne a découvert à Ephèse, dans une riche maison, une série de fresques datant de la seconde moitié du second siècle, et donnant des images de scènes de théâtre, avec chaque fois le titre de la pièce [1]. Parmi les mieux conservées, on trouve, sur le mur ouest, les Σικυώνιοι (*Sicyoniens*) de Ménandre, opposés à l'*Oreste* d'Euripide : la fresque représente peut-être, à gauche, l'esclave Pyrrhos, et au centre un homme en costume plus riche, portant un masque à pseudo-onkos plus haut, peut-être le soldat Stratophanès, et ce serait alors la scène de la lettre [2] (Kasser, *Menandri Sikyonius*, vv. 131 ss., fr. X). Sur le mur nord est figurée une autre pièce de Ménandre, la Περικειρομένη (Périkeiroménè) ; peut-être faut-il reconnaître dans les trois personnages une scène de l'acte V, dans laquelle Glykèra pardonne au soldat Polémon, tandis que Pataikos se révèle être le père de Glykèra et de Moschion. Ici encore, une pièce d'Euripide, *Iphigénie*, fait suite à la comédie de Ménandre.

Ainsi, les prototypes des mosaïques de Mytilène — les *Synaristosai* au moins le prouvent et très probablement aussi la *Théophoroumènè* — remontent haut dans le monde hellénistique ; la mosaïque d'Ulpia Oescus, les fresques d'Ephèse semblent indiquer de plus en plus clairement que, lorsqu'on

[1] F. R. Eichler, Die österreichischen Ausgrabungen in Ephesos im Jahre 1967, *Anz. d. phil.-hist. Klasse d. öst. Akad. d. Wiss.*, Jahrg. 1968, So 4., p. 86.

[2] Selon une hypothèse formulée par E. W. Handley.

souhaitait illustrer un comique grec, c'est Ménandre qu'on choisissait, comme on choisissait Euripide pour illustrer la tragédie. Lorsqu'on trouve, juxtaposées, des scènes comiques et des scènes tragiques, comme dans la Casa del Centenario à Pompéi [1], on est désormais tenté d'y reconnaître une alternance de pièces d'Euripide et de pièces de Ménandre [2]. Et on peut aussi supposer que beaucoup de mosaïques et de fresques romaines à prototype hellénistique figurant des scènes comiques se rapportent en fait à Ménandre. Une mosaïque de Sousse [3], par exemple, pourrait bien illustrer le début du *Dyskolos*: on y reconnaîtrait en effet l'esclave Pyrrhias à droite, son maître Sostratos au centre et, à gauche, le parasite Chéréas ; la situation correspondrait à peu près aux vers 92-95, quand Pyrrhias raconte, avec force mimiques, ses mésaventures lors de sa première rencontre avec Cnémon. Toujours pour le *Dyskolos*, on peut rappeler qu'une amphore conservée au Musée de Chypre à Nicosie porte deux graffiti (un sur chaque épaule) : d'un côté Dyskolos, de l'autre ME ; elle est datée du début du IIe siècle avant notre ère, et pouvait éventuellement faire partie du matériel utilisé pour la représentation, à moins qu'il ne s'agisse d'une simple plaisanterie, dont le sens n'apparaît plus clairement [4].

Il est remarquable enfin que deux fragments d'Oxyrhynchus, 2652-2653, datés du second ou du troisième siècle de notre ère, présentent chacun une illustration à l'encre en rapport avec une comédie de Ménandre : la première figure Ἄγνοια, l'Ignorance, et évoque le prologue de la *Périkeiroménè* ; la seconde montre le haut du corps d'un soldat, probablement le Polémon de la même comédie ; d'autres

[1] K. Schefold, *Die Wände Pompeis*, p. 41-42.

[2] Comme le voulait déjà K. Weitzmann, *Ancient Book Illumination*, 1959, p. 84.

[3] *Rom in Karthago, Mosaiken aus Tunesien*, 1964, p. 30, nº 9.

[4] Je remercie vivement Miss Virginia Grace d'avoir bien voulu attirer mon attention sur cette pièce curieuse.

exemples sont moins assurés, comme le papyrus *PSI* 847 [1]. Mais ces illustrations ont pour nous un autre intérêt encore : elles ramènent notre attention sur le problème des manuscrits illustrés ; car ces mosaïques de Mytilène, qui remontent, nous l'avons vu, à des originaux hellénistiques, même si leurs masques ou leurs costumes révèlent les transformations, adaptations, simplifications propres au IIIe siècle de notre ère, présentent une étonnante ressemblance avec les illustrations de Térence, dont les prototypes, pour certains manuscrits, remontent probablement à ce même IIIe siècle [2]. La disposition des panneaux de Mytilène semble indiquer qu'ils s'inspirent de séries d'illustrations ornant soit des manuscrits de Ménandre, soit des extraits illustrés des pièces, dont les artistes pouvaient tirer de véritables cahiers de modèles ; dans ces deux hypothèses, la série pouvait commencer par un portrait de l'auteur (portrait que l'on trouve effectivement en tête des manuscrits de Térence tels que le codex carolingien du Vatican), puis par l'image des masques utilisés pour la représentation [3], et comporter aussi un *Bios* du poète, dans lequel trouverait sa justification un panneau tel que celui des philosophes à Mytilène, ainsi d'ailleurs que celui qui présente la Muse Thalie ; les autres illustrations de pièces de Ménandre, à Mytilène comme ailleurs, se rattacheraient à des œuvres de ce genre. Et l'on est en droit de supposer, en remontant dans le temps, ce que les mosaïques de Dioscouridès nous permettent de faire, qu'à l'époque hellénistique il existait déjà de véritables versions illustrées de Ménandre (selon l'hypothèse formulée brillamment, dès

[1] V. Bartoletti, *SIFC*, XXXIV, 1962, p. 21-24.

[2] L. Jones et C. Morey, *The Miniatures of the Manuscripts of Terence*, 1931.

[3] Il suffit pour s'en convaincre de comparer par exemple les masques de l'*Andria*, sur le codex carolingien du Vatican, avec une plaquette en terre cuite d'époque hellénistique provenant d'Amphipolis, aujourd'hui au Musée de Cavala, *BCH* 83, 1959, p. 711, fig. 4 : les analogies sont frappantes en dépit des transformations inhérentes aux deux époques.

1898, par Wilamowitz, et reprise par Weitzmann [1]), ou, plus simplement, des livres d'images, extraits comparables aux prototypes qu'il faut supposer pour expliquer les « bols homériques » et les *Tabulae Iliacae* [2].

Quant à l'origine première de ces illustrations, on imaginerait volontiers qu'elles s'inspiraient directement de quelque représentation théâtrale : ainsi s'expliquerait le caractère éminemment dramatique de ces tableaux (qui illustrent chacun une scène capitale), la présence de trois acteurs principaux, l'absence de masques pour les personnages muets, en un mot le respect des conventions scéniques. Un élément intermédiaire pourrait d'ailleurs être un panneau destiné à attirer les spectateurs, et sur lequel on aurait représenté chaque fois la scène capitale de la pièce. Nous savons que de tels panneaux ont existé [3] : on comprendrait ainsi encore mieux la présence, sur les images de Mytilène, de l'indication de l'acte et la relation qui semble exister entre le titre de la pièce et le panneau figuré. Ces panneaux étaient-ils absolument fidèles à la représentation théâtrale elle-même? C'est une question à laquelle on ne peut donner de réponse certaine : nous avons vu en effet que les illustrations des *Synaristosai* et du *Phasma* posent des problèmes difficiles de réalisation scénique.

La longue tradition que révèlent les scènes des mosaïques de Mytilène ne permet pas d'inférer qu'à l'époque où elles furent réalisées les pièces de Ménandre qu'elles représentent étaient encore toutes jouées dans cette ville, mais les jetons

[1] U. von Wilamowitz-Moellendorf, *Über griechische illustrierte Volksbücher*, 1898 (repris dans *Kleine Schriften* V, 1, 1937, p. 500) et K. Weitzmann, *l.l.* p. 84 ss., qui parle de l'époque hellénistico-romaine.

[2] K. Schefold, *Vergessenes Pompei*, p. 45-46, et p. 78-79.

[3] Il faut peut-être reconnaître un panneau servant d'annonce à une représentation de cirque dans le fragment de papyrus plié et cousu *POxy* 2470, pl. XII, montrant un ours et un acrobate. Je remercie vivement E. G. Turner pour cette référence à l'appui de ma suggestion. Cf. *infra*, p. 254.

de la *Théophoroumènè* attestent des représentations de Ménandre au IIIe siècle à Athènes ; et le nombre d'images de scènes dramatiques que l'on rencontre sur des documents comme ceux de Patras [1] ou de Piazza Armerina où des chœurs dramatiques sont figurés, indique que le public lettré ne s'était point déshabitué de ce plaisir raffiné que représente la fréquentation du théâtre, et que la maison de Mytilène, qu'elle ait été la propriété d'un riche amateur ou plus vraisemblablement d'une association de technites, illustre brillamment.

[1] Pour la mosaïque de Patras, voir *Les Mosaïques de la Maison du Ménandre*, pl. 28, 1 ; pour Piazza Armerina, cf. G. Gentili, *La Villa Erculia di Piazza Armerina*, 1957, p. 19-20.

DISCUSSION

M. Turner: I should like to welcome Mme Kahil's pictures and her most fruitful explanation and investigation of them. They are of interest for many reasons. One is the evidence they offer of continuing interest in (and dramatic representation of) Menander. The jug from Achmim (cf. p. 234, n. 2) was made about the same time and perhaps in the same place as that in which M. Bodmer's codex was copied (for Achmim as its source see my *Greek papyri* pp. 52-53).

For the subject matter of the plays her sources (which give identifiable scenes, name of play, act number, and names of participants) are not of less value than either the papyrus book-texts or the indirect tradition represented by quotations. Her work is philological in the truest sense. It seems not to be excluded that the mosaics and frescoes derive from a different line of transmission than that of the book tradition. There are errors in the Mytilene mosaics (ΔΕΡCΙΠΠΟC for ΔΕΡΚΙΠΠΟC in *Enchiridion*; the confusion of CΥΡΟC and ΑΝΘΡΑΚΕΥC in *Epitrep.*). I wonder whether these errors are *not* the personal mistakes of the mosaicist laying the floors at Mytilene but errors in the model or pattern from which he was working. Mme Kahil has inferred the existence of a collected illustrated edition of Menander, with an illustration of the author as frontispiece followed by his life. The error in *Epitrep.* seems to support her alternative theory that the mosaics were based on "model" books or "pattern books" which illustrated certain scenes only and circulated among craftsmen. We know that certain scenes from the epic enjoyed a wide circulation (Anna Sadurska, *Les tables iliaques*, Warsaw 1964).

M. Handley: Could I put forward a very tentative suggestion about the *Misoumenos* mosaic? The *onkos*-like hair of the central figure looks rather like that of one of the characters in the Ephesus fresco of *Sikyonioi*, and might confirm the idea that both are soldiers. If the left-hand figure is a slave, the gesture he is making with his scarf may perhaps be a sign of agitation rather than anything to do with strangling—it seems something like that of the very agitated slave in the mosaic from Sousse. Can we then think that this scene gives the moment near the end of the play when Getas tells the crucial story of Krateia's consent to the marriage? If so, the girl is shown coming out from the house in the background for the bethrothal. In the text Demeas is of course present, from πρ[οάγετ' (?πρ[όαγε) 443. But the artist may perhaps have chosen to simplify by leaving him out, especially in view of his usual limitation to three major figures.

In brief, the suggestion is that the mosaic illustrates the action at 435-43.

The similarity in composition between the *Plokion* scene and the *Samia* scene is interesting. One wonders whether more analogies of the kind will be found as the number of these scenes grows, and whether there may not also be interesting analogies with scenes from tragedy. Possibly the composition itself, as well as the more concrete details of the gestures and movements, may have a bearing on interpretation. Thus it might be possible to think, from the analogy with *Samia*, that Laches is here quarreling with Krobyle, perhaps even threatening to divorce her.

M. Ludwig: Für Aktnumerierungen fallen mir im Augenblick nur Beispiele aus der lateinischen Literatur ein, z.B. Terenz, *Hec.* 39 *primo actu*, *Ad.* 9 *in prima fabula*, und die Fünf-Akt-Regel bei Horaz und in ihrer Anwendung bei Donat. Gibt es Belege für Aktnumerierungen aus der griechischen Literatur?

M. Handley: The μέρη of plays, in the technical sense of 'parts' or 'acts' are sometimes referred to by number in commentaries and the like. Examples are: *POxy* 2086, saec.ii-iii A.D. [Pack[2] 2860; discussion by Körte, *Archiv* 10 (1932) 226-8], scholia to a comedy, including heading μέρους δ'; *POxy* 2257, 'perhaps of the later second century' [Pack[2] 47], fr.1, 8ff, hypothesis to Aeschylus, *Aitnaiai*; *POxy* 2741, saec.ii-iii A.D., commentary on Eupolis, *Marikas*, with the phrase ἐπὶ τῷ πέμπτῳ μέρε[ι at fr. 1 B, col.ii,17; similarly ἐν τῷ δευτέρῳ μέρει in one of the hypotheses to Euripides, *Andromache*.

M. Turner: Miss Dedoussi called attention in her edition of *Samia* p. 3 n. 8 to the mode of citation in fr 206 Koe., Bekker, *Anecdota* 399, 24 and Phot. Berol. 135,26.

M. van Berchem: If we accept the idea of a collected edition of Menander, with frontispiece, portrait of the author and his life, would not the recording of the precise act of the play to which each scene belongs be most easily accounted for if only one scene from each play were shown?

M. Wehrli: Die einzelnen Szenen scheinen so gewählt zu sein, dass sie repräsentativen Wert bekommen, z.B. in den *Epitrepontes*.

Mme Kahil: I have also wondered whether the scenes might not have been chosen so as to make good "posters".

M. Turner: It is worth noting that a "poster" for a circus performance at Oxyrhynchus has probably survived in *POxy* XXVII 2470. But the idea of a "poster" may prove unhelpful to Mme Kahil's view that the scenes illustrated were actually represented dramatically before the audience. I can think of many posters of modern plays or films which display a scene never in fact represented in the play or film. In the mosaics the plays which have a present participle as title do not always show the subject of the participle. *Epitrepontes*, *Synaristosai*, probably *Misoumenos* do; *Theophoroumene* does not (though the scene is that which is intended to make her show herself: E. W. Handley in *BICS* 16 (1969) pp. 88 ff).

A. INDEX AUCTORUM

I. Auctores antiquiores

II. Auctores recentiores

B. INDEX NOMINUM

N.B. *Hominum mulierumque nomina minutis rectis, dramatis personarum minutis obliquis, geographica maiusculis litteris scribuntur; deorum heroumque nomina asterisco praeceduntur.*

PRINTED IN SWITZERLAND

ACHEVÉ D'IMPRIMER LE 31 OCTOBRE 1970
SUR LES PRESSES DE L'IMPRIMERIE DU
«JOURNAL DE GENÈVE», A GENÈVE, SUISSE